AF709913

Praise for *Navigating Bipolar Country*

"Hammond is a bipolar patient with clinical training and honed writing skills, making her an ideal guide when *Navigating Bipolar Country*. She has collected stories—compelling, heartfelt, distressing, and reassuring—from bipolar sufferers, family, and professionals. Kudos to her and all the contributors."

~S. Bruun-Meyer, Psychiatrist, Toronto

"Dr. Merryl Hammond's anthology, *Navigating Bipolar Country*, is a triumph in the field of bipolar disorder literature. Combining 42 essays told through the lens of individuals living with bipolar disorder, family members, and clinicians, she gives us an essential and unique read. These personal accounts provide priceless insights, comfort, and understanding of this complex disease. A rare gem, this book offers hope and is a must-read for anyone striving to learn more about bipolar disorder and its far-reaching effects."

~Sallie Crotty, author of *Out of the Ashes: A Story of Recovery and Hope*

"Should be required reading for all health professionals. As a fellow sufferer and mental health practitioner, I recognize myself as a traveling companion to those traversing the wilds of bipolar country. In this masterful book exist deeper and richer answers to truths you seek; gifts you didn't even know you needed."

~Caitlin Billings, LCSW, author of *In Our Blood: A Memoir*

"I love this book for so many reasons. Having dealt with bipolar issues in my own family, I can relate to many of the challenges that come with traversing the path to mental wellness. Whether you have family members navigating bipolar or live with it yourself, you will find hope and inspiration in these pages. It's important we openly discuss mental illness in all its forms so people can find the support they need, and we can work to remove the stigma. I highly recommend this powerful book."

~Stephanie Chandler, author, and founder of the Nonfiction Authors Association

"An engaging, powerful, insightful, and heartfelt anthology filled with creativity, determination, resilience, courage, compassion, and hope. Sure to inspire further exploration into bipolar disorder and its impacts."

~Debbie Sesula, MA, CPS

"These engaging and inspiring personal stories build empathy, provide comfort, and inspire hope. I recommend this book to anyone seeking a better understanding of mental illness."

~Karen Jensen, Librarian

"Hammond's memoir, *Mad Like Me: Travels in Bipolar Country*, helped me to understand bipolar disorder much better. When I learned she was compiling an anthology that included points of view from family members and healthcare professionals as well, I was excited to read it! I have relatives who struggle with bipolar, so reading other people's stories helped me to see what types of actions can help—and what not to do.

I recommend this book to anyone struggling with bipolar, any family members, and healthcare professionals who have patients struggling with bipolar. Well done!"

~Sue L. Canfield

"Merryl Hammond's latest project, *Navigating Bipolar Country*, is an insightful anthology about living with bipolar disorder. Her team of contributors has created an outstanding work and its quality lies in the well-rounded approach to the subject: we're given the essential perspectives of those living with the disorder; thoughts from family members; and contributions from medical professionals. I've come away so much more informed on what this disorder is and how it impacts people's lives. I encourage readers to pick up this educational book; I am sure they will come away just as impressed as I am."

~Chris Marsh, Librarian

"The fascinating intensity of bipolar sufferers pouring out their true-life experiences in candid, brutal, honest truths is spellbinding. Astonishing, shocking, horrifying. Hammond's 2018 memoir, *Mad Like Me: Travels in Bipolar Country*—so helpful, so insightful—was a great introduction, and now here, we learn much more. For bipolar sufferers and all who know them, this is easily the best book ever to have been compiled. Quite literally a lifesaver."

~Laurence Potgieter

"Merryl Hammond's latest book is an anthology filled with incredible stories and perspectives of people experiencing bipolar disorder. I learned so much, felt deep sadness as well as hope, was in awe of human resilience, and felt immense gratitude towards those who had the courage and generosity to share their experiences. This book is a testimony to hope, love and forgiveness."

~Anne Vrana

"*Navigating Bipolar Country* is an in-depth description of what it is like to live with bipolar, from the inside and the outside, and from many different perspectives. Well written, well-edited, and intensely personal. Each chapter can be digested as a short story unto itself. Congratulations to Dr. Hammond for another insightful book and to her daughter for a gripping poem, *My Bipolar Mother*."

~Jim Fyles

"This book is a gold mine of lived experiences to help those challenged with bipolar disorder develop insight and compassion for all those affected. An excellent resource, with additional insights from the professionals as well."

~Victoria Macdonald

"What an amazing anthology by so many talented authors! I don't think I've ever seen an anthology written so well and crafted so creatively by the author. In this book, you'll learn about bipolar disorder from people who live with bipolar, the families who care for loved ones with bipolar, and the clinicians who treat people with bipolar. Each contributor has a different bit of insight to offer. This anthology covers everything you would want to know about bipolar disorder. Bravo!"

~Kathy Day

NAVIGATING BIPOLAR COUNTRY

NAVIGATING BIPOLAR COUNTRY

Personal and Professional Perspectives on Living with Bipolar Disorder

Edited by Merryl Hammond, PhD

CAE Canada

Published by CAE Canada
Selection, Preface and Epilogue copyright © 2022 by Merryl Hammond, PhD
Foreword © 2022 by Candida A. Fink, MD

Individual contributions copyright © 2022 by the authors listed below (* indicates a pen name):

Janette Abramowitz • Dennis Barras • Paul Bearer* • Lara Beaulieu* • Kayla Behbahani • Anthony Berger • Sarah Boon • Sheryl Bruce • Amy Cox • David Laing Dawson • Jens Peter Eckardt • Julie A. Fast • Ellie Gainey • A-M. Ghadirian • Tami Hammond-Collins • Olivia Innes* • Barbara Jacobson • Minji Kim* • Isabelle Lipari • Tara Mandarano • Stephanie Marie • Victoria Maxwell • Catharine McKenty • Shauna Michaels* • Brionna Morse • Amy Dodd Pilkington • Gina Roitman • Diana Samuel • Bruce Saunders • Laurel Saunders • Janet Scott* • Eric Smith • Janet L. Stanley • Maggie Taylor* • Natasha Tracy • Felicity Vine* • Jayne Warren • Beverley Watkins • Wayfarer* • Gail Windsor • Tracy Windsor • Matthieu Zellweger

Earlier versions of three pieces were previously published:

Black Garbage Bags by Julie A. Fast was published by Martin Baker and Fran Houston on their website, GumOnMyShoe.com, 2020; *Yup, It's an On-going Process* by Victoria Maxwell was published as *On the Road Again* in *Visions*: BC's Mental Health Journal. Employment. No. 13, pp. 12–13, Fall/Winter 2001; and *Bipolar Stories* by David Laing Dawson was published on Marvin Ross's blog *Mind You*, 16 September 2019.

All rights reserved. No part of this book may be reproduced or transmitted in any form or by any means, electronic or mechanical, including photocopying, recording, or by any information storage and retrieval system, without the written permission of the publisher, except in the case of brief quotations embodied in reviews.

Disclaimer: This is a collection of true accounts, many about an author's own experience with mental illness. Bipolar disorder is extremely serious, so please always consult your health care provider before using any information or advice in this book. Using ideas from this book is at the sole discretion of the reader. The anthology editor, authors, and publisher are not liable for any damages resulting from the use of advice or information in this book. Nevertheless, the editor hopes that the accounts included here will be helpful to readers who are "navigating bipolar country."

Editors: Tami Hammond-Collins—tamzhc@gmail.com and Nina Shoroplova—NinaShoroplova.ca
Cover art: Robert Bogdan Choma
Cover Designer: Pagatana Design Service—pagatana.com
Book Interior and E-book Designer: Amit Dey—amitdey2528@gmail.com
Production & Publishing Consultant: Geoff Affleck, AuthorPreneur Publishing Inc.—geoffaffleck.com

Archived at the National Library of Quebec
Hammond, Merryl, 1956–
Navigating Bipolar Country : Personal and Professional Perspectives on Living with Bipolar Disorder / edited by Merryl Hammond

ISBN 978-1-989298-04-6 (Paperback)
ISBN 978-1-989298-05-3 (eBook)

SEL020010	SELF-HELP/ Mood Disorders / Bipolar Disorder
PSY022030	PSYCHOLOGY/ Psychopathology / Bipolar Disorder
SEL011000	SELF-HELP / Mood Disorders /Depression
MED102000	MEDICAL / Mental Health

First Edition
merrylhammond.com

Dedication

For all who have navigated—or are navigating—bipolar country, whether as an unpredictable driver of the bipolar bus, or an unwitting passenger being dragged along for your family member's ride into unmapped territory, or as a concerned professional trying to prevent your client's bipolar bus from going off-road.

For each of you.

Contents

Foreword

Candida A. Fink, MD

Author of *Bipolar Disorder for Dummies* and *The Ups and Downs of Raising a Bipolar Child*

Writing about bipolar disorder (formerly called manic depression) traditionally fell to professionals publishing textbooks and articles in academic journals. That changed in 1995 when Kay Redfield Jamison, PhD, a psychologist, originally published *An Unquiet Mind*, a memoir about her struggle with bipolar disorder. As both a professional and a person with lived experience, Dr. Jamison's work resonated for millions of people living with bipolar disorder and for the many people who wanted to know more about it. It riveted me early in my career as a psychiatrist to hear—with such clarity—the pain of the disorder and of the treatment journey.

Since then, memoirs about living with bipolar disorder have exploded, coinciding with the growth of the internet and social media. Whatever the downsides of these digital platforms may be, they have created spaces for people living with mental illness to connect with each other, to tell their stories, and to chip away at the deeply entrenched stigma that has kept mental health in the shadows. Knowing that one is not alone with a life-changing illness can alter the whole trajectory of healing and recovery.

In 2018, Merryl Hammond, PhD—the editor of this anthology, and herself a health professional—wrote an extraordinary memoir, *Mad Like Me: Travels in Bipolar Country,* documenting and detailing her own journey with bipolar disorder. Her storytelling engages the reader with grace and powerful details, bringing her experiences to life. Her story has deeply impacted readers. When I read it the first time, I was struck by the pattern of recovery and relapse, over and over, that disrupted her life and the lives of her family members with renewed intensity at every one of these junctures. In my work with patients with bipolar disorder, these patterns are familiar, but each story is unique and heartbreaking in its own way.

For Dr. Hammond, the act of writing, of storytelling, has been part of her path to process and manage her life with bipolar disorder. Her idea for this anthology grew out of her generous spirit—from her desire to help others tell their own stories and to help readers hear first-hand what living with bipolar disorder feels like. She could find only one previously published collection of lived experience narratives about bipolar disorder. So she set to work collecting true accounts and reflections and editing them into this anthology that you are about to read. This book, *Navigating Bipolar Country,* is the result of her dedication and skill, and it provides a unique and powerful range of perspectives and a spectrum of experiences.

The book contains 42 contributions divided into three parts: reflections from people living with bipolar disorder; family members' reflections; and contributions from professionals who work with people with bipolar disorder. While most of the pieces are directly written by contributors, two of them—*A Gift or a Curse* by Amy Cox, and *It's Hard to See the Light* by Wayfarer—are excerpts from email exchanges between them and Dr. Hammond. Both these authors' struggles with symptoms of bipolar disorder and other stressors interfered with their ability to write their reflections independently. Dr. Hammond's flexibility and creativity in approaching these types of challenges gives this anthology a genuine voice. In the process of gathering these contributions, she did not give up on people who were struggling: she had compassion for their difficulties and worked to find solutions so that readers could hear stories from people who were actively managing some of the most difficult symptoms of bipolar disorder and would otherwise have been excluded from the project.

Another example of Dr. Hammond's flexibility was her use of telephone interviews to gather contributions. For example, Catharine McKenty's piece, *In the Storm and the Sunshine*, was gathered in phone interviews during which she recalled living with her late husband's bipolar disorder. She was 89 at the time of the interviews and didn't have access to a computer in her senior care centre, so she would have been unable to participate and share her immense experience without the use of interviews. Phone interviews were also used for the powerful daughter-mother contributions by Tracy Windsor (*A Bumpy Road to Recovery: Worth the Ride*) and Gail Windsor (*Traversing Volcanoes*), among others. Some busy health professionals also chose the interview option to save them the time of writing a piece from scratch.

The authors' birthdates range from 1930 to the late-1990s. Most wrote under their own names, while a few used pen names. Storylines include parenting with bipolar disorder, parenting a child who has bipolar disorder, navigating marriage and partnership with bipolar disorder, managing a job and career with bipolar disorder, and growing up as the child of a parent who has bipolar disorder. There are tales of medications, hospitalizations, and incarcerations, as well as psychotherapy and electroconvulsive therapy (ECT). There are vignettes, life stories, factual accounts, and even some poetry, along with a high speed, high intensity collection of musings over the course of one hypomanic, sleepless night.

The last part of the anthology is a collection of pieces by psychiatrists, licensed social workers, psychologists, counsellors, and others who work with people who have bipolar disorder. It includes a range of topics from basic information about bipolar disorder, to how it's diagnosed (and sometimes misdiagnosed or undiagnosed), to available treatments. Several pieces peek into hospital units, psychiatric consultations, and family sessions. I especially enjoyed the piece *Let Me into Your Mind* by Matthieu Zellweger, a photographer with a prior career as a research scientist. He describes working on a project for the medical journal, *The Lancet*, and the challenges he encountered trying to accurately portray people who were actively manic. This final part of the anthology provides a range of perspectives on treating people with bipolar disorder—with the focus on treating the person, not just the condition. As someone who cares for people with bipolar disorder, I think this is our most important goal: to focus on people and their stories, not just symptoms and numbers.

One of Dr. Hammond's greatest challenges in compiling this work was the onset of the COVID-19 pandemic in early 2020, just as she was beginning to collect contributions. While writing and communicating virtually are tasks that can be done from home, the situation remained extremely stressful for most people—especially those living with pre-existing mental health challenges, including bipolar disorder. Fear, unpredictability, changes in routines, therapists and treatment programs going online, having to figure out how to get medicine delivered, coping with loneliness and isolation from loved ones, navigating too much together time with family, losing work, and financial stressors all intermingled to put deep pressure onto established systems of survival and support.

Kudos to Dr. Hammond for compiling this moving collection and for bringing together this wide range of stories that will draw you in, touch you deeply, and remain with you long after you have finished reading. I am honoured to be a small part of this endeavor, and I look forward to more unique and important stories and anthologies from Dr. Hammond in the future.

Preface

Merryl Hammond, PhD

Editor of *Navigating Bipolar Country*
and author of *Mad Like Me: Travels in Bipolar Country*

Welcome! Whether you yourself have bipolar disorder—or another mental illness, perhaps—or whether one of your family members or friends has the disorder, or whether you are a health or other professional who works with bipolar patients and their families, you are sure to find insight, sustenance, and inspiration in this extraordinary collection.

For those—like me—who have bipolar disorder, I hope you will learn from the experience of your peers in part 1, but equally from the candid reflections of family members in part 2. Their dedication and commitment often go unnoticed and unappreciated. As well, the insights of health and other professionals in part 3 should be of great interest. For family members, I hope you will gain greater insight into your loved one's disordered world when you read part 1, into the challenges of fellow family members, and into the constraints faced by health professionals who treat your family member, both in hospital and in the community. Finally, for professionals, may the true accounts in this book help you to better understand the struggles of your patients or clients, their family members, and your colleagues on the multidisciplinary health care team.

There is something here for everyone!

It's been an honour for me to edit this anthology, and it's now an honour for me to share it with you. May it give a small taste of what it's like to navigate bipolar country.

Trigger warning

Many of the essays in this collection will, of necessity, deal with such sensitive topics as depression, mania, family breakdown, self-harm, suicidal ideation and completed suicide. Some readers may find other subjects not mentioned above upsetting. Given the nature of this anthology, I have decided not to include specific trigger warnings at the start of each relevant piece, but rather to issue this general trigger warning here. If you're at all concerned that these accounts may adversely affect you, please ask a trusted friend or relative to screen the pieces for you first.

Definitions

Bipolar disorder—formerly called manic depression—involves significant changes in mood, energy, and activity levels. It's often described as a rollercoaster with a high mood (called mania or—when somewhat less severe—hypomania) alternating with a low mood (depression). Bipolar I features manic episodes and depression while bipolar II is characterized by hypomanic episodes and depression. (Please see the essays by Dr. Behbahani and Dr. Abramowitz in part 3 for details about diagnosis and treatment.)

My background with bipolar disorder

I was diagnosed with rapid cycling bipolar I in 2008 at age 51. (Rapid cycling means that a person has four or more bipolar episodes in a year.) At times, my mania got so bad that I experienced psychosis: mainly visual hallucinations.

Many have asked, "What's it like to have bipolar disorder?" Imagine: you never know if you'll wake up the next morning and be able to function normally or not. It's quite possible that you'll be utterly paralyzed; unable to move at all. That's depression, of course. Or maybe your legs will suddenly take it upon themselves to speed up, so that you can only scurry, run, dance, jump and skip, but not walk (like a "normal person") or stand still. That's either hypomania or mania. Either way, you just never know. You cannot make firm plans, not knowing what your legs will be doing on any particular day in the future. You're simply not in control. Your legs, your body, your mind now have minds of their own!

What an incredible relief, what a monumental gift it is, then, when you're finally correctly diagnosed, and they find some magic combination of medications in the right dosages to gradually coax you back to stability. To mental health. To *yourself*.

But even then, there's the overwhelming stigma to deal with. People who've heard that I have bipolar but don't know me well (or don't know that I've now been mentally stable for several years) often pull back in open fear when I enter a room or sit beside them. I feel like a leper! And the worst is that I then check myself: am I walking normally; speaking at a socially acceptable volume; smiling appropriately—not too much, not too little? Like Goldilocks looking for the perfect bowl of porridge, or bed, or whatever. It's exhausting, and I resent having to do it. I hope this anthology will help to build understanding and break the stigma that affects us all.

How this anthology came to be

In 2018, I published what became a bestselling memoir about my experiences, *Mad Like Me: Travels in Bipolar Country*. Many people who read it said they really related to my story and appreciated the honesty with which I told it. Their comments and reviews made it clear that many of them had experiences of their own that they were willing—even anxious—to share.

My mental cogs started turning, and once the initial work of launching and promoting my memoir had settled, I started researching the possibility of editing a bipolar anthology with multiple writers from a variety of distinct groups: people like me who are living with bipolar, family members, and professionals.

How I got from the initial idea of editing an anthology to the finished product you are now reading is quite a story. As I explain in the Epilogue, I reached out to many bipolar memoirists, authors, and experts to invite them to participate in this project, and several agreed. I felt that their collaboration would lend a certain credibility to the work.

But while the involvement of these renowned writers was reassuring, I also wanted to hold space for emerging writers to express themselves: I knew from their initial emails that they had amazing accounts to share. And I'm so glad I did. As you'll discover, some of the most poignant and profound submissions are from previously unpublished writers who were struggling, for example, to come to terms with their new diagnosis, or trying to make sense of their own or a loved one's destructive bipolar behaviours.

Each essay shines a light on specific aspects of the complex, complicated, and infuriating entity that is bipolar disorder. And the individual pieces build on each other to starkly illuminate the reality of life lived with bipolar. In many cases, contributors bravely step out of the wings to centre stage, bearing the glare of the spotlight, emotionally exposing themselves for our education and understanding.

What a privilege it's been to be taken into the confidence of all these contributors; to have the darkest corners of their bipolar experiences exposed to the light; and now to share their hard-won lessons, their painful mental wounds and scars, and their hopes for recovery with you. I offer this exceptional collection to you hoping that these profound accounts will engage, enlighten, and inspire you—as they did me.

Welcome to bipolar country!

PART 1

Reflections by People Living with Bipolar Disorder

… in which people living with bipolar reflect on how it feels to experience bipolar episodes from the inside out; how the disorder has derailed their formerly ordered, successful, and productive lives; and in some cases, resulted in new perspectives, a fresh start, and hope for recovery.

A Bumpy Road to Recovery: Worth the Ride

Tracy Windsor

Editor's note: Tracy's mother, Gail Windsor, has written about her experiences as a family member in a piece titled Traversing Volcanoes *in part 2. You may want to read that account immediately after this one.*

I was diagnosed with bipolar I with psychotic features when I was 19, about 12 years ago now. I'd been struggling with anxiety and depression for about two years before that. And much earlier, as a young child—around the time my parents were getting divorced—I had therapy for trichotillomania (hair-pulling disorder).

My parents had been concerned about me for over a year by the time I was finally diagnosed with bipolar disorder. Here's what happened:

- In 2006, after graduating high school in Nova Scotia, I moved to Vancouver to live with my mom. I was incredibly lonely in Vancouver and experienced my first real depressive episode during my first semester at university.
- A few months later, for Christmas 2006, I went to visit my dad in Nova Scotia. I was excited to see my family and friends there. My "cup" was refilled, and I was inspired to go back and make my life in Vancouver one that I would enjoy.
- When I returned to Vancouver, I had what we now realize was my first manic episode (starting in January 2007).

- In June 2007, I went back to Nova Scotia, still manic. I remember feeling unusually irritable and even aggressive about minor things my dad said and did. I guess I was overreacting during the mania, because he phoned my mom and told her about what he called my "bizarre behaviour." (None of us yet had the vocabulary of "mania," "hypomania," and so on.) By the time I got back to Vancouver, the mania had subsided, so my mom didn't really understand what my dad had been complaining about.
- When I returned to Vancouver in July 2007, I became depressed again.
- This depression continued for four months as I struggled through my third semester at university. There were days when I would go to class, commuting over an hour each way, and not speak to anyone all day.
- In December 2007, I went back to Nova Scotia again. Again, I was inspired to take control of my life in Vancouver and make it an enjoyable experience.

Then, from January to April 2008, I failed two courses because mania reappeared, this time with gradual development of psychosis in April. This deserves a section of its own.

Second manic episode with psychosis: early 2008

I was 19 when I experienced an elated mood for a couple of months in early 2008. It was then that my mom first saw me in a manic state and understood what my dad had been talking about the previous year. She too started referring to some of my behaviour as "bizarre" or "strange."

I remember feeling euphoric and having grandiose ideas. For example, I was on the bus and believed that all the passengers could hear my thoughts, and that they were all reacting to my presence.

It was as if all these strangers were acutely attuned to and aware of me, based on the way they were moving and shifting in their seats.

Another example: at Science World in Vancouver, there's a large globe, about five feet in diameter. I was convinced I could make it spin—and then stop spinning—entirely at my command.

Since I believed my thoughts were so powerful, I decided I should think only *positive* thoughts so that nobody would think I was a bad person.

Around this time, Mother's Day was coming up, so my mom and I went to visit Nana in the care home where she lived. I decided to test my hypothesis that people could read my thoughts. At the florist, when my mom asked me which flowers we should buy for Nana, I didn't reply at all. I figured she should be able to read my thoughts! My mom was very concerned that I was behaving oddly, and out of character. She got so concerned she called my dad. He suggested she take me to hospital for drug testing.

> *On that point, I had been using quite a bit of cannabis for a few years by then, and maybe that did play a role in my mental illness, but who knows? All I do know is that I absolutely cannot use it at all now: I tried it once recently and it precipitated psychosis right away. Looking back, I'm aware that I used more cannabis than most of my friends, so maybe I was self-medicating for anxiety and depression at the time? I also sought out people who tended to use more than my other friends. In large groups, I would drink a lot, and become a kind of clown in the group. In small groups, I'd get high. Then I'd feel freer to express myself. I'd also use cannabis on my own.*

First hospitalization and diagnosis: May 2008

It was at the hospital, during this manic episode, that they gave me the diagnosis: bipolar I with psychotic features.

The mania lasted about six months in all, and psychosis about two months.

I was hospitalized in Burnaby for about two weeks. The psychosis was still raging. I remember at one point being in a relaxation class, lying on my back on the floor. I looked up and saw all those small holes punched in the ceiling panels: little black dots. And as I stared, the dots expanded, changed shape, and came down toward me. It wasn't a scary hallucination; rather pleasant, actually. The dots morphed into the shapes of farm animals that came closer to me with each inhale: cows, chickens, horses, sheep…

At one point, the psychiatrist asked: "Are you hearing voices?" I got quiet and focused on my hearing. I said that I could hear people talking on the other side of the door. He said: "No, that's not what I mean. I mean do you hear voices when nobody is around?" I truthfully replied, "No," because voice-hearing was not—and never has been—part of my experience. I think perhaps because I did not hear voices, he didn't ask me anything else about my psychosis experience. If he had asked me things like "Do you think people can hear *your* thoughts?" or "Do you believe you are special in any way?" then I may have said "Yes," and my psychosis may have been diagnosed sooner. Instead, I was prescribed a mood stabilizing medication, and sent on my way, not feeling any different than I had when I went in.

> *On the one hand, I wore that as a badge of honour. You see, I was ambivalent about whether I really had bipolar or not, and now here it was that their treatment had made no difference to me, so maybe I was right to deny the diagnosis. On the other hand, it was a bruise to my ego that they had given me this diagnosis and admitted me to the psych ward. So, I felt simultaneously validated and invalidated, if that makes sense.*

Somewhere around this time, my mom decided to leave her job so she could take care of me. We spent a lot of time wandering in the woods together. And she'd take me to my various psych appointments.

Lead-up to second hospitalization: psychosis continues

The single medication they prescribed in hospital was not at all sufficient to control my symptoms. My psychosis persisted and progressed.

I saw the community psychiatrist weekly. As my delusions progressed, they became increasingly strange and engrossing. I started to believe that every thought that came into my mind would come true. Because my last name is "Windsor" like the Queen of England, I thought I was a princess being raised outside the royal family for some classified research or intelligence reasons. As I continued to believe that everyone could hear my thoughts, I started to see myself as an exceptionally good person, which soon progressed to thinking I was a Saint. One evening, as I lay on my bed, I felt a warm light wash over me from head to toe. I interpreted this as God blessing me and anointing me as the Messiah, sent to prevent World War III.

One day, however, my thoughts crossed over to what I call the "dark side." As people passed by on the sidewalk, for example, I would see them turning into Zombie-like characters in my peripheral vision. I imagined that everybody I thought about would be killed. I imagined corpses rising from the dead, and zombies roaming the streets.

My psychosis also made me believe that all the men of the world were killing all the women because I, the Messiah, was a woman who had failed humanity. I thought that the appendages of the dead women were going to be attached to my body and I would become a huge, grotesque monster. I would be tortured and progressively robbed of all my senses, except touch. I also believed that scientists had discovered how to make people live forever and so I would feel nothing but pain and agony for all eternity.

During the first few weeks that I saw the community psychiatrist, I didn't say anything about my delusional thoughts. I thought that if I let on that I knew about the Royal Family Experiment, then it would be called off and I wouldn't be allowed to become the princess. Once my "dark" thoughts became so scary, however, everything poured out during a session with the psychiatrist. She said that I was experiencing "psychosis," and that I needed to be hospitalized immediately.

I didn't know anything about psychosis; my understanding at the time was simply that it was synonymous with "crazy," and people who had such experiences were "psycho." I didn't want to believe this about myself, and I didn't want to go back to the hospital. My mother continued to take care of me—or, rather, manage me, and make sure I didn't run away and put myself in danger.

But I don't recall any suicidal thoughts at that stage.

Those came later.

Now, when I try to explain what psychosis feels like, I write the word like this, with the letters all confused and warped looking:

psyChOSis.

Doesn't looking at that make you feel a bit disconcerted and off-balance? Well, that's exactly how I felt—all the time.

Second hospitalization: June 2008

After several unbearable days, I asked Mom to take me to the hospital. I thought that of all places in the world, a hospital would keep me safe—or at least study my special body and mind in a responsible way for science. I was taken to St. Paul's Hospital. I remember speaking very quickly and fervently to a nurse in the emergency ward. He left the room, returned moments later, opened the door a few inches, and handed me a small white pill in a little cup. I took the medication, which was likely Ativan to help calm me down. I was soon admitted under the Mental Health Act and transferred to an assessment unit that was more like a prison than a rehabilitation unit. The room consisted of a thin mattress on the floor, a steel toilet, and a steel sink. There was nothing that could be used as an improvised weapon.

The hours or days I spent in the assessment unit is mostly a blur, but I do remember my mom, a friend, and my uncle coming to visit me on my 20th birthday. They had brought a cake, which we quietly ate while crouched on the floor, careful not to disrupt the other patients on the ward.

I mentioned that a fiend came to visit me in hospital for my birthday. I didn't realize at the time that this was the beginning of the end of this friendship, and many others. I think that my mental illness and my having been in a psych ward freaked people out. I also had a drinking problem, which had led to blackouts and some unsavoury behaviour. As well, I stopped going to university and playing sports, which minimized my regular contact with people, so my lack of friends was probably due to a combination of things.

My mom had done some research on treatment for psychosis and asked to have me transferred to University of British Columbia (UBC) Hospital, where I could be referred to an Early Psychosis Intervention (EPI) program. The psychiatrist at St. Paul's agreed, and I was taken in a transport ambulance across the city of Vancouver to UBC Hospital. I stayed there for a month or two. I vaguely remember attending a group therapy session, but my mind was very foggy. I doubt that I could have actively participated. They tried me on other meds: Wellbutrin and Celexa, and this time, I was discharged on lithium and Olanzapine.

For outpatient follow up, Mom had insisted that I get a transfer to the EPI unit at UBC, so that's where I went.

Third hospitalization: October 2008

I tried to re-start my university studies in September 2008, but just a few weeks into the semester, I had to withdraw. I was experiencing unmanageable depression, and the EPI team encouraged me to go to hospital. I was there for two months, this time.

Three admissions in an eight-month period. There's something wrong with this picture.

I can't even remember what meds they tried this time, or what I was discharged on. They had tried so many meds and combinations, and my depression was no better at all. I just gave up and decided to be discharged anyway.

Weight gain

Growing up, I never had to worry about what I ate—I was thin and lithe without really having to try. Food was never a preoccupation for me: I ate when I was hungry and didn't think about food the rest of the time. When my world became small, and everything else in my life that held meaning was severed, food became the one thing that gave me pleasure; the one thing I could look forward to. Apart from that, my meds caused increased hunger, so weight gain was a definite side effect.

About once a week, Mom and I would go to a sushi restaurant that had the most delicious special rolls. They were delectable! I am salivating just thinking about them. This visit to the restaurant became a ritual for me. The moment they put the food down in front of us was exulting. Food was my salvation from the bland monotony of my meaningless life, and I began to pack on the pounds.

I gained at least 50 pounds (23 kilograms) in six months. Dark, crooked stretch marks began to show up on my hips, arms, and thighs. The stretch marks on my breasts looked like red starfish, clinging to rocks. One of the medications I was on caused rough scales on my scalp. My hair became extremely dry and started to break off in clumps. In addition to feeling like a shell of the person I once was, there was also a completely different person looking back at me in the mirror.

Suicide attempt and fourth hospitalization: January 2009

I tried again to resume my studies in January 2009, but after my third discharge, the depression worsened. For the first time, I experienced suicidal thoughts.

I felt totally hopeless about the future:

- It seemed the depression was never going to lift, and I would never have a life worth living.
- I felt isolated and rejected by my so-called "friends." (I had only lived in BC for about two years by then, so I didn't have a strong network of like-minded people; everyone I met in Vancouver before my diagnosis was no longer a friend after it.)
- I did want to be in a long-term relationship, but after my first hospitalization, and my erratic and somewhat-stalker-like behaviour, the guy I'd been seeing had stopped taking my calls.

This all added up and made me feel desperate.

I made a serious suicide attempt about a month after the thoughts first set in. My depression had dragged on for over four dreadful months by then, and I was entirely without hope.

They tell me I was found unconscious by my sibling's partner. A couple days later, I woke up in the middle of the night at Vancouver General Hospital. It took me a minute to figure out where I was, but I soon put the pieces together. My suicide attempt had failed, and I was nowhere near grateful for having survived; instead, I was a failure, and would now have to continue living my pathetic, worthless life.

They tried various meds to treat my depression, but three months later I was right back in hospital with depression.

I was kept in hospital for ages this time. About three months. I ended up having electroconvulsive therapy (ECT). I don't remember much about this period: my mom's account of this will be more reliable.

I was discharged back home to live with my mom, and then a few months later, in July 2009, I was accepted to Watson House, a group home for young adults with a mental illness. I was 21, and needed more independence, but couldn't afford my own place. I was ready to work on my recovery, and this was a very supportive setting.

In September that year, I again registered for school, this time at Langara College, just taking one class at a time.

Fifth hospitalization, December 2009

Almost a year after my suicide attempt, I was back in hospital with depression again. I only stayed two weeks this time and was discharged in time to start the January semester at college. I grinned and bore it through the Olympics in Vancouver. Even though I lived downtown, I rarely went out to any Olympics events.

Sixth hospitalization: March 2010

In March 2010, I was back in hospital, for depression again. This was my sixth hospitalization in less than two years. While there, I made another suicide attempt. It was actually an incident of extreme self-harm during a fit of outrage at my illness. I felt so hopeless, so desperate.

> *My first suicide attempt was pre-meditated: carefully planned several weeks in advance. This second attempt was impulsive.*

I was kept for about three months, and this time, with the depression still stubbornly lingering, they suggested a second round of ECT. I was so desperate for relief, I agreed.

The ECT finally made a difference, and I was eventually discharged on the same meds as I take now: Seroquel SR, lamotrigine (Lamictal), and Zoloft.

After discharge, I had several months of relative stability. It seemed that the right combinations and dosages of meds, plus the second round of ECT, had really worked for me.

I was able to continue my college studies, one course at a time.

> *Around this time, I started feeling well enough to get involved in peer support initiatives including support groups and a speaker's bureau, where I shared my story with others. The last thing I wanted to do was to share my experience publicly; however, it turned out to be a very healing experience. Later, I got interested in social work, which I am now studying.*

Seventh hospitalization: July 2011

In July 2011, two things were happening at the same time. First, I was getting ready to leave the group home to move into a shared house with roommates, and I was anxious and uncertain about that. Second, the new drug Abilify was being heavily promoted, so I was started on it. But I had awful side effects: my appetite became voracious, leading to even more weight gain, and my mood started to crash again.

I felt overwhelmed, and I was collapsed on the couch of the group home, feeling suicidal again. The staff called a Car 87 (an unmarked car with a plain-clothes police officer and a mental health worker). They were empathetic and kind, and we talked. They encouraged me to go to hospital, which I agreed to do. At St. Paul's, they took me off Abilify, and kept me for about two weeks.

More suicidal ideation

A few months after that discharge, I was in another depression. I had just seen a movie with a friend. It was about a man with cancer, so I guess that could have triggered thoughts about my own mortality. Afterwards, my friend and I parted ways and I started walking toward the Lions Gate Bridge. To jump. I called my mom, and she lived about 45 minutes away at the time. I was crying, and I said, "I'm heading to the bridge." She knew exactly what I meant and said, "Rather go to the SkyTrain Station; I'll come straight there and pick you up." She raced into town by car to fetch me.

Update since then

Since mid-2011, I've been more-or-less stable—no further hospitalizations, thank goodness. With luck, the seventh will be my final hospitalization! I never tinker with my meds or dosages: changes are only made in consultation with my care provider.

In 2011, I started Peer Support Worker training, and am still actively involved with peer support and advocacy work. In 2012, I was discharged from EPI and referred to a mental health team in the community. I continued my college studies, and in 2015 started a Bachelor of Social Work, doing a maximum of three courses at a time. I graduated in November 2019. Also in 2019, I got a part-time job as a Consumer Initiatives Support Worker. Right now, I'm in the first year of a Master's in Social Work program, studying part-time, by distance education.

Since initially moving out of my mom's home, I have experimented with several different living situations. After the group home, I've lived with roommates, alone in a studio apartment, in BC housing, and in 2019, I moved into a house with my brother and his partner, who are away most of the time.

All-in-all, I live a full, meaningful, and interesting life, and I have goals I believe I'll be able to fulfill while I keep my bipolar under control.

After the COVID-19 pandemic, I'd like to get back into teaching spin classes (I became a spin or indoor cycling instructor in 2016), and maybe start teaching other forms of group fitness. I also want to travel to different parts of the world and attend conferences related to mental health.

Insights for people with bipolar

Somewhere in your research online, you're bound to come across references to the "anti-psychiatry movement" which opposes the conventional medical model. They don't believe in "mental illness" or the need for people to be "fixed" by taking meds. They ask: "If we pathologize certain behaviours, why not all behaviours?" This approach can be helpful for some people, but I think it can also be harmful. I say: do whatever works for you. Find a baseline where you can function and have meaningful relationships and find a community where you feel respected and accepted. I don't think there's only one way to live.

You decide whether to take meds or not take them, engage in therapy or not, change your lifestyle to accommodate bipolar or not… It's your choice. But you must think about what kind of life you want to live, and whether your illness gets in the way of that or not, and what you can do to manage your bipolar so you can live the life you want.

Like many, I am curious to see what would happen if I were to go off my meds, but I'm not willing to risk it. I've finally found a regimen that works for me, and I would hate to lose the stability I now have.

I personally am more middle-of-the-road: I favour a biopsychosocial model using a combination of meds, therapy, family and community support, together with lifestyle adjustments including exercise, nutrition, sleep, relaxation, and so on. Spiritually, I'm agnostic, but open-minded. Philosophically, I'm intrigued by existentialism, and there is a lot more I look forward to exploring over the course of my life.

Suggestions for family members

To family members, I'd caution: Don't value your affected loved one's compliance with a treatment program over your relationship with them. Instead of focusing on the "problem to be fixed," remember there's a real person in there, needing your love, support, and attention.

Work together on a safety plan, directed by the affected person when they are well. Give them as much autonomy and decision-making power as possible. This is *their* life, after all.

Encourage them to talk to their mental health professionals about issues they've shared with you as family members. Professionals need to know what's truly going on in the person's life (symptoms, side effects, medication non-compliance, drug or alcohol use, suicidal thoughts, and so on) if they're to treat the disorder effectively.

Suggestions for health professionals

Know that your clients may feel very isolated and will need social interaction. So, you need to be familiar with local resource centres and community support networks. Peer support resources can be a lifesaver.

> *I got involved in peer support work before discovering the study of social work. I've met my closest friends through support groups and hospital stays. Most have been inpatients in psychiatric wards. The shared lived experience bonds us together. Because I don't use substances anymore, I've surrounded myself with people who also don't use substances—or at least not very many, and not around me.*

Looking back, I can honestly say the only time I felt stigmatized or that my voice didn't matter was in the psych ward. I empathize that it could be because the nurses are tired and don't want to deal with people who have alternative views of what constitutes reality. I imagine that could be quite exhausting, day in and day out. It was horrible to be treated that way, though. There seems to be quite an "us-versus-them" attitude on inpatient wards, and I'd like to see that change. Nobody deserves to be treated like that, no matter how little sense their words seem to make. In the group home and in various services provided in the community, on the other hand, the staff made me feel very much seen, heard, and respected.

Conclusion

Bipolar is a spectrum disorder, and different people have so many different experiences with it. For example, I have friends with bipolar who can work full-time, just push through, and can "pass" for people without a mental illness. Others are very much affected by it—as I was in the early years.

It's a day-by-day process. It can take quite some time to find a new baseline, and it's crucial to learn what helps you feel good—especially if you've been feeling not good, or too happy, or too sad for a long time.

While bipolar might totally disrupt your life goals, you'll probably be changed by the experience, and it's entirely up to *you* how you react to that change.

Only you can determine that.

Tracy Windsor

I was born in Sydney, Nova Scotia, in 1988. After moving to British Columbia (BC) in 2006, I received a Bachelor of Social Work at the University of British Columbia and am doing a Master's in Social Work at Dalhousie University. I live in Squamish, BC, work part-time at Sea to Sky Mental Health & Substance Use Services with Vancouver Coastal Health, am President of the Kaleidoscope Mental Health Support Society, and teach Standard Mental Health First Aid. At age 19, I was diagnosed with bipolar I with psychotic features. I enjoy studying peer support and mental health, walking my dog, and playing Scrabble.

First Anxiety and Depression, Now Bipolar

Minji Kim*

** Editor's note: This is a pen name.*

I am using an alias for this piece, as I don't want to be identified as someone living with bipolar disorder. I am a doctoral student in a counselling psychology program in the US. I was born and raised in South Korea and moved to the US when I was 12 for better educational opportunities.

Anxiety and depression

I don't even know where to begin with my story. I was always an anxious child from as far back as I can remember. Perhaps it's genetics. (None of my close and extended family members are officially diagnosed with a mental illness but there are a few of my extended family members on my paternal side whom I suspect have bipolar disorder. Their moods vacillate and they make poor choices about finances and in other areas of their lives.)

I have always worried to the extreme over things that do not warrant anxiety. I have perfectionistic tendencies and am compulsive about achieving excellence. I've always gone above and beyond: I was raised always to try my best to succeed. This attitude and some neurological imbalance in the brain put me into a depressive spiral that was paralyzing.

I was first diagnosed with major depressive disorder at age 16, but really, depression has always been a part of me. It ebbed and flowed throughout my life. I was depressed and anxious about my academics and was eventually put on an SSRI antidepressant shortly after my diagnosis of major depressive disorder to manage my mood in conjunction with weekly therapy. The psychiatric nurse who I saw at the time was an immense help in overcoming my issues. I don't remember exactly but I think I was on the SSRI for a little over a year. It seemed to help treat my depressive mood. I think it was the combination of both the SSRI treatment and therapy.

I became interested in psychology and the helping professions around this time when I was in counselling in high school.

My second episode of depression set in shortly after my master's program. I studied for a master's degree in Counselling, to become a therapist. After I got my degree, I was unsure of my future career path and despondent about how grim my future seemed. To manage my depression, I was once again treated with an SSRI, which improved my mood slightly.

Various stressors leading up to bipolar

It seemed like everything was going well. I was employed after I graduated with my master's degree and worked as a mental health therapist and subsequently transitioned into being a drug and alcohol counsellor at another agency. Then my dream came true: I was accepted into a PhD program in Counselling Psychology. I'd wanted to become a psychologist since high school, as my own experience in therapy was invaluable to me back then. So I uprooted my life and moved to the Midwest, where it was less culturally diverse and predominantly white. This move appears to have been a risk factor for the onset of my bipolar disorder. I spent the first two years very productively, plowing through all the requirements of my training. I had an overload of coursework plus 20 hours a week of clinical work all while preparing for my dissertation proposal. Looking back, I don't know who that person was. And I do not think I could repeat what I did back then after getting the diagnosis of bipolar disorder.

It was the summer of 2019 when the ball dropped. I'd just come back to the Midwest to continue my training after being back home for a visit. My parents still live in Korea so I don't get to see them as often as I would like to. But it was a challenging visit. There was a lot of discord at home at the time. I guess that also had an impact on the onset of bipolar as well. My brother was trying to get married to this girl who he had just met a couple months before so he could get a green card that would allow him to stay in the US. I was baffled and helpless in the situation because he had disclosed this information in confidence, so I was not able to tell my parents or get any assistance from others. However, I decided to intervene by paying his tuition so he would not go through with this marriage. Another stressor I assume had an impact on me was the Comprehensive Exams I had to take to proceed with my degree. This is when I started to lose sleep due to anxiety and worries surrounding exams, compounded by other life stressors at the time. With all this going on, I also had to start preparing applications for a pre-doctoral internship, which is a partial fulfillment of the degree. I was stretched thin. It's astonishing I did not see how burned out I was. I was kind of thriving in a stressful situation, I guess. Yes, it was challenging and hard, but I saw it as rewarding and motivating as well.

Until I was hospitalized …

First mania and hospitalization

I don't remember much detail about my first manic episode, as it was severe enough that I had to be hospitalized twice. With everything going on, I was stressed out to the max and at one point I became delirious and delusional. I don't exactly remember the rationale and logic for calling one of my friends, but I called him very confused and distressed. I was bawling and not making any sense. He helped me get myself together and drove me to the hospital. At the time, I was resentful toward him for hospitalizing me: I felt I just needed someone to talk to. But looking back, I was totally psychotic. I was paranoid and delusional that people were after me and surveying me. I felt I was being watched in secret, like through a nanny cam, by my doctoral program directors.

Because I thought I was being secretly observed, I acted so I would be seen in a positive light. I acted extremely socially competent and friendly with other patients. I befriended many patients and engaged with them very closely, which was totally out of character for me. Also, the psychiatrist told me that I became flirtatious with one of the patients, which I still deny to this day. Until half-way through my hospitalization, I didn't know what was going on. One day, I asked my psychiatrist what my diagnosis was, and she said: "You have bipolar disorder." I was in complete denial. I thought this diagnosis was assigned to me by the doctoral program director, as I was still convinced that they were watching me. I thought the whole process of being hospitalized was part of the Comprehensive Exam and that I had to meet certain standards to pass. Upon discharge, I went back to school, and because I lacked insight, I stopped taking the medication they had prescribed. Why would I need medication if this diagnosis is fabricated? In retrospect, the manic episode was inexorably worsening and waiting for its apex.

After discharge, more mania

My delusions became more severe after I was discharged from hospital, as I was not taking my medication as prescribed. I was still in denial and convinced that I did not have any mental health issues. I wish I had more insight into bipolar so I could have gotten the treatment I needed and avoided all the things I did.

I became more paranoid and delusional: everyone was against me, and I believed I was being persecuted. I became extremely wary about my surroundings, and I avoided being seen in public. For example, I wore sunglasses and used a sun visor in the car to avoid traffic cameras, as I believed the police were after me. I purchased a luxury car I couldn't afford, believing that it would protect me from being exposed, which makes absolutely no sense now. At one point, I was sleeping in the car, as I was convinced there was an intruder who came into my apartment while I was getting what little sleep I did get at the time. I was severely manic. Of course, my academics were set aside, neglected. But this was not yet the peak of my mania …

One night, I decided to de-clutter and clean my apartment. I couldn't stand how disorganized and uncared for my apartment was. My decision to clean the apartment was also influenced by this delusion that one of my friends—who is immaculate and clean—was judging me for how cluttered and disorganized I was. The cleaning spree started in the early evening, in the bathroom. I scrubbed the bath and organized the vanity, including all the manicure tools and cleaning brushes. Next, I started to clean the kitchen, vacuuming and scrubbing the floor. I don't remember exactly when and how I lost my temper and my mind. I just remember I got overwhelmingly frustrated during the process of cleaning and started to throw my belongings out of the apartment. I was on a rampage and completely trashed the place. All the while, as I was incessantly throwing things and destroying my property, I repeatedly yelled, "Call the police; call the police!" One of the neighbours called the police and I was arrested. I was facing a felony charge.

After my rampage, my mother came from South Korea to fetch me so I could get the treatment I needed. I took a leave of absence for a year and went back to South Korea with her. Back home, I was just resting and dealing with the stress that had accumulated over the last year or so.

Second hospitalization and recovery

My manic symptoms were still unmanageable and caused another hospitalization. For most of the time, I had no insight into my disorder. However, as my mood became stabilized, I became more cognizant of what had occurred, and my insight increased. I became filled with shame and regret about what I had done and the pain I had caused my loved ones.

This second inpatient experience was a long haul: a little over a month. Throughout the hospitalization, I was on a cocktail of medications that I don't really recall, as they were changing them constantly. Also, mania-induced amnesia did not really help me remember details. I believe I was on high doses of Depakote and Abilify.

Looking back, however, I can compare my experiences as an inpatient at a psychiatric hospital in South Korea and in the US. Overall, the US hospital staff had a better understanding of what group therapy is and were more systematic about it. Group therapies there were run by counsellors or counsellors-in-training, and I felt comfortable engaging and sharing with the group. Things were different at the hospital in South Korea. Endless "group therapy" sessions were somewhat forced and slipshod: I didn't see the point of them and actually found them unhelpful. The staff there just slapped the label "therapy" on basic activities that did not have a therapeutic effect on anyone—well, at least not on me and several patients I was acquainted with. It just felt like a way for us to pass time in activities that the nurses or psychiatry interns threw together at the last minute.

In addition to the group therapy in the US, there were other activities for patients to participate in. For example, I used to love occupational therapy sessions, where we were encouraged to colour or make knick-knacks with beads, and so on. It kept me busy and gave me a sense of accomplishment during that period of confinement. There was no occupational therapy in South Korea. For much of my time in hospital there, I just sat staring numbly at the wall. I was so thankful when I was finally discharged.

Upon discharge, I was home, in recovery for about seven months. Although I was excited initially, and pleased to be out of hospital, I found this time to be very boring and unproductive. I spent most of my days reading—which I do not enjoy—and watching TV. Toward the end of the recovery period, I started playing golf, which I found somewhat interesting.

Picking up the pieces

After a year's leave of absence and taking my prescribed meds religiously, I came back to the PhD program. I'm concerned that my cognition is not the same as it used to be. For example, it is a struggle for me to read and to concentrate on schoolwork. I'm not functioning at the same level as I used to anymore. I feel cloudy and lack critical thinking skills, which are imperative in graduate school. But I'm trying to stay hopeful that my cognitive abilities will return as I continue with my recovery.

One day at a time toward recovery, despite my awful nightmare caused by bipolar …

I was born in South Korea in the 1990s and moved to the US at age 12. I have a bachelor's degree from an East Coast university, a Master's in Counselling from a university in Pennsylvania, PA., and am currently working on my PhD in Counselling Psychology in the Midwest. I was diagnosed with bipolar disorder in my late twenties, having suffered from anxiety and depression since childhood. Prior to the onset of bipolar disorder, I enjoyed cooking, running, and socializing. I am in the process of recovery while working on my doctoral program. I hope to become a hospital-based psychologist doing testing and therapy to help patients with psychological issues.

My Kids Saved My Life

Stephanie Marie

My sons mean everything to me; I'd take on the world for them. I know this because I have. This is our story.

I am a mom of two young children, and I have bipolar II. My sons are now nearly seven and five years old, but when I was first diagnosed, they were only about two-and-a-half years and six months. Trying to capture memories from that time is like trying to grasp water, so I've confirmed a timeline and factual details of my story with my husband and my then-psychotherapist to be as accurate as possible. How I *felt*, though, that I remember vividly.

I had my second son in Jupiter, Florida on December 17, 2015. My husband Darren and I are Canadians and when we got the opportunity to live in the USA on a work visa for a few years, we jumped at the idea of warm weather, swimming, and palm trees. I was about three months pregnant when Darren accepted the job. We already had a toddler named Van and a quirky English bulldog named Mac Daddy. We sold our newly purchased home mere blocks away from family in Canada and stayed in hotels and Airbnb rentals for a few months while we waited for Darren's work visa before we could begin our southern adventure.

One of my fondest memories of my pregnancy with my second son was Halloween 2015. I was quite heavily pregnant; due in January 2016. It was a hot October and sweat dripped down my back as we trick-or-treated through our new Floridian neighbourhood. I was hot, swollen, and happier than I'd ever been.

Gunnar's birth, complications, and impact on me

Fast forward about six weeks and I got a call from my doctor that my amniotic fluid was dangerously low, and I'd have to deliver my son ASAP, three weeks early. Without family, with a brand-new nanny I'd recently vetted watching Van and Mac the dog, and with Darren by my side, I gave birth to our beautiful 5-pound, 9-ounce son Gunnar Clarke. I found a definition of Gunnar that meant "bold warrior," and he is very much that. He had laryngomalacia—an underdeveloped larynx—and we found this out when we brought him to the ER at barely two months old to have a doctor assess his lingering jaundice. In the ER waiting room, he choked on formula in a bottle with a fast flow nipple and went dark blue. He'd stopped breathing. I screamed wildly, nurses and doctors ran out to grab him, rushed him behind closed doors, resuscitated him, and sent us to St. Mary's hospital in West Palm Beach, which was better equipped to care for an infant with his condition.

We stayed at the pediatric ICU for five tedious days, during which he stopped breathing a few more times. I didn't leave his side or sleep nearly the entire time. At one point, I saw a figure at Gunnar's bedside and believed it was my deceased uncle watching over him. I was incredibly depressed, anxious, and felt like a failure of a mother for not knowing he had this condition sooner. I was lost, and deep down I knew it was about even more than my son being unwell.

Gunnar was soon released to a general floor and then home, thank God, and a couple of months passed with us feeding him in tiny doses and upright, constantly rocking him sitting up. I got next to no sleep as I watched him breathe every night on the monitor they sent home with him; we'd hook him up to it with electrode pads across his torso and the machine set off a sound similar to a smoke alarm if the pads slipped off as he slept. Thankfully, his laryngomalacia resolved as he grew out of it, and he never again stopped breathing like the times he had in the hospital.

I know how fortunate we were for him to be well, and to be able to hire a nanny who looked out for all of us during this time; her name is Toni, but we called her Titi. She would drop in like an angel during many weekdays and let me go lie down alone and sleep for hours without ever asking questions or making me feel inadequate. I was so low and so sleep deprived I could hardly get myself out of the bed in the mornings and it was a sweet release when I had the freedom to wallow in my depression alone in my room. The times I didn't have Titi there, I'd slog through the minutes trying to extract joy from my time with Gunnar; his drooly little smiles got me through the more difficult moments, hours, and days. (We had signed Van up for daycare because I simply couldn't manage two kids at home at the time.)

After a complete breakdown in front of Darren during which I admitted I was having suicidal thoughts and was consumed with how worthless I felt and what a failure of a mother I thought I was, he begged me to talk to a therapist. He was convinced I had postpartum depression and said he couldn't continue carrying the full weight of our family on his back. I understood, so I complied. I did it for him and I did it for my kids. I didn't see much value in it for myself at the time. I'd done brief stints with other therapists throughout my life, but none had matched me until Holly, the psychotherapist I saw in Palm Beach Gardens.

First hypomania and diagnosis

It was during the first couple of months with Holly that I experienced my first clinically observed hypomanic episode. I swung from being in an all-consuming depression to having more energy and creativity than I knew what to do with. I started boxing classes, a new nutrition program, often worked out twice daily, started writing a novel, and I invented baby products—four in one week in my heyday. I spent hundreds and hundreds of dollars at craft stores (I'd previously hardly stepped foot in one, never having been crafty) and at Home Depot trying to make my mental creations come to fruition. I even had a welder develop one of my products. I remember the day I went to meet him at his warehouse to talk shop decked out in short shorts, a tiny tank top, and fire-engine red lipstick. I wanted—no, I needed—to be noticed. I didn't know the meaning of hypersexuality back then. I sure do now.

In hindsight and with the knowledge I have today, I can see that our big move from Canada and giving birth to Gunnar and all the dramatic events surrounding his health struggles triggered mood swings from a pre-existing bipolar disorder. Today, through much therapy and introspection, I can cautiously identify other depressions, mixed episodes, and hypomanias that I'd experienced in my twenties and early thirties. (I was 34 when I was diagnosed with bipolar.) I didn't have the understanding or language to know what they were before I was eventually diagnosed.

My diagnosis of rapid cycling bipolar II was an awakening—it was the key that unlocked revelations about who I was and why I'd done some of the things I'd done in my past—but I was also deeply ashamed by the label at first. My maternal grandfather had been diagnosed with bipolar late in life, in his seventies; he experienced depression, mania, and psychosis, but as a family we tucked that away and barely talked about it. My Grampie, a phenomenal man, coped the best he could throughout most of his life, struggling with a mental illness he didn't have a name for, let alone effective treatment.

I had one major advantage over my Grampie: I had been given a name for my disorder. To me, this meant hope. During the period when I was diagnosed, I dipped from my hypomania back into a depression; these moods flip-flopped for several months before I agreed to try medication. I had a stigma in my own mind about it. I thought if I was strong-willed enough, meditated, worked out, and ate healthy I could manage this thing called bipolar on my own. I was wrong; for me, these were only parts of the total equation. I tried one medication only to get a rash so was quickly pulled off it. Then my doctor found a cocktail that has worked for me ever since, as long as I take my medication religiously. But that's an ongoing uphill mental battle in itself.

Despite the learning and personal growth I've experienced to date, a part of me is still in denial that I need medication. I don't know if this critical internal voice will ever be completely silenced. I've gone through prolonged periods of stability, sometimes thanks to being consistent with my meds. Ironically, these periods of stability lead me to question once again if I do in fact need the medication. There's an almost constant internal battle going on between the rational part of me that knows I benefit from meds, and the idealistic part of me that wishes I didn't require them. Because, of course, I wish I didn't have bipolar disorder. Coming to terms with having bipolar is something I may always struggle with.

Mixed episode

In November 2019 after being off my medication for nearly five months, I experienced one of the worst mixed episodes I've ever had. I was intensely agitated yet depressed and felt an almost uncontrollable compulsion to just RUN AWAY. Having since returned home to Canada, I fled solo back down to Palm Beach Gardens, got a hotel room, and was tortured with thoughts of worthlessness as a mother (a common lie my brain tells me during difficult episodes), self- loathing, and ultimately self-harm.

I recall sitting on my hotel bed journaling as tears flowed: "I'm failing my kids. There are two paths I can take at this point. I could end it, relieving them of the burden of trying to please me. But in doing so, I'd then be handing them the burden of wondering for a lifetime if they weren't enough for me to try. Or I can wake up every single day and work to be better… I just can't stand the thought of damaging these perfect boys."

As the words spilled out of me, I made a conscious decision: I was going to fight to be better; I was going to war for my mental health. I was *not* going to give up. I saw my Floridian psychiatrist and psychotherapist. I spoke to my mom and was fortunate to have her and my aunt drive up a couple hours from their winter homes in Naples to be with me. We spent time going for lunches and dinners, and I had introspective heart-to-hearts with both my mom and aunt separately, who listened patiently. I'll never be able to thank them enough for that time spent together; I needed the quiet, non-judgemental support they lent more than they knew.

Conclusion

The driving force behind my search for wellness has always been, and will always be, my love for my two wild, rambunctious, sweet boys. And the biggest factor in my ongoing quest to come to terms with bipolar has been education and proactively seeking answers to questions. I also know that I've been beyond fortunate to have privileges like being able to hire Titi and afford daycare for Van; these variables were lifelines for our family during my diagnosis. My mental health has also blossomed thanks to my husband who has tirelessly sought answers, as well as my being part of an extended family that constantly researches and supports me unconditionally. Not everyone has these relationships or privileges and I'm hyper-aware of this.

I tell my story here for a few reasons. One is because I wouldn't wish for anyone to be diagnosed and live with bipolar in a bubble of isolation. If I can provide even a single person a story in which they find commonalities so they can know they're not alone in their struggles, I'll do it. Another hope is to help normalize the conversations we need to have around bipolar so that one day the stigma will no longer exist. I believe stigma persists is in large part due to fear of the unknown. And finally, I tell my story to continue my own personal healing process: every time I tell it, I peel back another layer of revelations.

I'm making the best of this messy, medicated, perfectly imperfect life I've got. I'm a mom with bipolar disorder, and my boys have quite literally saved my life.

Stephanie Marie

I was born in Guelph, Ontario, Canada in 1982. I attended Carleton University in Ottawa and graduated with a Bachelor of Arts Honours degree, majoring in English. I was diagnosed with bipolar II in 2016. I am currently a freelance copywriter living with my family in Cambridge, Ontario. In my spare time, I enjoy tennis, singing, and playing guitar. I also host a podcast available on Apple Podcasts and Spotify called *Cutting Through Chaos*, in which I interview guests with bipolar disorder, hoping to help normalize important conversations about the disorder. CuttingThroughChaosPodcast.com

When Motherhood and Bipolar Disorder Collide

Tara Mandarano

"Come in the pool with me, Mama!"

I glance at my three-year-old-daughter smiling and splashing in the water. She looks tiny in the large inflatable pool my husband and I bought this summer, once we realized she had outgrown her small plastic kiddie one.

"Please, Mama! Play with me!"

Her big blue eyes, overwhelming cuteness, and invitation to bond are impossible to ignore.

"Okay, I'm coming in!"

She squeals in delight and watches me approach.

The grass is hot, and the sun is strong. A refreshing dip with my daughter is exactly what I need.

The tank top I'm wearing is sticking to me from the blanket of humidity in the air. My sweat has also seeped into my shorts, and suddenly I long to be free of them.

Without any hesitation, I pull my top off over my head and throw it on the patio chair. Next, I shimmy out of my shorts.

There, that's better, I think, already striding toward my daughter.

As I swing one leg over the side of the pool, I catch my husband looking at me out of the corner of his eye. He looks mildly surprised, but I refuse to let him spoil my fun.

The water is shockingly cool, yet exhilarating, and I eventually lower myself all the way down.

"Here's a boat for you, Mama," my girl says, and I take it, chasing hers around the water and laughing when we crash.

It feels wonderful as a mother to be making good memories with her. To be present. To be the fun one, for a change. I revel in it, because so often I am not up to parenting her the way she deserves.

As we find other toys and take turns splashing each other, it doesn't occur to me that I would never normally sit in a pool in my backyard—where any neighbour could look out their window and clearly see me—in my black bra and underwear. This stripping down is wildly out of character for me. I'm not usually so free of inhibition. Normally, I feel self-conscious about my body, and I'm a dedicated follower of social conventions.

Later that night, I will realize that hypomania has raised its euphoric head again. In this state of bipolar disorder, I feel giddy and abnormally upbeat. My self-confidence is exaggerated, and my judgment and decision-making skills are impaired.

But I don't care about any repercussions when I feel an emotional high coming on. I crave it, I welcome it, and I never want it to end. It gives me more energy to play with my daughter, and for that benefit alone, it seems worth it.

I was diagnosed with bipolar II in my early forties. It came as a total shock. It was difficult to process, since I had already been living with a few different mental illnesses by then: anxiety, depression, and premenstrual dysphoric disorder (PMDD), a more severe form of premenstrual syndrome (PMS). But bipolar was something else; something altogether more serious sounding. And I really didn't need another psychiatric diagnosis stamped into my mental passport.

My psychiatrist prescribed Prozac to see if it would be more effective than Zoloft for my blues and worries, as I was still experiencing severe mood swings and anxiety. We had tried increasing the Zoloft dosage, but it resulted in me sweating profusely and experiencing hypoglycemia on a regular basis, so I couldn't tolerate it.

I only lasted about a week on Prozac; my brain and body found it too activating. I learned after the fact that it was meant to work differently in that way. It made me feel even more anxious, on edge, and restless—totally the wrong fit for me. It also made me angry that I had to learn the hard way that this medication was the *opposite* of what I needed to get through my days psychologically intact.

Eventually I resumed taking the Zoloft, but the short trial on Prozac seemed to have flipped a switch in my brain. Soon I started to notice episodes where I would feel unusually happy and high-spirited for a few days in a row—sometimes a week. My blood seemed to be racing in my veins. My thoughts came tumbling and swirling, and ideas for poems and essays filled my mind to overflowing. Often, they would keep me up at night and I would furiously type them into my phone, afraid I would forget them come morning. The fewer hours of sleep didn't bother me at the time.

As a writer, I felt a huge boost to my creativity. I also became more social, an extroverted version of myself, speaking to strangers, video-calling friends and family members at odd hours. I had an abundance of positive energy that I had to get out, and I began to talk faster, more animatedly, and for way longer periods than usual. By nature, I am an introvert, but I didn't think too much about it.

After living with lows for the past couple of weeks, this episode of hypomania was exhilarating.

At the time, it just felt *so good*. Like a high.

I never wanted it to end.

But of course, it would.

And then I would crash.

Hard.

My daughter is innocently dragging a toy car along the walls of our living room, over and over. It sounds like nails on a chalkboard to me, and I feel my stress level about to spike. Each time she passes me, my irritability rises up like hot-red lava, threatening to explode.

She is not deliberately trying to annoy me, but the effect on my shattered nerves and depressed mood is just the same. I take a deep breath and try to ignore it, but I can't take it. I have no interest in playing with her or distracting her into doing another activity with me. All I want to do is escape to my bedroom and be alone with my gloom.

Once there, I feel sad and empty, like I have nothing to give my daughter. I can't resist the pull of sleep. I lie down, pull the covers over my head, and quietly sob. I don't want her to see or hear me when I am in this state, when I feel so hopeless—both as a person and a mother.

The guilt is suffocating. I'm failing at my most important job in the world.

This disheartening scenario comes with the territory when you're a mother with bipolar disorder. One minute I am extraordinarily wired and twirling my daughter around the kitchen as we enjoy a spontaneous dance party. Or I'm suggesting we build a fort in the basement, speaking in a Southern accent, giggling, and wildly waving a flashlight in the dark.

But these pleasant, lovely interludes in my parenting journey never last.

Because the next minute, it's as if my mind just flickers and then goes black.

The fact that bipolar disorder affects everything—including my mothering—breaks my heart. Whenever I envisioned having a child, I never dreamt there would be hours or even days where I wouldn't feel up to looking after her. I never imagined the unpredictable ups and downs I would constantly have to navigate, with a little girl watching me with anxious, observant eyes.

I don't want my emotional instability to disrupt her life, so that is why I'm committed to regularly speaking with my psychiatrist and taking my prescribed medications. I also keep track of my moods and reach out for help when I need it. If I feel myself starting to crash or become melancholic, I contact family members to help me out. Sometimes that means arranging playdates where my daughter can spend time with her cousins, and I can focus on self-care until I feel a bit better.

Being a mother with a mental illness is extremely challenging, but when you add a marital separation into the mix, the situation instantly becomes much more complicated. (How much my mental illness contributed to my separation is something I ruminate about, but it's not healthy for me to obsess about it. I'm sure it played a part in the disintegration of my marriage, but I know there were several other factors at play, too.)

As a newly single mother, I am now learning how to handle solo parenting on the days my daughter stays with me (which is half the week). It's never been more important for me to reach out to my village and seek out their support when I need it. My co-parent and I also speak honestly and openly with each other about how I'm doing emotionally. Being on good terms with him makes being a single mother with bipolar disorder much more manageable.

Now that I'm a single parent, there is so much more pressure on me than before.

Clashes with my daughter regularly wear me down emotionally, and I must force myself to push through these parenting struggles. For example, when she refuses to eat any of her dinner and insists on chips instead. Or when I try to brush her hair and she runs in the opposite direction.

This is when I have to pull myself out of a puddle of self-doubt and self-blame about my mothering role. Every time my daughter runs through the door to greet me or asks me to build Lego or play with her dolls, I might not be feeling my best psychologically. My mood stabilizer and antidepressant keep the worst of my mood swings in check, and professional help also keeps me calm. But no medication is perfect. And kids notice everything.

As a parent who's also lived with chronic pain, I've done my time being bed-bound. Dealing with bipolar disorder has made me determined to help myself as much as possible, and it's also made me a stronger mother. I've had to reach down deep to find my core inner strength and trust myself to do the best I can.

Instead of avoiding all the potential emotional landmines that accompany mothering a strong-willed seven-year-old, I feel better equipped to deal with the inevitable parenting storms that come my way.

I can't afford to be out of the parenting picture anymore, or on the periphery. I've lost a couple years of my life already due to my physical ailments and mental illness, and I don't intend to mother on the sidelines anymore if I can help it.

Bipolar disorder may affect everything in my life—including my relationship with my daughter—but it doesn't define it.

Tara Mandarano

I was born in Ontario in 1977 and have a degree in journalism from Ryerson University. I'm a Best of the Net-nominated writer and editor, and an advocate for patients in the mental health and chronic illness communities. My work is featured in the anthology *BIG: Stories About Life in Plus-Sized Bodies*. I have also been published in *The Washington Post*, *Huffington Post*, *Motherwell*, and *Today's Parent*, among others. I was diagnosed with bipolar disorder in 2016, and I also struggle with fibromyalgia and endometriosis. I live in Ontario with my young daughter. Follow me on Instagram and Twitter @Tara Mandarano to learn more about my journey.

From Missed Diagnosis to Misdiagnosis to Bipolar Diagnosis

Felicity Vine*

This is a pen name.

Some people fall into madness, others drift into it, still others spring from one degree of sanity—or insanity—to another. The last is the beast I know, the beast that has become my life's work to tame. Part of that life's work and processing has been to write: to write about my journey into and relationship with mental illness, which has been both long and dramatic. This writing is not only for cathartic personal reasons, but also for a wider audience. In this essay, I want to give you a glance into my world and to highlight the problems that emerge when a diagnosis is delayed or missed altogether. I want to add to the voices working to break down taboos surrounding mental illness, with the hope that these voices are heard, understood, and accepted. I also want to share a message of hope with readers that things really do get better.

Beginnings

It's difficult to pinpoint when it started, given that I had a stable, loving, and privileged upbringing. There was the scream, at age 14, the scream that broke through the day and pierced the night, that pieced my heart, broke it, perhaps? Perhaps there were cracks before things had been chiselled away by life's meandering circumstances, but the break began with that scream. As my teenage self was evolving into adulthood, I began to realize that life could not be controlled and contained. This triggered a deep reaction in me, one of grief and panic. It was as if I opened my mouth but could not find words and instead found a sound, a guttural instinctive animal sound, only meant for childbirth, but something else was birthed in that scream: a madness, a descent from sanity, the losing of my mind, the losing of my "self." I did not understand this reaction at that time; there were no words to explain that scream; no frame within which to position that moment.

Life then became a frantic search: a search for self again, a search for meaning, a search for sanity. Could self and identity be found in other people, in reams of boyfriends, in sexual exploration, in the stars, in drink, at parties? The search became a hunger, a desperation, a means of survival. Where was meaning? Where was hope? I was lost, I was falling, I was getting further from my self; every search empty, a void forming in my mind that threatened to engulf me.

There was the cut, at age 16, the sweet surrender of my arm to the blade. A strange sense of calm as scarlet beads bubbled onto my skin. Then instantly the shame, the fear: this isn't the way. But the calm, there was a calm to be found.

There were the tears, at age 17. Tears that opened a floodgate of shame, of desperation, of knowing I was lost, of knowing I had fallen far short of what I'd hoped for my self. My self, where was I? I was trapped between two lives: one life at home where I was loved and held and nurtured, and one life in my mind where I was dangerously pivoting on the edge of sanity, trapped in my own mind, unable to hold myself steady, unable to tether the swirling thoughts inside my head.

My tears drew me to a door that when opened changed my life forever, provided me with an anchor that would hold fast in the storms that would continue to haunt me throughout my adult life. The anchor was the hope for my soul, the understanding of my spirit, the knowledge that no matter what, it is well with my soul. This path of pain has been walked before, tears of blood have been cried before, blood has been shed, skin split open, pain borne, the cross lifted high. My God, my God, what words have I for you? I believe. I believe. And my heart will sing: "Here I am to worship, Here I am to bow down, Here I am to know that you're my God" (Tim Hughes).

And so it began. My journey of faith started and a line in the sand was drawn to separate that which came before from that which was to come. I came to learn that in storms, sand could be blown, that line could be hidden, life could blend into itself, and my mind would forever carry the thorn of the grief of the scream. I learned that my mind would warp and twist and turn and that the anchor would be pulled as the ship of my life tossed in the waves inside my head. And yet the anchor, the anchor remains, hope remains, it is well with my soul, "and all shall be well, all shall be well, and all manner of things shall be well" (Julian of Norwich).

Missed diagnosis, ages 14 to 26

My first doctor's appointment in which my mind exposed a fragment of fear was at age 14. The fear was obsessive in nature: I was certain that I would be raped and bear a child. The timeframe was consistent with the scream, a madness had begun, and I cried out for help. I expected reassurance, hope, a turning around of my mind; not a reinforcement, not food for insanity, not the offer that came. The offer was not for therapy; the cracks of my broken mind had been papered over, rendered invisible. The offer instead was for the contraceptive pill in case my fears came true. And so it was then, at 14 years old, with my broken mind and fears poured out, that I started the contraceptive pill. Not the last medication to be presented as the solution to this fragmented life of mine.

With the option of medical help shut down, I crawled inside my mind to sit it out. Nevertheless, thank goodness for the National Health Service (NHS). Thank goodness I was born into this generation. A generation earlier and I would already be passing through the doors of an asylum, possibly held for years against my will, even subjected to electroconvulsive therapy. Perhaps no therapy was better than that? Perhaps a fight to have my voice heard—the fight that followed—was better than that? For madness can disguise itself when it's not institutionalised. It can pose as "one of us," it can hide in the crowd, it can be curtailed and dressed up and policed by itself, just bursting through in moments of life and dear God, let those moments not be life-damaging.

In the 12 years between that first doctor's appointment and the second, life moved at a pace. University came and went and with it a move across counties; love was found and lost and recognized not to have been love in the first place; relationships were built and forced and controlled; faith was stretched into a submission to people rather than to God; new love was found that lasted and blossomed and produced babies. And in all that time my mind crouched like a ticking time bomb inside itself, making good decisions, making bad decisions, but affecting no one other than me.

It wasn't until I had a family of my own that I needed a second doctor's appointment. After the birth of my first child, the cracks became breaks, and the breaks became dangerous. I was 26, had a one-year-old son and was expecting my second when I finally realized that no marriage would ever be strong enough to contain a breaking wife, and that no friendship could bridge the gap either.

At the time, I had no words to describe what I was experiencing, and only later learned about bipolar mood swings. Looking back, I can clearly see that I was experiencing episodes of mania, periods of depression, and again months of euphoria following my first son's birth.

Undiagnosed hypomania and mania

Hypomania didn't feel like illness—I felt like "Super-mum" at her finest and I'd laugh when others suggested I was burning the candle at both ends; as my husband says, I was unstoppable. It wasn't that I was determined to be a good mother; rather, I was stuck in the grandiosity that I was the best mother. I was driven to do everything with excellence. That became the red flag—my obsessions and resolute mindset. The drive to excel took over like a golden calf. These weren't just good intentions: this was my reality, and nothing could stand in my way. I was convinced that through everything I did, I would change the world.

Hypomania felt good. Fun! It was great to be the life and soul of the party, to be the driving force behind a project, to have dreams and ambitions, to achieve and be creative. It was difficult within that moment to notice that dreams became manipulative, that sleep routines slipped, that contact with reality became fragile.

A creative force can achieve great things, but there was a subtle shift from hypomania into mania and I lost sight of the hearts that were on that journey with me; lost all sense of their humanity and personality and fragility. I look back and cringe, not at what I achieved, but at how I achieved it and how my grandiose ideas undermined those around me. I know now that what we need in our bipolar lives is something to hold us down, someone to provide a reality check, someone to be an embodiment of the anchor for our souls.

Hypomania and its progression into mania followed a destructive path. The urge to spend became relentless: for me, that urge related to the urge to buy a better life; to escape from what I had. I lost all appreciation for my home, my husband, my family. It all felt urgent: what I had to say; what I chose to buy; what I wanted to achieve. A dream turned into an idea, which turned into action, which turned into hypomania, which turned into mania.

The mind can unravel in an upwards spiral. Like a kite without strings, we can quickly lose control and the fun of freedom can be transformed into a dangerous fear that hurts not only ourselves but those around us. There is, of course, a glass ceiling and what goes up must come down, and inevitably for the bipolar life it comes down with a crash. The bubble bursts.

And after the crash, what then?

After the crash there's an aching pain, a debilitating grief, a deep shame, an empty depression. That which was busy and fun and vibrant is stripped away in one fell swoop.

Undiagnosed bipolar depression

Where mania is expansive and vast in scale, depression renders everything withered and bleak. Where hypomania is resolutely focused on achieving and creating, depression loses all focus and eyes wander to the ground.

When depressed, the world around me seemed noisy. Stress levels spiked beyond control, and this caused me to despise myself. Sometimes it seemed everything was shouting at me, squashing me into a tiny hole, and making my voice so meaningless that I was just ignored. Or perhaps I was ignoring myself? I wished that my world would shrink, and I could curl up in the womb. My body huddled into a fetal position. I dreaded opening the door back into my life. Maybe I could just cease to exist?

I hate my mood swings. Hate them. HATE them. Every time I'm depressed, I feel more depressed than the last time. I'm a victim of my own head and in that moment, I feel this is completely ruining my life and I'm furious that I am who I am. I'm fighting my brain; I'm my own worst enemy. Why, oh why God, do I have this stupid head? I could just bang it against a wall until my brain comes out and all my unspeakable thoughts pour on the ground.

I'm trapped in my mind. Confined to my bed. My terrifying and muddled thoughts circle around in my head endlessly and there's a weight of dread that shrouds me. Tears flow until there are none left, so my heart weeps instead.

After some months of this mental anguish, I went to the doctor—a new doctor—and once again poured out my fragmented self, spewed her up in all her ugliness and struggle, desperate for comfort, desperate for a solution, desperate for this pain to be named and healed, for my unfurling mind to be stitched together again. But to my horror I was told, "You are tired." Tired! I was fobbed off, misunderstood. How could I have made myself clearer? My ten minutes was up. The moment was lost. The pain inside my mind threatened to overtake me and bear down on the fetus I was carrying and impose itself on him.

Misdiagnosis: Postpartum depression

Finally, in the wholesomeness of himself, my second son was born. He was held and cherished and loved but my brain would not release that love; it greedily held onto my maternal hormones as if to punish me. I couldn't connect, couldn't comfort, couldn't put him first. I couldn't put myself first. What even was first? I was unravelling at a speed of knots. Sails flapping in the wind, the storm intensifying, my anchor pulling, pulling, pulling. I received a song as a gift to my soul and I grasped the anchor and held fast: "I need you more, more than yesterday, more than words can say" (Kim Walker-Smith). And once again, I was grateful for the NHS. Within weeks, I was diagnosed: postpartum (post-natal) depression. There were pills and visits and friends and meals and love and acceptance and sleep, and gradually I crawled out of the cave that had carved itself inside my mind and suddenly my son was 11 months old, and my hormones surged, and I loved him, and I was well.

Two more years ticked by during which I declared myself well, but frighteningly fell back into periods of illness, springing from one degree of madness to another with level playing fields in between. It was exhausting. My life was exhausting. My house was exhausting. My head was exhausting. I was exhausted by the exhaustion. And things people said drilled down into my inner core and the scream threatened again: "Well, it *is* exhausting having two young boys," they said. "Motherhood is exhausting." "Life is exhausting." But these platitudes didn't sit true. I was misunderstood. I was unhinged.

But once again, thank goodness for the NHS. At my second son's 2–3-year health check, a professional finally asked, "And how are you?". I talked about the pills I was taking for my post-natal depression, the highs and lows inside my brain, my fears, my hopes, and my lost sense of self. "That's an awfully long time for post-natal depression to last," she said, encouraging me to visit a different doctor.

And finally, 16 years after the incident with the contraceptive pill, I was listened to. Finally, my voice was heard. Finally, I shared about the exhausting highs followed by debilitating lows, the pain of years trapped inside my head, the inability to express myself, my late grandfather's diagnosis of manic depression, the struggle to keep my life in balance for my two pre-schoolers. I shed tears of relief, of having found my voice, of being heard.

Bipolar diagnosis, aged 30

After two meetings with a psychiatrist, my diagnosis was confirmed: bipolar II. Two meetings. But a 16-year fight. And a lifetime ahead. Still a lifetime ahead. It hits me now even as I write this, a further seven years on. A lifetime. A life sentence. But the relief, oh the sweet relief of having been heard, of finally being understood, the jubilation, and the desire to gloat to all who'd said I was just exhausted: "Ha! See? See! Something is wrong; I told you so; your experience is not mine; this goes way beyond exhaustion. How dare you tell me that 'mothering is exhausting'? How dare you be exasperated by this broken mind of mine? How dare you watch my mind unfurl itself and call it 'motherhood'? How dare you?"

And so, I receive the diagnosis, I breathe it in for the sweet relief that it brings, for the explanation, the justification. I receive the treatment of medication and therapy. I eventually settle into a rhythm of taking daily doses of Quetiapine and Aripiprazole, with Diazepam and Zopiclone on hand for emergencies. I attend courses on cognitive behavioural therapy (CBT) and peer support but find that regular appointments with a Christian counsellor work best for me. And I resolve that this will not be my curse, that it will be my life's work to make bipolar my friend and not my enemy, that I will take this news and become the very best version of myself, that I will hold onto the anchor of my soul and know that despite all this, "It is well with my soul" (Horatio Spafford).

Conclusion

I've lived with my bipolar diagnosis for seven years now and it feels both new and old. My moods are generally well-managed through a combination of medication, ongoing counselling, and supportive people, but there are times, at least once a year, when it flares up and emergency medication and strategies are needed. My family has learned to talk and share about my bipolar life and also when they need to step in and when they can step back again. I would say that now I thrive rather than merely survive. I work part-time running my own successful home-based business, and I love looking after my children and engaging in artistic hobbies.

I remember the tough times before I had a proper diagnosis and effective treatment. What I'd like to end with, for the benefit of any readers who are feeling desperate, is a message of hope. Whenever I feel trapped and drowning, I look for a break in the clouds and tell myself: "This is not it; this is not how my life always is. It's just been a storm; a storm that engulfed me, but a storm that will end." Shivering, faint, weak, but with hope, with medication, with therapy, and with support, I cling to the truth that "thus far the Lord has helped us" (1 Samuel 7:12) and I know in that moment of the storm that it will eventually pass.

May you find an anchor in your storm and may it pass soon.

I was born in England in the 1980s. I have various post-graduate degrees and was diagnosed with bipolar II in 2014. Since writing this essay, however, and mere months before this anthology was published, my bipolar diagnosis was removed as it was felt that I no longer meet the criteria for that diagnosis. I am currently weaning off my medication under supervision and will see how I might respond without it. I live in England with my husband and two children and work part-time as a self-employed businesswoman.

Yup, It's an Ongoing Process

Victoria Maxwell

Editor's note: An earlier version of this essay titled "On the Road Again" was published in Visions: BC's Mental Health Journal, *No. 13, Fall/ Winter 2001: 12–13. This piece builds on and updates that article.*

It's 1990. I'm dancing with John Travolta. No, really; on the set of *Look Who's Talking Too*. For those of you who aren't old enough to know who John Travolta is, this is like a really big deal for me. My dream of working as an actor has come true. I have no idea that in two short years I'll be strapped to a gurney fighting bipolar disorder and psychosis with my livelihood disintegrating.

Back in 1988, I graduate from the University of British Columbia's theatre program and begin my acting career. I split my time between cashiering at the Safeway grocery store and acting on local television and film sets. Hollywood North is kind to me. By all accounts, I'm a working actor: movies, commercials, TV shows. I also happen to be spiralling into a dangerously deep "funk." What is it actually? The severe depression side of bipolar disorder and the generalized anxiety disorder I'll eventually be diagnosed with. But I've no clue that this despair, this all-encompassing fear, this soul-damaging fatigue I'm experiencing are part of illnesses, let alone treatable ones. I've nothing to compare it to.

As a kid, I frequently felt "down," on edge and worried. From age 17 onward, I struggled with an eating disorder: compulsive overeating and exercising. The out-of-control bingeing, the food and calorie obsession created a caustic self-loathing. What I didn't realize at the time was that my undiagnosed bipolar depression and anxiety fuelled both my binges and my relentless over-exercising.

Eventually, I start seeing a therapist to uncover the roots of my unhappiness. Perhaps because I "present well" as psychologists say, no one realizes how hopeless I feel. The mask I put on keeps the severity of the depression and anxiety hidden, even in counselling. I talk about it, but still manage to function fairly well—at least in public. At home, weeks of dishes and laundry pile up, messages from friends go unanswered; I easily sleep 10, 12, even 14 hours a day but still wake up unhappy and unrefreshed.

I continue battling mood swings shifting, sometimes in a matter of hours, from numb depression to frustrated tears to giddy euphoria. Until one day in 1992, I become so manic I catapult into a psychosis (literally a break with reality) and land in the hospital. The psych ward to be exact.

I have what ...?

"You have," explains a pale, humourless doctor, "rapid cycling, mixed-state bipolar I with psychotic features, mild temporal lobe epilepsy, generalized anxiety disorder and disordered eating."

Easy for him to say.

At 26 and with four years of therapy under my belt, my dynamic, albeit chaotic life as an actor has now completely gone off the rails. After six weeks in the psych ward, I'm released. But I reject the diagnoses and refuse medication. I deny the illness for another four years and during that time experience innumerable manias and depressions until a final psychosis propels me to run through a genteel neighbourhood naked. Ambulance. Police. The whole shebang. I land in the psych ward once again—this is my fourth time.

I'm barely working now and stand at a crucial crossroads. I can continue living in denial and plummet further into illness, or I can accept the diagnosis and begin to carve out a life. I choose the latter.

Why? Largely two reasons. First, since I started wrestling with this inexplicable emotional pain, I've tried everything to untangle myself from it. EVERY. THING. You name it, I've done it. Prayer, meditation, affirmations, reiki, colour therapy, healing touch, aromatherapy, tarot card readings, and more. But none of it really made a lasting difference. I keep finding myself a regular guest of the psych ward. With gritted teeth, I begin to see that my way is not working.

Second, I'm frightened. Terrified really, that I'll continue spiraling in and out of psychosis and the psych ward, watching any dreams I had for my life dissolve.

Why not accept this label and try the medically accepted treatment options? It can't leave me more suicidal than I already am. So, I capitulate and begin seeing a psychiatrist and taking medication, both on a regular basis.

At this point, I've accumulated a hefty debt and my auditions aren't quite what they used to be—psychosis and depression does that. I live in a rooming house with a two-burner hot plate and a shared bath, and I buy groceries on my credit card. I rarely take shifts at Safeway. My agent doesn't call. Neither do most of my friends. Both my financial and artistic reserves have evaporated.

Career change

I move in with my folks; comply with treatment; quit my Safeway job and apply for disability benefits. And I leave the world of acting to those with a higher tolerance for uncertainty and rejection.

(My psychiatrist doesn't encourage or even suggest I leave acting. I do. I need to. For the sake of my sanity, I need to walk away. Acting is a punishing career regardless of your resiliency. I don't need stardom; I need stability.)

I face an intimidating blank page: what the heck to do with the rest of my life? Dr. Dillon, my "no-nonsense-tell-it-like-it-is" psychiatrist, has the uncanny ability to make the sensible sound tantalizing. His suggested goals? Find a new career, learn to support myself and stay self-sufficient and stable (as much as reasonably possible). Something I can barely imagine.

The very act of undergoing vocational testing helps me recapture some of my former chutzpa. After several weeks, exams are complete. Yes, I've a knack for acting, but also marketing and interior design. I focus on marketing. I haven't worked in over four years and am petrified I won't manage even a four-hour shift. Then I happen upon *Gastown Vocational Services (GVS)*, a pre-employment program for those with mental illness. I investigate: a wait list. A long one. But because I live in North Vancouver, I don't have to wait as long. Something about regional quotas. *GVS* is pivotal in getting me on my employment feet and rebuilding my loss of confidence and sense of self. The three-month program forces me to be punctual and committed. It gives me a schedule, objectives, and purpose. Bipolar disorder, especially depression, has an insidious way of making structure seem pointless and goals unfathomable. But with fellow students—ones who empathize, offer support, and expect to see me—I'm compelled to attend.

The supervised work placements *GVS* coordinates are invaluable, but nerve-racking. My job coach is a godsend. When anxieties reach their typical zenith, he's my bridge to reality. He listens to my panicked cries of "I can't do this" or "what the #*%@ do I do now?" and gently gets me to breathe so we can tackle the problem at hand—if there is one at all. Usually, it's a case of insecurities running wild.

During my work placement at a marketing firm, the owners offer me a full-time position. I don't know whether to jump for joy or jump out a window. But with quiet reassurance from my wise parents, psychiatrist, and job coach, I say "yes." As my time on the clock accrues, so does my self-assurance. I discontinue welfare, settle my debt and about a year later, move out on my own.

Next stage includes being on the stage

But once the acting bug bites, the itch usually stays. I crave—no, need—more creativity in my life. I begin writing about the very illness that put me on this path. Then in a local newspaper I see a call to present at KickstART, a festival dedicated to celebrating the talents of disabled artists. In my application, I explain that I could read some excerpts from my book. I get accepted. But I don't yet have a book! I barely have any excerpts. Holy crap! Regardless, this will mark my initiation back into the arts. I write and write, then rewrite and rewrite some more. I finalize pieces and read excerpts from what will eventually become my first one-woman show, Crazy for Life. It's well received, so much so that I'm invited to other festivals: other parts of Canada, England, even New Zealand.

I might be able to perform this thing in more places than I thought and get paid for it! I stay with the marketing company until I'm sure I can support myself with speaking and performing. I pledge: if I return to the arts, I must be able to maintain not just my emotional health but financial health. It's essential to my sanity—literally. Slowly, slowly I move toward my dream of running my own business.

I begin performing the play as a keynote at conferences, from small local ones to large association ones to in-house corporate events. I offer workshops about the been-there-done-that experience of psych wards, shrinks and hospital gowns; about how to recognize workplace mental health issues and what to do about it.

Through word-of-mouth, requests to speak and lead breakout sessions start to flow. In January 2003, *Crazy for Life Co.* is born. I use a lot of humour in my story to help people feel comfortable talking about the still rather taboo subject of mental illness. My speaking and coaching business took off in large part because of good timing. In the early 2000s, I was one of the first 'Joe/Josephine Averages' to so transparently (and irreverently) share their story. At this time, most peoples' reference point for psychiatric illness came from tragic or sensationalized stories in the news, or experiences told by celebrities who few could relate to. People were hungry to hear something more relatable. My lived experience fit the bill.

I've written two more solo shows: one about returning to work; another about family and stigma. I perform them and my original play across Canada and in the States. I work with managers, health professionals, associations, and companies from all industries, as well as the public to raise awareness and understanding of mental illness and diversity, particularly workplace mental health issues. I teach how to recognize the early signs of mental health issues and how to help someone, whether it be a co-worker, employee or loved one.

Through these performances, keynotes, workshops and online education sessions, people discover what many of us who live with mental illness already knew: mental health issues are treatable, and we are as valuable as any other employee in their company.

The more we dismantle the stigma of mental health, particularly in the workplace, the less people will stay silent and the easier it will be to reach out for support and for others to reach in to help.

Living well with my illnesses

I have a healthy respect for the conditions I live with. I know I'm not cured, but I can live well with my illnesses. The daily choices

I make support my mental health and allow me to live symptom-free much of the time. I still grapple with episodes of depression, hypomania, bouts of severe anxiety and even the occasional psychosis; but they aren't as debilitating as they once were.

Today I take medication (several actually), see my psychiatrist, do psychotherapy, exercise, meditate, get the right amount sleep, and eat well (okay; maybe potato chips and ice-cream doesn't count as "well," but overall, I eat a pretty balanced diet).

And one part of me, that observer within, gently watches for unusual darkness or too much light. Not putting on make-up when I normally would, always wearing track pants, bingeing on bread, butter, and cheddar cheese, buying fistfuls of *Scratch n' Wins* with my credit card. I've memorized these signs. Likely it means something's brewing. So, I change course, try to head it off at the pass. See my psychiatrist, check my meds, have a shower, put on jeans, go for a run, breathe, pray, practice mindfulness, practice self-compassion. The adjustments don't always stop the mood swings, but they do at least lessen their blow.

As I lay strapped to a gurney during one psychosis, just before the jab of a straw-sized needle, I thought: "I've gone crazy." Images of what I believed my life would be like shot through my mind. Those images didn't include recovery, a career, marriage, a welcoming house to call home, or any amount of fulfillment. I wish I'd understood then how many people with bipolar disorder have deeply rewarding lives and enriching relationships. With the encouragement of those around me when I felt like giving up and, yes, hard work on my part, I discovered I could reclaim my joy and sense of self. But it's an ongoing process. I still need support from my husband and friends. And I have to put in effort every day to stay well.

For you, who are reading this right now and are perhaps struggling with bipolar disorder, or for you who are loving someone with bipolar, this is my hope: know that recovery is possible (however you define recovery—whether that's living in a group home, or on your own; whether it's working full-time or volunteering occasionally).

Recovery *is* possible and contentment is within reach.

Victoria Maxwell

I was born in Victoria, British Columbia in 1966. I got a Bachelor of Fine Arts from the University of British Columbia and was diagnosed with bipolar disorder in 1992. I also live with anxiety and psychosis. I am a top speaker in Canada and internationally about the lived experience of mental illness and recovery. I teach people how to effectively speak to someone who might have mental health issues. I'm also a self-proclaimed Wellness Warrior and Bipolar Princess. In 2013, the Mental Health Commission of Canada named my theatrical keynote, *That's Just Crazy Talk,* one of the top anti-stigma interventions in the country. I live with my husband Gordon in British Columbia. VictoriaMaxwell.com

Jailed Body, Imprisoned Mind

Eric Smith

What you are reading here is the most thorough account I have ever provided about my experience as a person with severe mental illness in jail. From this, I hope you will gain a better understanding about the intersection of mental health reform and criminal justice reform, and why this demands urgent attention and change.

Diagnoses and attempts at treatment

I have a long and complicated history with mental illness.

I was about 13 years old when the first psychiatrist I saw suggested to my parents and I that I was possibly "manic bipolar" at the time. At age 15 or 16, I was then seeing a different psychiatrist who suggested I be tested for bipolar disorder, and the tests yielded results suggesting I met the criteria for bipolar disorder. My symptoms included periods of high highs (mania), followed by low lows (depression).

Since then, psychiatrists who saw me at my worst diagnosed me with schizoaffective disorder, and those who did not see me at my worst diagnosed me with bipolar disorder.

My "worst" looks like someone who appears to be awakened from a dream, as my thoughts and words were far from aligned with reality. I recall looking up at the daytime sky and thinking snipers were hovering directly above the clouds, and I sometimes saw and heard shots fired at strangers who were miles away from my physical position. I recall looking up at the nighttime sky and thinking there were aliens in cloaked ships trying to determine if the people of earth would be valuable allies or savage enemies as they observed all the daily conflict around our planet unfold. My "worst" was also permeated with delusions (especially during my psychiatric hospitalizations), as I repeatedly called the FBI, various consulates, and embassies to provide what I sincerely believed to be actionable intelligence about threats against world leaders. During my hospitalizations I was also convinced I was hearing orders directly from the mouths of senior CIA staff but not in the context of hearing voices as can be attributed to a symptom of mental illness. Rather, I believed I was hearing their orders by way of a cranial implant developed by the Defense Advanced Research Projects Agency (DARPA) that allows covert and undetectable communications to exist between clandestine assets and mission leaders. In addition, I believed spies from other countries were looking for a way to kill me that would not be tied back to them and their respective governments. In short, at my "worst" I had textbook psychosis with delusions, hallucinations, and paranoia.

Conversely, when I'm not at my "worst" I tend to have no psychosis, delusions, hallucinations, *or* paranoia. For years leading up to my first psychiatric hospitalization, I had a history of having far too much energy (mania), followed by some deep crashes (depression), but other than the high highs and the low lows there was no psychosis to speak of. As a result, I was initially diagnosed with bipolar disorder. In the years since my last hospitalization, schizoaffective disorder is again not considered a likely diagnosis for me. Psychiatrists now think I have bipolar disorder with psychotic features, although I have had no form of psychosis since the beginning of 2012.

From the late 1990s until 2012, I went through about 15 years of failed medication regimens. I had been prescribed virtually every

Selective Serotonin Reuptake Inhibitor (SSRI), antidepressant, benzodiazepine, antipsychotic, and other types of medications that a person with mental illness is prescribed. The list is extremely long, and none of the meds adequately managed my symptoms. Not only did the medications not work, but they also all ran the gamut of untoward side effects: persistent hunger, rapid weight gain, upset stomach, fatigue and lethargy, insomnia, abnormal dreams, agitation, and so on.

My arrest for criminal trespassing

I was arrested once and only once, on a charge of criminal trespassing.

In the weeks and months leading up to my arrest and subsequent first psychiatric hospitalization, the reality was that a long list of medications had failed to help me, and none of the counsellors or psychiatrists I had seen up to that point could help me make any sort of meaningful progress. This, coupled with the fact that psychosis, delusions, hallucinations, and paranoia were noticeable for the first time in my life was of the greatest concern to my parents at the time. While I had been diagnosed with bipolar disorder for about a decade at this point, I was truly losing the ability to experience and process reality. I started believing that I was working on behalf of the FBI and CIA to gather intelligence that would prevent assassinations of world leaders and the next major world war.

On the advice of one of my former psychiatrists, my parents had me arrested in the hope that it would result in me being transferred from jail to a psychiatric hospital where I would receive the inpatient care I desperately needed. The psychiatrist who made this suggestion was doing so with an expert understanding that this would be my best chance at finding sanity. When my parents told me that they were going to call the police and have me arrested, I was in a delusional state in which I believed I had power over the police, so I said: "Sure, go ahead and call the police!" I then calmly sat on the front porch waiting for law enforcement to arrive.

When the police pulled up, I was still calm. I recall thinking that if I were taken to jail, it would only be because it was part of my mission to be there. In my mind everything I was experiencing and was yet to experience was a product of a clandestine mission plan, and it was my duty as an asset to follow through.

In the holding cells

I was taken to a local police station and stripped of my clothing, watch, and shoes. I stood naked in a holding cell, where an officer searched my naked body for anything dangerous or contraband. After what seemed like 30 minutes, I was then ordered to put my clothing and shoes back on to prepare for transportation to the Bexar County jail.

Another officer arrived to transfer me to the main county jail, and he put me in the back of his patrol car to do so. When I arrived at the jail, I was convinced I would be set free because of some delusion-based power that police would follow my orders if I gave them any. Because I also believed I was an agent of both the FBI and CIA, I was not eager to leave the situation at the time because I had a responsibility to follow through on my mission. At this point, I started to believe I was at this jail for a reason, namely, to gather intelligence about threats to world leaders from inmates in the jail.

After being placed in a temporary holding cell at the county jail, I was taken in for processing by an officer. He ordered me to place my fingers on a scanner to confirm my identity, and so I did. The officer then looked at me and said the person my fingerprints showed in the system was clearly not me: I am Caucasian, was in my mid-20s, and weighed about 180 pounds at the time, but my fingerprints returned a result of a middle-aged male who weighed at least 250 pounds and appeared not to be Caucasian. In short, my fingerprints matched someone else's identity, and the officer let me see the screen he was looking at to confirm that. He said: "This needs to be fixed." Regardless, the fact that my fingerprints produced someone else's identity only fed into my delusions and psychosis. I was even more deeply convinced that my job as a CIA and FBI agent was either to find the person my fingerprints incorrectly matched to get information about my next mission, or to assume the identity of that person as part of my mission. In any event, I believed the Bexar County jail was the right place for me to be as my (not real) clandestine mission unfolded.

Planning my escape

Not long after, I was moved to an area of the jail with holding cells for large numbers of males. I recall approximately five of these holding cells filled with probably 20–25 people each. We were moved from one cell to another after waiting for a while, and I started to feel the onset of impending danger that was not a result of anything specific other than my mind's decompensated state. I felt like I needed to leave the situation, so I planned my escape to take place during the next mass transfer from one waiting area to another when that happened.

During the hubbub of the next transfer, I waited for all the officers to take their eyes off me, and I then started walking closely beside one of the jail's staff who was passing by at that moment to make it appear that I was with them. I got back to the main entrance of the jail but saw several police cars parked directly at the entrance so I knew I couldn't escape at that time. There was a bench right next to that entrance, so I sat there and waited for an opportunity to escape.

Some time went by, and then an officer approached me and asked: "Are you Eric Smith?" "Yes," I said. He said officers had been looking for me, and I said I had been directed to wait here. I then told him I had a history of mental illness and that I was on psychiatric medication. He took me back to a cell with a large group of other males and told me I would get to speak with medical staff at some point.

Jail's medical staff and hallucinations

I was taken to speak with the jail's medical staff for what seemed like less than five minutes. They asked what my mental illness diagnosis was, and if I was prescribed any medication. I told them I had bipolar disorder and named the various types of medication I had been prescribed. They wrote some things down on paper that I could not see, and then an officer took me back to the holding area to wait. I began to hear voices in my head, and I started to feel I had developed an ability to hear the thoughts of others unbeknownst to them, so I assumed those were the voices I was hearing.

The voices informed me that in my holding cell were members of various criminal organizations tasked with getting arrested for the sole purpose of finding out why I, an agent of the FBI and CIA, was there. These voices were uneasy about me, so I believed I had to calm their suspicions and let them know I was on their side. Some officers walked by, and I yelled, "Fuck the police!" right at them, as loudly as I could. The officers glared at me, and I shouted, "Your jobs are bullshit!" I started feeling confident this was the right course of action as the other arrested people clapped and laughed at my brazen rebuke of the officers.

"Judge and jury" in the holding cell

After my anti-police rant, the looks on people's faces around me confirmed that I had gained their respect and eased their suspicions. I sat down in the crowded cell and a large inmate sitting on the other side of the cell addressed me. When he spoke, I saw that he had the attention of every inmate in the cell.

Inmate: "Why were you arrested?"

Me: "For trespassing at the address listed on my driver's license, which is my parents' house."

Inmate: "Have you been to court yet?"

Me: "No."

Inmate: "Okay, so I will be the judge and these guys *(indicating all our fellow cell mates)* will be the jury. Now, tell us the story of what happened up to the point of your arrest."

Me: "Well, I'm an agent working with the CIA and FBI trying to gather information about threats against world leaders. I'm not here to interfere with you or anyone else in the jail." *(I believed this self-proclaimed "judge" to be an influential figure among the various gang members in the jail, and felt I had to make him understand my presence was in no way a threat to his—or any other gang's—power or control.)*

Inmate: "And what world leaders are you protecting?"

Me: "All of them, but more specifically President Obama and the King and Queen of Jordan are in danger. Assassination attempts are being planned that will destabilize the entire world and lead to World War III."

Inmate: "Okay, I've heard enough. Now listen—all of you—no one is allowed to hurt this guy! Got that?"

Our cell mates all nodded in agreement. I went over, shook the "judge's" hand, and thanked him for his "ruling."

Transfer to a communal cell

I was eventually transferred to a cell with several showers, toilets, and rows of bunk beds all within the same communal room. As soon as I got there, I believed I was to make contact with a person in that room, because I saw no other reason why I was there. I didn't know who I was supposed to contact, so I kept my eyes and ears open for a sign about who I should speak with next as part of my mission.

Nighttime came around, and I realized this large cell with bunk beds and more than two dozen inmates is where I would be sleeping. Rather than sleep, I stayed awake all night because I believed that was how I would earn the trust of every other inmate, using my power and influence as a CIA and FBI agent to prevent police from messing with other inmates. Next morning, the person in the bunk next to mine woke up and asked me if I had been awake all night. I told him I had not slept at all because the police wouldn't mess with anyone while I was watching them. "You're crazy, but I appreciate what you did," he said.

At lunchtime, that same person said not to eat the yellow cake if it showed up with my lunch. I figured this mention of yellow cake was my sign that he was my next point of contact as part of the mission, thinking of yellowcake uranium that would be of interest to both the CIA and FBI.

The person sleeping in the bunk on the other side of me practiced voodoo and would draw intricate pictures of people to place hexes on them. He was regularly drawing pictures and showing catastrophic events to me telling me that some could be prevented, but some had already happened. I viewed this inmate as my source of news from the outside world and he had me believing nuclear war had struck and that World War III had indeed begun. There were no windows anywhere near this cell, so my hallucinations and delusions were running amok with vivid images of the apocalypse, supported by this inmate's drawings. I woke up one morning a few weeks later, and this man had been removed from our communal cell. I asked other inmates what happened to him, and they told me he was removed for practising magic against others, but I'm not sure what actually happened to him.

I started to think some inmates could hear my thoughts. I felt like that could put me in danger, so I told the officer watching our cell (there was always an officer at the front of this cell) that I needed to speak with a doctor because I was having a psychiatric medical emergency. I figured a hospital would be a safer place for me to be than a jail. The officer told me to calm down, and then said I didn't have the right to call 911 for an emergency of any kind. After a lot of arguing, he finally called a superior to speak with me.

When the superior arrived, he took me into the hallway right outside the communal cell. I placed my hands above my head against the wall to let him know I was not a threat to him, and I demanded to speak with a doctor about a psychiatric emergency I was experiencing. I also told him what I had told someone else earlier, that I believed President Obama and the King and Queen of Jordan were in danger and that assassination attempts were being planned to destabilize the entire world for what would become World War III. The officer told me he would set up a meeting with the jail's doctor.

Visit to the jail's doctor

Not long thereafter, I was called out to meet with the jail's doctor for the first time. (Earlier, I had discussed my diagnosis and medications with a nurse who was part of the jail's staff.)

I didn't have my glasses with me when I was arrested, so I would squint whenever I looked at something out of arm's reach the entire time I was in jail. This is relevant to know, because the female officer who came to get me to bring me to the jail's doctor called my name and I looked up at her with squinted eyes.

Officer: "Hey! If you don't quit mean-mugging me right now, you and me are going to have a big problem!" (I understood this to mean that she would physically hit me to un-squint my eyes. I didn't view this officer as a part of my mission, so I didn't bother too much.)

Me: "Yes, ma'am." *(Politely.)*

Officer: "Did you just say 'Yes, man'? Do I look like I have a pair of balls?" *(Aggressively.)*

I just shook my head to indicate "no" to her question, and she then escorted me to the doctor.

As soon as I saw the doctor, I told him I was not being given any medication and that I was diagnosed with a mental illness that required medication. I said that if something happened to me because I wasn't getting medical care or medicine, that it would reflect badly on him as the jail's doctor, and that could be a problem for his job security. He asked me if I was threatening him, and I said that I was just speaking factually, not threatening him. He asked what medication I was on, and I told him a list of medications I had been prescribed. He said the jail didn't have a wide variety of psych meds, and that I wouldn't be able to get the specific meds I had previously been prescribed. Then he said: "We're done here."

At that moment, I instantly believed this doctor was yet another reason I was there at that jail on behalf of the FBI and CIA. I figured he had taken his position at the jail specifically to prescribe a very narrow array of medicines that would only benefit one or two major pharmaceutical companies. The way I saw it, if only a few select medicines were used inside this jail (and many others like it), then the jails were intentionally generating revenue for specific pharmaceutical companies as part of a plan to devalue the competition. In turn, I also believed jail doctors were receiving enormous monetary kickbacks from the relevant pharmaceutical companies. It then became part of my mission to expose this corruption and I believed my ability to read thoughts put me in a unique position to confirm my suspicions about the doctor, the medications, and the drug companies as true, which is why the CIA and FBI chose me to finish out this mission.

To be clear, I was not given any medication throughout the entire time I was in jail.

Moved from communal cell to single occupant cell

When I was taken back to the communal cell after the doctor's visit, I began to loudly explain how the officers were not in charge at this jail, but that the doctor was actually in charge, placed there by the powers that be to strengthen the bottom line of major players in the pharmaceutical industry. I was yelling about how the officers were pawns of the jail's doctor and pharmaceutical companies, and that every person in the jail was being experimented on with medication in their food and water. I was making everyone nervous, so eventually I was transferred to a sparse cell with just a bed, a sink, and a toilet.

Initially, jail staff didn't allow me to see my parents because that required me to leave my cell. In fact, my parents had come down to visit me, and after waiting there for a few hours they were told I wasn't allowed to leave my cell to visit with them. This caused my mom to cry, and a ranking officer who caught wind of this then pulled rank and allowed me to see them. Apparently, this ranking officer had a family member with some form of severe mental illness, and that allowed him to be empathetic.

The visit with my parents was visibly unnerving and sad for them. I recall sitting down and seeing them through the thick glass window, and my mom looked like she had been crying, and my dad looked exhausted. I didn't want them to be sad, so I stood up and loudly proclaimed that I was in charge at the jail. I was yelling about various things, like how all the illicit drugs being smuggled into the jail belong to me, and how I was untouchable because of the ruling by the inmate/judge who told the other inmates that I wasn't to be harmed. I also remember yelling about how the King of Jordan was sending a jet to transport me to his country so that I could provide him the intelligence I had gathered up to that point. My memory of this visit with my parents is mostly me yelling about things that are attributable to the symptoms of my illness and did not include much of anything that would fit the definition of a conversation.

Pleading my case

At some point during my stay in jail, I was directed to appear before a judge tasked with hearing cases of people in jail. When I got to the small room the judge was in, a woman introduced herself to me as an attorney assigned to my case. I had never met nor spoken with her before. We sat down in a corner of the room, and she asked me to explain why I'd been arrested. The cramped room was crowded and loud, with many different conversations occurring between inmates, attorneys, officers, and the judge. A few short moments into my explanation, a police officer came over and yelled: "Hey! You're speaking way too loud. Quiet down!" I was confused by this because the entire room was noisy, but the officer only targeted me. I began to speak in a tone I thought was much quieter, and a few seconds later that same officer said: "You're refusing to follow my orders! If I have to warn you again to speak more quietly, I'll send you back to your cell without the judge hearing you."

At this point I began speaking in a virtual whisper, and explained to the attorney: "I was arrested for trespassing at my parents' house, and I'm in jail because I am gathering intelligence for the FBI and CIA. I am innocent, and the charges against me are just a cover for a mission I am on while in jail."

She didn't react in any way to my statement. I guess she had heard it all before.

The attorney said the judge would ask me how I plead to the charges, and I was to respond with the words, *"Nolo contendere"* (Latin for "I do not wish to contend"). At the time I thought this phrase meant I was pleading not guilty, but only later learned that it means one accepts punishment but does not admit guilt. I did not feel I deserved to be punished, so I would never have said *"nolo contendere"* if I had known what it truly meant. I felt like I should be honoured—not punished—for allowing myself to be brought to jail to gather intelligence that would prevent assassinations and war.

When my name was called for the judge to hear my case, my attorney directed me to stand.

Judge: "How do you plead?"

Me: "*Nolo contendere.*" (Dutifully, speaking as quietly as I could because that officer had twice ordered me to speak quietly.)

Judge: "Speak up; I can't hear you."

Me: "*Nolo contendere.*" (In a somewhat louder voice. The officer glared at me and shook his head as if to warn me not to speak any louder.)

Judge: "I said speak up so I can hear you. If you keep wasting my time by not speaking up, then you will be ordered back to your cell to think about how you are wasting my time before being given another opportunity to plead."

Me: (Genuinely confused about whether to speak loudly for the judge or quietly for the police officer, I paused a moment before responding. Then I figured the judge outranks the police officer.) "*Nolo contendere.*" (Loudly! The officer looked at me menacingly as if I were using the judge's directions as a tool to try to diminish the officer's authority over me.)

The judge then sent me back to my cell having heard my plea of "Nolo contendere," which I truly thought was a plea of innocence.

Transfer from jail to hospital and Assisted Outpatient Treatment (AOT)

Toward the end of my stay in jail, which lasted about 30 days, a court liaison came to speak with me while I was in my cell to determine if I would be a good fit for inpatient care at a hospital followed by an assisted outpatient treatment (AOT) order. Just as I was about to be discharged from the jail, a judge created an order to move me to a hospital for psychiatric care. I stayed in hospital for about three months. From there I entered AOT after being stabilized.

Fast forward through a few more hospitalizations, the last of which ended in early 2012, and I have now graduated *magna cum laude* near the top of my class with a BA in psychology, and I am currently a graduate student diligently preparing to help others as I have been helped. I am also a mental health advocate, public speaker, and consultant with Treatment Advocacy Center.

I credit AOT with rescuing me from the downward spiral that used to be my life. AOT saved me from the criminal justice system, and from insanity. AOT recognizes mental illness is not a crime and allows for civil proceedings and treatment to help remedy many of the complex problems associated with severe mental illness (SMI). The criminal justice system is in no way equipped to meaningfully address what I was experiencing, and that holds true for everyone else drowning in the abyss of SMI from the riptide of arrests and incarceration.

Conclusion

Looking back, I can say from personal experience and with absolute conviction that the criminal justice system is not designed to treat people with mental illnesses. Criminalizing mental illness and the people diagnosed with it is the wrong thing to do; it doesn't work, and it is a waste of money. Civil (non-criminal) proceedings and programs like assisted outpatient treatment (AOT) are among the best ways to help address many of the complex issues stemming from severe mental illness.

The last psychiatrist I had as an inpatient was astounded that I was able to recall so much of what I experienced from when I was in a decompensated state of mind and told me that is incredibly rare. I can recall all the emotional turmoil that my family and I experienced and doing so is often traumatic enough that I find myself in tears as I recount the journey to others. Being able to relive this trauma is taxing on my mind and body. When I revisit how tragically it all could have turned out (serious harm, injury, even death) versus how it actually turned out, a rabbit hole of dark thoughts haunts me.

However, this curse of being able to remember the turmoil I experienced while psychotic is also a blessing of sorts, in that it allows me to tell my story to help others through changes in legislation, policies, and practices. I am hopeful my advocacy helps society evolve toward a recognition that civil, compassionate, and evidence-based care must replace mechanisms of criminal justice in cases of severe mental illness. In the meantime, countless people desperately in need of medical care continue to live a life like I experienced: jailed body, imprisoned mind.

Eric Smith

I was born in Phoenix, Arizona, in 1983, was diagnosed with bipolar disorder in my mid-teens, and with schizoaffective disorder in 2009. I have a BA in psychology from the University of Texas at San Antonio and am currently pursuing post-grad studies in social work at that same university. I am a mental health advocate, public speaker, and consultant with Treatment Advocacy Center, and I hope to continue this work after graduating. I enjoy spending time with my family and dogs.
TreatmentAdvocacyCenter.org

Learning to Manage My Triggers

Amy Dodd Pilkington

I have bipolar I with psychotic features and have been stable for years now. The fight to gain stability was tough. That fight continues every single day, and I will continue fighting that same fight every day for the rest of my life. Living with bipolar disorder is a constant battle, even during stability.

When I was first diagnosed in 2006, it was somewhat of a relief. By then, I had spent more than a decade searching for answers. My initial diagnosis was depression, and the antidepressants I was prescribed only worsened my condition. The pills triggered psychosis and fuelled bouts of mania. I knew something was not right because the treatment was all wrong. Every antidepressant I was prescribed only increased my symptoms. Receiving the correct diagnosis—bipolar disorder—was scary, but it was also exciting. Starting the correct treatment would surely make a difference.

I assumed I would be prescribed the right medication, and everything would go back to normal. I did not know that it would take so many med changes to find the right one. I spent a few years avoiding medication altogether because I thought it was useless. In doing so, I suffered much more than I should have. I prolonged my pain because I was not stable enough to understand the consequences of trying to ignore the problem.

After dealing with several psychotic breaks and more periods of suicidal ideation than I care to remember, I realized that my mental illness would be terminal without treatment. My life was at stake, and I had to keep trying or I might as well lay down and die. I was determined to fight for my life. I just had to figure out how.

I went through nearly a dozen medications before I found one that worked for me. Some meds did not work at all. Others worked too well and left me emotionless. A few triggered psychosis. Something as simple as finding the right medication was a battle in my war against bipolar disorder. I persevered until I eventually found one that helped me achieve stability. That first period of stability was important.

While my judgment was not clouded and I could think clearly, I realized that more work needed to be done. I was still having minor issues with mania and depression from time to time. These bouts were mild, but I knew that could change at any time. I kept thinking there had to be something more I could do to remain stable. It was a therapist who helped me realize what was needed.

I had been to therapy many times in my life, and not once did I feel it was helpful for me. When I started seeing this therapist, I went in assuming it would be pointless. I was there because my family wanted me to be there, not because I felt it would be beneficial. I had no way of knowing that this man would be the one to make a difference. During our sessions, he never made any suggestions. He asked questions, but he never gave solutions. He just kept asking me how I thought these issues could be resolved.

At first, I didn't understand why he was doing this. I honestly felt he was less than helpful. When I finally started coming up with solutions for different problems on my own, a light bulb turned on inside my head. This man was teaching me that I had all the tools I needed to figure things out, and all I needed was to learn to use them. It boosted my confidence and taught me that I could assess issues and work to resolve them on my own. That is exactly what I decided to do.

Within a few weeks of my realization, I started a blog. This blog was never intended to have an audience. It was more of a journal to allow me to write down my feelings along with everything that happened that day. I blogged whenever I felt a strong emotion, and that was fairly frequently. When depression would sink in, I would browse my posts and find the bad days. It was comforting to know that I made it through all those days. It gave me the strength to keep going.

Eventually, that blog intended for my own benefit started attracting attention. I suddenly had followers cheering me on in my fight. It was empowering and having an audience that had faith in me kept me going through the worst times. I did not want to let them down. I needed to succeed to show those who were also struggling that it could be done. It was not just my own life that was in my hands. I felt I was responsible for everyone who contacted me to discuss their struggles. Somehow, I had to find a way to save all of us.

That pressure became a bit much after a while. After realizing that a manic episode was the fuel for my saviour complex, I knew I needed to get to work fast while my mind was still sharp. I read everything I had ever posted. Day after day, I read my blog from start to finish and started trying to put the pieces together. About a month of reading led to another light bulb moment. When I first noticed the patterns, I had no idea if any of it would be helpful. I just knew there was too much to ignore. There was no harm in trying, and if it turned out that this idea derived from mania, I will have lost nothing but time. Swallowing a pill every day was not enough, and I knew it. That pill was very necessary, but it only cleared my head so I could put in the work needed to stay stable. I decided to give it a try.

I realized there were certain things that affected my moods more than other things. Looking back through the posts, I could see that days with manic episodes had events and occurrences in common. It was the same with days of depression. Of course, I knew none of those things caused the episodes. I also knew they certainly did not help. I made a list of potential triggers and decided to start my experiment.

One of the biggest problems on my list was bouts of psychosis. The worst episodes were the most terrifying experiences of my life. If I could avoid them, that would be a huge weight off my shoulders. Coping would be much easier if I could rid myself of them, even if only for a short while. I checked my list and noticed that a common element on days when I heard voices or had other hallucinations was horror movies.

I stopped watching horror movies, and the voices in my head got fainter until I could not hear them at all. It did not happen overnight, but it did happen. A few years later, I watched a film that bordered on horror. My reaction was quick and harsh. The voices and other hallucinations came back. Since then, I have never watched anything even remotely resembling horror. And I have not had any issues with psychosis since that time. Could it be a coincidence? Perhaps. Perhaps not. All I know is I have not had a bout of psychosis since I stopped watching horror.

The second most troublesome symptom on my list was depression. For me, depression was far more dangerous than mania because it always led to suicidal ideation as the episode progressed. I scoured my posts to find any common elements. A lack of routine seemed to be a big trigger. Staying up late, being overscheduled, participating in unplanned events and outings, and travelling were all on my list of suspects.

Having multiple things to address, I started with the simplest item on the list. I decided to set a regular bedtime for myself. Even if I don't go to sleep, I am in bed at a certain time almost every night. It is part of my routine, and it makes a difference. I also started making sure my schedule wasn't too hectic and required advance notice of any outing. When I travelled, I made an itinerary. Having a set schedule and maintaining the safety of routine made a tremendous difference. My stress levels dropped. I felt more secure, and that security led to a reduction in symptoms of depression. I have developed a reputation for being a control freak, but it works for me.

Last on my list was mania. It was more complex than the other issues. I had noticed that anger, which is a common symptom in mania, was also how I dealt with fighting off depression. Rather than feel sad, which scared me, I would convert my emotions to anger. You can project anger, but you must fully experience sadness and depression. I projected. It was a coping mechanism I had developed out of necessity. It became a survival tactic. I knew this was something that I needed to address: I was becoming isolated and was pushing people away. I knew this would only lead to the undoing of all my efforts, so I had to find balance. This was by far the hardest thing for me. I had to find an outlet for my emotions that allowed me to let some steam off without having the pot boil over and cause major issues. But I also knew I had to tread very carefully when dealing with something that kept me from falling into depression.

I noticed that sensory overload often preceded anger. Multiple voices blended together to sound like a foreign language. High-pitched sounds felt like something tapping on my brain. Loud noises were often bothersome, but sometimes even the slightest bit of noise was too much. During those times, the mere sound of the seal on the refrigerator door releasing its suction as it opened was enough to make me cringe. Everything was too much at times.

Whenever I started to feel overwhelmed, I sought quiet. I need time alone to clear my mind and get myself together. After more than a few days without alone time, I get agitated. My family knows I need this time to balance myself out, so they allow me the time I need. It has helped me stave off a lot of anger. Taking time to unwind and relax helps me sort through every emotion I am feeling before it translates to anger.

From the moment I wake up until the time I fall asleep each day, I take care to avoid all my triggers. I take the time I need to collect my thoughts, and I carefully monitor my moods to catch any changes before they become bigger issues. Every single day, I still take that pill, but it is only part of my wellness routine that keeps me safe and stable. This hard work has kept me stable for many years now.

While I am under no illusion that I am cured or that I will never have another bipolar episode, I have—at the very least—enjoyed many years without the complications of major episodes. I have experienced a few minor episodes, but their severity was far less than previous episodes. A short-term supplemental medication was required just twice in all those years, and both times I was able to avoid major issues and get back on track. Careful monitoring of my moods allows me to catch potential problems before they become big trouble.

On my quest to find ways to manage my mental illness, I developed a lot of coping mechanisms. I write a lot, and I listen to music. Sometimes I paint, but I prefer to peruse the art of others. I fidget when I have nervous energy. It is not unusual to catch me fidgeting with my rings or the zipper pull on my jacket. I have learned to redirect my attention by finding something more interesting to focus on instead of dwelling on something dragging me down. Being able to distract myself is a huge win in my war.

My life is different now. It is much simpler, and it feels easier to just live. After spending so many years fighting to stay alive, it is so nice to be able to just live. I do still fight every day. I take my medication, avoid my triggers, and try to keep to my routine. It's a different fight. The daily battle has become a part of my routine, and I am winning the war against bipolar disorder. I am not just staying alive. I am enjoying living.

Amy Dodd Pilkington

I was born in Memphis, Tennessee, in 1974, and was diagnosed with bipolar disorder in my thirties after suffering with its symptoms for more than a decade. I live in Bolivar, Tennessee, with my husband, four children, and our beloved dog. I have authored more than two dozen books and my work has appeared in various publications. I enjoy camping, photography, reading, and spoiling my adorable grandchildren. I love a tall glass of sweet tea and aspire to be a beach bum when I grow up.
AmyDoddPilkington.com

Black Garbage Bags

Julie A. Fast

Editor's note: An earlier version of this story was previously published on the mental health website, GumOnMyShoe.com by Martin Baker.

I lived in Japan for several years in the early 1990s. I was often so depressed I would go out on the roof of the gaijin (foreigner) house where I lived just to be in the sun and the fresh air. It was obvious I had depression, but there was so much more than depression affecting my life.

There was, for example, the wildness that would come before my extreme down swings. I had enormous creative surges and an incredible focus on work followed by weeks or months of serious depression and a body that could hardly get out of bed. I remember one weekend where I woke up in a man's bed and didn't know where I was. I walked through the streets of the small Japanese town and couldn't find the train station. I was mortified and filled with shame. Life would then get back to normal and I would be myself again for a while.

I felt possessed by this out-of-control behaviour and swore I would stop it each time, but I couldn't control it at all.

I often believed that friends and coworkers were out to get me, and I saw and heard things that were not there. This is the benefit of hindsight of course. At the time, I didn't have any insight into what was happening. I just lived through it.

I do remember asking myself, "*What is wrong with me?*" over and over again. I never got any answers.

When I first moved to the *gaijin* house, I rented a *tatami* mat room that included a futon, bookshelves, and a closet. I heard from the other women that the former renter was picked up by her parents and taken back to Australia the week before I showed up. When I walked into her room, I saw that the windows were covered with black garbage bags. The room was incredibly warm and there were books strewn all over the place. We all talked about her as though she were a ghost. I never met her, but I knew that something must have been very wrong in her life to lead to the black garbage bags and her parents having to take her away. Was she trying to keep something out, or keep something inside? It all felt bizarre to me and a bit scary.

The black garbage bags represented someone out of control, and yet I didn't recognize my own behaviour in her. I didn't make the connection that I also had a black garbage bag story that was equally bizarre and scary.

The year before I moved to Japan, while going to university in Seattle, Washington, I parked my car quite far from campus and had to walk on a trail in the woods to get to my classes. I have very clear memories of being anxious on rainy or dark days while on that trail. One day, I looked to my right and saw a large black garbage bag and could immediately tell there was a body inside it.

I could SEE the body.

I could FEEL the body.

I heard a voice that said, "You need to call the police! There's been a murder!"

I experienced this with all my senses; with my whole being. It freaked me out and I turned away. When I looked back, it was suddenly perfectly obvious it was just a big bag full of leaves.

On other days, I would see something on the ground that looked exactly like a severed hand. When I turned away in fear and then looked back, it was obvious it was just a leaf.

I didn't tell anyone about these experiences, not even my therapist. I just assumed it happened to everyone.

It's incredible to me now that the story of the young woman who put garbage bags on her windows and my own black garbage bag experiences didn't lead to any kind of self-awareness. "She's clearly crazy. I'm just depressed. It's not the same thing at all," I thought. (Of course, now I am embarrassed at my lack of awareness and compassion for a fellow human being.)

I spent four years in Japan going through these elated and then depressed mood swings without any help. I had a fabulous job in Tokyo that allowed me to really use my brain—and then the brain that could be so amazing would just SHUT DOWN. And I would end up back on my futon crying or going out on the roof to lie in the sun. It made no sense, but not for one minute did I think of myself as mentally ill. I thought I was the cause of my problems, and that I just needed to learn how to control myself. I kept asking for help from very uneducated therapists who would try to get me to figure out why I made such "poor decisions."

I once told a therapist about the experience of waking up with a strange man in the small Japanese town. I explained that this was SO out of character and so shocking to me that I needed help. She said, "Maybe you need to address the lack of Christian values in your life."

That is an exact quote. How could I know what was going on with me if the "professionals" who were supposedly trained to help people with mental illnesses were this ignorant? This lack of awareness about serious mental illness is still present today. We don't know what's happening with us and when we finally do tell a therapist or family doctor what happened, we need them to have answers. Often, they don't.

I wonder what would have happened if I'd told the therapists in Japan, "I see dead bodies in garbage bags and leaves that look like severed hands." I finally disclosed this to a psychiatrist in 1995, along with all my out-of-control sexual behaviour, work problems and deep, suicidal depression. I was told, "You have ultra-rapid cycling bipolar disorder with psychosis." Eventually, I received a revised diagnosis: schizoaffective disorder. This means I have bipolar disorder and a separate psychotic disorder.

The garbage bag with the body and the leaves that looked like severed hands were visual hallucinations. The voice that said I had to call the cops about the murder was an auditory hallucination. The paranoia I felt all through college and often during my time in Japan was a delusion. My uncharacteristic sexual behaviour was caused by mania, and the crushing sadness that led me to sit in the sun was depression.

Between the ages of eighteen and thirty-one I saw at least twenty health care professionals to ask for help. Not one asked me the right questions.

I'm sharing this story to shine a light on how and why people with serious mental illness like me can see mental illness symptoms in others but not for a minute recognize those same symptoms in ourselves. The young woman with the garbage bags was obviously sick. Her roommates knew this, as did her parents who came to take her home. She was paranoid—using garbage bags on the windows to block out the world, or prying eyes, or people "out to get her"—just as I was paranoid walking through the woods to my school. I never made this connection until I was finally listened to, asked the right questions, and properly diagnosed.

Everything—and I do mean everything—was explained by a correct mental health diagnosis. This diagnosis gave me insight.

Insight is something we can grow in ourselves once an accurate diagnosis gives us a clear direction for care.

I still experience mania, depression, and psychosis. I have an illness! But I know how to manage my symptoms and I am no longer scared. Two years after I was diagnosed, I created the bipolar management system I share in all my books. It is now used around the world.

I hope that the young woman from Australia got the help she needed as I finally did over twenty years ago. We are the sisters of the black garbage bags.

Talking openly about mental health and getting a correct diagnosis saved my life.

I hope that my story helps you find peace and support as well.

Julie A. Fast

I was born in 1964 and lived with untreated bipolar disorder and psychotic disorder symptoms until I was finally diagnosed correctly in 1995. Medications were not the answer I had hoped for, so I created the plan that is published in my books and is now used around the world. I believe in using a management plan for most symptoms in combination with the judicial use of medications for symptoms I can't control on my own. I am the bestselling author of *Take Charge of Bipolar Disorder, Loving Someone with Bipolar Disorder, Getting it Done When You're Depressed* and *The Health Cards Treatment System for Bipolar Disorder.* I currently live in the United States. You can read more about my work on JulieFast.com, BipolarHappens.com, on Facebook at Julie A. Fast and on Instagram @JulieFast.

Hypomania,
This Beautiful Condition of the Mind

Paul Bearer*

* *This is a pen name.*

> *Editor's note: This piece was originally written as one long paragraph of rapid thoughts just flowing out of the author. Anyone who has experienced (hypo)mania will identify with that! To make it easier to read, I have shortened and edited it very slightly (e.g., by adding punctuation, paragraph breaks, etc.). However, to communicate the author's rapid thinking and flight of ideas in hypomania, I have deliberately left some parentheses unclosed as they were in the original submission. After reading this edited version, Paul emailed me:*

I feel good about this! I have to say, however, that I think the piece has lost some of the power and strength that the original raw text had. I see your intention of adding punctuation for comprehension, but it really takes away from the expression and feel. I also see this punctuation as a function of how society so typically wants to put us into boxes and keep us neat and organized. Bipolar is not neat and organized; it is messy and that is okay. It's as if the edits are trying to make readers more comfortable. I don't feel I need to change myself to make others more comfortable; I think they need to loosen up and work harder to see differences and accept them. I don't feel good about us having to continuously medicate and edit ourselves to be more "normal." Why aren't they taking drugs to be hypomanic instead? I do think the edited piece still gives insight into the state of hypomania, but without the true essence of the blurring of thoughts and ideas from one moment to the next that I was experiencing. But I understand why you made the edits, and this is your book, so I give you my permission to do as you please as it is not being published under my [real] name. Which says a lot. I hope one day I can share and advocate for bipolar folks without fear of future repercussions and risk to my professional career.

February 5, 2013; 2:13 a.m.

I just woke up sweating. My t-shirt, the pillows, and the sheets are soaked. My thoughts are lightning fast: I can't tell if my heart is racing because I feel simultaneously calm, at peace, and as though I am white-light speeding between buildings in a lightning-fast urban motorcycle race. I think this is what people feel like on amphetamines, or cocaine. I can see why they do them.

There have been a lot of drug references that parallel the feelings I've been experiencing the last few days. Yesterday when I was sitting in front of my computer screen at work, before I had a panic attack, I felt serene and blissfully happy. Joy rising. I almost began to cry and then suddenly completely understood what Nirvana was and if anyone felt as good as I did at that moment through any spiritual quest that they would want nothing but to pursue that feeling. It made sense to me why people dropped out of society to become monks. The thought was white and pure and this thought had full space around it: everything stopped for a moment while I pictured Buddha in a cave inside a lotus flower with nothing but beauty and space surrounding him and his thoughts. I almost had tears of joy run down my face, wanting nothing but to cry in that moment in my office. (My friend is writing to me on gmail chat now, so I'm writing this and talking with her simultaneously. It's great to hear from her. She moved to the Yukon. [2:21 a.m.] We spoke for about 30 minutes; I stopped writing this after the first ten minutes.

2:50 a.m.

My heart rate seems to have come down. I feel much calmer now than when I first woke up. I was dreaming/thinking (sometimes I don't really sleep deeply when I'm in this "inspired" state for days but my eyes are closed and I continue to run through ideas while my body charges up enough to keep going again. After a few hours the batteries in my body are re-charged and I wake up like a child, excited and WIDE awake on Christmas morning, although physically my body aches from lack of sleep (like you do when you wake up without sufficient sleep to catch an early morning flight or bus. Somewhat sore, and disoriented, but jazzed and excited [side note: I just took the earplugs out of my ears. I sleep with them, but forgot they were in when I woke up. The silence of the night is soothing and deafening. It is helping to calm me and relax me out of this ultra-excited state that has my body aching. It feels good. My fingers are starting to hurt from typing. I think I will get out of bed soon and leave my laptop to give them a break and try to do something physical. Work on some art. I'd really like to work out right now and do some pull-ups on the chin-up bar in our apartment, but my roommate is sleeping and I don't want to wake her up. She just finished hosting a work event two days ago and had been in full-stress mode coordinating its production and man did she ever do an excellent job! It was for a non-profit organization and she (You know what? This thought just came to me. I think James Joyce must have been hypomanic as well. I have tried to read Ulysses before, but I found it was like trying to wade through someone else's emotional molasses. Now I could see how someone could write a novel like that in stream-of-consciousness if they were feeling and thinking as clearly as I am right now. I would also wager that Nicholas Baker (I think that's his name? I am usually terrible at remembering people's names, but these days names have been coming to me without hesitation; it makes me feel very together. It can be frazzling when you are trying to remember a name, or a street name, and you can't remember, I'm always trying to describe it to people, ha ha. "You know that tall building in Paris. The one in the park that is in almost every movie?" "You mean the Eiffel Tower?" "Yes! That one!" Sometimes I forget very, very good friends' names at the second I'm about to say it to another person who I am introducing them to. It can be so embarrassing. Consequently, I've just stopped introducing people, I let them do it or I say "introduce yourselves, please" if it is awkward because I don't want anyone to feel badly if I should forget their name in that moment. (I also sometimes have a brain glitch when I'm signing my own name. For example, on a cheque. I will get half-way through signing it and my brain goes blank and my hand stops moving. I have never understood that, except that it must be neurological. It is a little disturbing when it happens though.

Alright, that has been a lot of thoughts. I am going to return to my original one about describing the way I've been feeling, and also draw parallels to drug use. But first I need to close a lot of brackets. You know what. Closing all of those brackets right now seems like it won't be that helpful but will require a lot of my energy and too much focus for no reason, so I am just going to leave them and I will come back and edit this in a couple of days or a week when I am no longer hypomanic. I trust that my thoughts are composed, they usually are when I'm in this state.

3:07 a.m.

I can't believe how fast I am typing, and I am hardly making any errors. There is almost no difference between my hands and the keyboard, thoughts are pouring out of me so fast. But my hands are really starting to ache. I think that is one thing about computers and typing that has been good for me: for a long time I could think faster than I could write and so I would constantly have to stop writing when I was doing it by hand to flex my fingers. My hand would be so cramped and aching I would just have to stop and do something else. But right now, I really just want to get some of this down to make sure I don't forget it.

Oh yes, I have been meaning to say here as well, but I've had to hold that thought in the background while I collected it during the day today and composed it better, that I think my psychologist Lyn and I should write a book about hypomania and what this is like. In fact, while I have been writing this, I have thought it would make a good introductory chapter to let people know what it is like to think and feel this way. It feels great! I was thinking the title of the book should be *Hypomaniacs*, and it should be in bold black text, like that British author who writes books with intense, emotionally raw content. He wrote *Trainspotting*, and also *Porno*. Not Nicholas Hornby ... *(I pause here to enjoy the blank space momentarily in my head and to rest my fingers.)* Irvine Welsh! That took ten seconds to remember, during which I had the most delicious moment of pause in my head—all the simultaneous thoughts stopped momentarily. That said, you should understand that I don't find this exhausting, it feels great right now. It feels like it must feel when Lance Armstrong is on a bike, or what Oprah must feel like when she is filming TV. Complete serenity and oneness with what I am doing.

Right, so as I was saying, I believe I should write a book about this with my psychologist, Lyn. She is a great woman, I really feel like she understands me without any judgement, she just wants to help me. It feels so great to have people behind you! She really believes in me. Ha ha, today I had to go all the way across the city to track her down when I suddenly realized at work that I was in a hypomanic state and I wanted her to see what it was like, live. Finally got to her office and when we finished talking (we only had ten minutes between two of her patients—clients?) she said "thank you" and it was funny because I had come to her office across the city so she could help me plan my way forward with this [3:19 a.m.], but she said "thank you" to me when we finished talking, and that was when I knew she understood that I had come all the way across the city to share this feeling with her so she would fully understand, and she did. In the hour that I was waiting for her, I took out a piece of paper and started mapping the last 5 years of my life, charting it in a graphic way with notes related to my [wait. I have to go pee. It is 3:20 a.m. I don't want to stop writing this because I really feel like I'm onto something good at this point. If I were just "freeflowing" right now (that is what I call it when I let my brain pause and go to artistic projects and float from one thing to another) I would go to another activity after I peed, but I am going to wait as long as I can and try to get this out, try to focus.

Okay, I do feel like I need to re-read this because I can tell there are now many, many unfinished thoughts above that got stuck in parentheses. I think this is why I "freeflow" because when my brain gets forced into a corner, I just let it out and let it run free. It feels cornered right now and that is uncomfortable.

I'm stopping, I am going to get a drink and come back to this and re-read it from the top, perhaps edit it a bit, and collect and complete any unfinished thoughts that I come across.
(Pause at 3:24 a.m. to get a drink.)

3:27 a.m.

When I stood up, I could feel the residual lactic acid build-up (I just signed out of g-mail chat so that I don't get into another conversation with someone. I want to finish this a little bit, I feel like I'm onto something here and it's coming out nicely. I think I can type faster than I can talk when I feel like this. For a moment I considered getting a voice-recorder, but I am enjoying the silence of the night so much that I know it's not the right thing to try. I like to type. I can pause with an idea and return to it later if I want.) in my body from the lack of sleep and I really had an urge to exercise. I stretched a bit, and thought about looking into 24-hour gyms in my neighbourhood, but it's February and very chilly outside at this time of the year, and a little too scary in the dark night alone in the cold, so I am just going to stretch a bit, maybe do some push-ups, and then work on turning the sketch that I did for Lyn today of my moods during the last five years;

I would like to turn that into a beautiful graphic. Hmm, just now I pictured that graphic wrapping the full cover of the book (jacket) with the Helvetica bold black Hypomaniacs text layered overtop. I think that will work well. I'm excited to draw it up in a few minutes in Adobe Illustrator. Thank god I learned all of the creative skills I learned in art and design school, so that when I am feeling "high/inspired," I can completely resolve full ideas from thought, to sketch, to final product. I also want the cover, under the dust jacket, to be embossed, I think maybe with neon. I know that is really "on trend" right now, and I usually hate doing trendy things, but who gives a fuck.

3:36 a.m.

Ok, I think my brain is getting a little tired now, because the thoughts aren't just flowing out now. They are still coming, but I just had a sentence that I had to stop and correct for the first time without it first being fully formed in my head. But I know better than to try to sleep yet, I should wait a few more hours if I can so I can relax a bit more.

3:38 a.m.

Right, so what I was trying to say above (I'll just summarize, because I really want to work on the graphic of my moods during the last few years. It's sort of becoming like an itch that I am just dying to scratch—drawing that up on the computer in Illustrator. It is going to look divine—I can see it now in my head. I can't wait to work on it) is that:

1. I want to write a book with Lyn about how this feels so people can understand; and
2. I think drawing parallels to drug use (ecstasy, cocaine, etc.) will give some insight into hypomania.

[Editor's note: For reasons of space, I have removed about 800 words here, in which the author describes his experiences with street drugs.]

Right, so I was trying to say that if I write a book with Lyn, I thought it should be half diagnosis and analysis and half of my writing, or just sharing of my writing without the analysis. I would also like to include some (all?) of the letters that I have been writing to myself and mailing to my parents' address for the last ten years without opening them. I have no idea what is in those letters, or how many there are, but I think they will give insight into this beautiful condition of the mind. (I am going to read this from the top now and try to complete any points I forgot. I feel like I have got out most of what I wanted, and also some fun stories in there along the way! Freeflowing is fun, ha ha!)
(I edited from the top down starting at 4:00 a.m.)

4:42 a.m.

Minor editing and clarification where necessary to complete most thoughts. I think there were surprisingly only two that weren't completed and were really only missing a couple of words or an additional sentence for clarity. It felt like it was going to need a lot more work as I was writing it. It is validating to know that I can trust my judgement about my abilities when I am feeling "inspired."

4:47 a.m.

I just went to pee again and realized that I still had my mouthguard in my mouth that I wear when I'm sleeping to prevent me from grinding my teeth. I know when I spoke with my supervisor today at the architecture firm he thought it would be fine for me to stay in the office and work through creative projects when I am in this state, but I had reservations. Mainly I felt like I just need to do whatever I need to do in the moment when I'm feeling "high/inspired," and sometimes that means stretching or walking around a bit as I freeflow between projects. I sometimes pace a little bit in the apartment while I let ideas build on themselves until they are ready to be written down or drawn, and I think this would make people uncomfortable in the office. The same way that I forgot that I had my retainer in my mouth—because it wasn't important to pay attention to—I think I might forget that I am pacing a little bit or doing mildly erratic behaviour that other people would find strange. I don't need to be judged when I feel like this, I need to be encouraged and allowed to flow freely, and it feels best to do this in my own space or wherever I feel like I need to go. Being constrained or forced to do something non-elective feels wrong and bad in this state. It felt wrong at work today trying to write an email and work on very formal, mundane tasks, and that made me feel uncomfortable and backed into a corner. Explaining how I felt to my supervisor then leaving to find Lyn was the right thing to do.

4:55 a.m.

I am going to stop writing now. I have a bit of a headache, feel restless in my body, and want to stretch and move around. I've been lying horizontal in bed while I wrote this. I think I will work on the graphic of my moods or just lie and think restfully for a while.

Five years later; July 10, 2018

I'm 34 now and have certainly had high and low points my whole life. It is just the way my brain works. It wasn't until 2013 in a moment of crisis that warranted a visit to the psychiatric hospital that I began to look for some way to take the edge off the high points—those times where the solid distinction between me and the universe transforms into a permeable membrane where anything is possible, like the night I was writing the piece above. Anyone with bipolar knows what I'm talking about. I got some simple tranquilizers that knocked me back to my baseline and let me sleep after 11 days of bliss, toward the end of which I started to tap-dance on the rickety edge of exhaustion and the perfect white truth where everything is amazing… but where I may collapse at any moment if I do not soon get more than three consecutive hours of sleep.

It was several uneasy months of waiting before I finally had an answer to what was going on. (My biggest difficulty in all of this has been the *months* of waiting to get any psychological aid when suffering. It is a travesty of our system.) I was finally referred to my first psychiatrist who promptly diagnosed me with bipolar after one brief meeting and refused any further discussion or access to group meetings unless I agreed to go on drugs to treat it, saying it was progressive and would only become worse. What I really needed in that moment was a chance to talk with others who had similar realities to mine and full access to the group meetings so I could understand more clearly what the options were, not to be pushed out the door with zero help or consultation unless I agreed to take pills.

I needed time to process what the doctor had told me. I felt like damaged goods and that this was something I would need to hide as best as I could. The stigma of the diagnosis weighed heavily. It took me some time to digest (and some exploration of bipolar group meetings in the city) and I came to the realization that our society tries to pathologize any non-"normal" behaviour, but luckily as an artist and creative person I've never felt "normal" at any point in my life. I eventually embraced this aspect of myself and put in place some measures for self-care when I hit my extremes, including getting a family doctor and a psychologist who I see regularly. It also took some reading to realize that I identify most as hypomanic, my periods of "inspiration" (as I call them) never lasted more than two weeks and then I return easily to my baseline. My "introspective" (depressive) periods were also less than two weeks and bleak, but I always knew I would come out of them as it has been this way my whole life, so I just plodded through or spent a few days in bed reading.

Up to this point it has been a real exploration of self. I've learned that noise drives me to a feeling of irritation almost immediately and visual stimulation can exhaust me very quickly, but just having the knowledge of this helps me manage it. Ultimately, in the time since 2013, I've realized that I am just a very sensitive person and I need to respect that—if that means rejecting the "normal" way of others for what makes me feel better and be more myself, that is okay. Consequently, reducing my work week to four days per week has been the best thing I ever did. It gives me time to be by myself and get the distance that I need to help stay balanced.

It hasn't all been perfect—I've had some longer depressions since 2013—but I'm figuring that out too and realizing that ultimately stress management is key for me to being okay and balanced.

We'll see what happens in the future!

Two years later; September 5, 2020

I suppose it is the future now. It has been about six months since the start of the COVID-19 pandemic, and it's been fascinating to observe how reliant people are on each other for support. After the first month of quarantine, people were fraying: I watched friends implode with worry and anxiety and depression and others explode with rage at the things they couldn't control happening around us and to us. I feel like I was lucky: the tools I have developed over the years for self-care and self-observation allowed me to know when it was necessary to talk with others and when I was okay. Feeling very alone at times in the past equipped me well for the periods of isolation—but I admit, I really did miss hugs. What I found surprising was that many friends turned to me during this time. Over the years, I had spoken with them about my mental health experiences and for them these feelings were new and terrifying as the pandemic became very real. They suddenly understood. I was able to be a solid support and point people to resources as I saw them hit crisis points because I knew how to navigate troubling times.

My life has been a winding road with many twists, but I'm developing wisdom from my experiences that I can now use to help others, and for this I am grateful.

I was born in Ontario in 1984, and studied fine art, design, and architecture, completing three degrees at the Ontario College of Art and Design University, Dalhousie University, and McGill University. After passing the French language exam, I completed my professional examinations to become a licensed architect in Quebec in 2019. I was diagnosed with bipolar disorder in 2013 at age 29 but have experienced mood swings all my life.

Finding the Words

Sarah Boon, PhD

I have been having trouble writing lately, seized in the grip of a bipolar depression that seems to pull me underwater so I have to hold my breath and can't let any words out. When I try to write, I am confronted by a completely blank brain, like a two-stroke engine that won't turn over—it just keeps grinding and sputtering until the battery dies. Any words I do produce are stilted and stiff—I don't have the ability to inspire.

My psychiatrist says this is a normal response to getting over a bipolar high episode and can last up to twenty-four months after the high itself. Yes, you read that right—twenty-four months after a high, provided you have no additional highs in between, you could feel better. *Could.* After two whole years. Forgive me my skepticism when I'm just trying to get through the next twenty-four hours. Given that my last high was in September/October 2019, I'm only one year in as I write this. He tells me the story of a patient who couldn't find things in her kitchen after having a bipolar high. I'm not sure if the story is intended to be sympathetic or educational, something to show me that others suffer cognitive decline as well. Sometimes I think he's giving me false hope by talking about patients who have managed their bipolar and have an okay quality of life after two years.

I also suspect I'm feeling the effects of COVID-19 that, as many have noted, is making us grieve how our lives have changed during the pandemic. As David Kessler writes, "The loss of normalcy;

the fear of economic toll; the loss of connection. This is hitting us and we're grieving. Collectively. We are not used to this kind of collective grief in the air."

To break the grip of this depression (with added COVID-related stress on the side), I've decided to try counselling again. I did it for two years when I was first diagnosed, then we moved from Alberta back to British Columbia and I did phone counselling for a few months, but I let it fade because I no longer found it helpful. Now I do counselling by Zoom, so I can see the counsellor even if I can't shake her hand or meet in real life. We talk about paying attention to where your mind and body are at with regular "check-ins." We talk about cognitive distortions that mess up our thinking, and core beliefs that make us interpret the world in set—and often unrealistic—ways. And while these things are helpful, I want to know the *important* stuff. What can I do when I wake up feeling too depressed to function? How can I cope when the depression persists and deepens? What do I have in my toolbox that will help me deal with it?

I manage to salvage some days partway through, taking time lapse photos of the garden and writing in my garden notebook. I have several weeks of daily photos, ready to be put together to see the garden change over time. Other days aren't saved until after my afternoon nap. And some days continue to fester unproductively well into the evening, so that I just want to go to sleep and hopefully feel better the next day.

It is the writing—or the lack of it—that has bothered me the most, though. I am a writer. That's a fact, even when I'm not physically writing. But not being *able* to write is a different story. I have always been able to write, even if I wasn't always at my best. But it is frightening for me to have nothing—absolutely nothing—in my mind. No writing ideas. No nuggets that I could flesh out into a blog post. No random words percolating up from the depths to generate new ideas. This is particularly galling because last year I had a surfeit of ideas and wrote many essays for publication. I feel like this year I have succumbed to my illness and not fought hard enough against it. Even though I know that fighting bipolar is a losing battle: my mind will do what it wants, regardless of what I try to force it to do.

It is scary, this lack of words, that seems connected to the proverbial black dog of depression tripping along at my heels throughout the day. I try to chase him away, but he prefers to be a faithful companion. He is loyal and stays close. He is a dog, after all.

Sometimes I think my real dogs sense that something is up. They follow me around the house and come for petting and cuddles when I sit down. They lie on me on the couch or in bed. They check in regularly to see how I'm doing with this dark shadow they sense but who never makes himself visible to anyone but me.

Some days, the black dog bounds off after a ball or another victim and I am left feeling unexpectedly lighter. Like on the evening we had a backyard campfire and life was good. But those moments are rare, so I seize them with both hands—like a drowning swimmer might grab at their rescuer and almost pull them under in the process.

I have tried to get around not writing by doing timed writing. Well actually, at first, I gave in to my brain's inability to focus on writing. I didn't write for a few weeks, except to do my mental check-ins. But otherwise, I let the writing be and didn't—or tried not to—think about its absence. Then I decided one Sunday that it was time to do something about it, so I tried timed writing to basic prompts. For example, this essay that you're reading now emerged from the prompt "essay for bipolar anthology." And it looks like I've managed to chip a tiny piece off the non-writing block. Sort of.

For my work, so far, I've written about the Canadian Rockies and my experiences there during my undergraduate degree: Parker Ridge in Banff National Park; Elizabeth Parker, whom the ridge was named for; our field camp back in 1997; and the hike we did to Saskatchewan Glacier during that field camp. These topics are all part of my work-in-progress book, so it's important that I write them to get my second sample chapter done. I have mulled over the book structure enough that it's time to edit the chapters and make them sing. I will pick out a section of each chapter and try to bring it to life, so that it's not just words on a page, but so that they spring out from that page full of energy and enthusiasm. I will break the back of my wooden writing by cracking it open with regular writing exercises. It's the only way I know how to do it.

I just have to take it slowly, hoping the black dog doesn't reappear and that I can stay above water and keep on writing my way out of this. Maybe I need to keep in mind these wise words from Lauren Groff, "…the vast majority of the time one spends writing a book isn't spent in writing the book, but rather reading, dreaming, running, walking, experimenting, restarting, writing things that gradually bring you closer to the book."

Fingers crossed that the writing impulse will return—and remain—sooner rather than later.

Sarah Boon

I was born in Alberta in 1977. I studied geography at the University of Victoria and glaciology at the University of Alberta and hold BSc and PhD degrees. A former environmental science professor, I am now a writer and editor, and have published interviews, book reviews, and essays in numerous magazines and outlets. I am working on a book about my research adventures at remote sites in the Arctic, Rocky Mountains, and Coast Mountains. I was diagnosed with bipolar disorder in 2013. I live with my husband and dogs on Vancouver Island, British Columbia, and enjoy photography and fabric art.

A Gift or a Curse?

Amy Cox

Editor's note: Amy contacted me via my website in March 2020, just as the lockdown for the COVID-19 pandemic was starting in her US state. As the email thread below shows, I encouraged her to write for this anthology, but she didn't feel well enough to do so at the time. We kept up an informal email correspondence over the next five months, however, and she gradually wrote more and more, filling in details that had previously eluded her or would have required too much energy to share. Together, we agreed that publishing our emails would be the best way of giving her a voice in this anthology.

March 26, 2020

Hello Merryl,

When the universe and our governor told us to prepare to be at home, I ordered some books online and just yesterday began reading your memoir, *Mad Like Me: Travels in Bipolar Country*. It already mirrors my experience in key ways and I look forward to reading the rest and retaining it for reference.

I wish I had a support system like yours, because as an older, single, working woman with no family and few friends, I need to rely on myself to monitor my illness. It's almost never a good idea to leave the fox in charge of the henhouse!

Your late diagnosis after a stressful life event gives me hope that I, too, will be able to have a fairly stable future if I pay attention to my own triggers.

Humour is often my best defense, and my love of reading, particularly books about the lives of just about anyone, means I always have company.

Thank you, and be well.

On the same day, I responded and asked Amy to clarify if she personally has bipolar. If so, I invited her to consider writing something for this anthology. She replied within the hour.

March 26, 2020

Thank you so much for the kind invitation. Yes, I do have bipolar disorder. I also have a master's degree in music. Unfortunately, my creative self, which also includes writing and art, is rarely accessible when I'm stable, a source of grief for me. I currently work in a grocery store, which isn't a place for self-expression anyway. An anthology is a wonderful idea, and I will keep it in mind in case my brain activates itself again by the deadline for submissions.

I'm reading your memoir right now on my day off from customers who may or may not have COVID-19.

The same day, a few hours later, I replied, "I do hope that you'll feel inspired to write something for the anthology. Even just a couple of paragraphs about how frustrating it is for you to have 'lost touch' with your creative self ... e.g. Before bipolar, I used to love .... (music, art, etc.). My favourite memories are of ... But then, in (year) I was diagnosed, and things changed.

"Describe how things changed for you as a creative person. How do you feel now? What do you wish for? What do you need others to understand about your disorder, and why?

"Each small contribution to the anthology is like a single square in a beautiful big quilt that we can then share with others to help them understand what it's like to live with bipolar. Maybe you can challenge yourself to share a small piece of your own story? Just see how you go!"

Again the same day, March 26, 2020

Merryl, your encouragement is much appreciated. I also worry about getting ill, as in the past being prescribed steroids for respiratory infections has resulted in (hypo)mania, hospitalization, and job loss. To that end, I spoke with my relatively new nurse today to discuss a plan, should I happen to catch the current virus. I mentioned your book to her.

I'm still a bit leery of creativity, since I was just in the hospital last year following a wonderfully productive period. It scares me to think of sitting at the piano and feeling my fingers being too agile, or taking up my pen to express my thoughts in case they should come so quickly that I can't keep up with them. It takes so long to get my sleep back in order again that I've almost resigned myself to simply living without the things I truly love.

On that note, I spent one of the best months of my life in your birthplace, South Africa. My late brother Ken, a brilliant trumpet player, was principal trumpet with the Natal Philharmonic in the late 1980s. He invited me to stay with him after a particularly difficult depressive episode, and Durban was the perfect place for the two of us to be our quirky selves, something he could never do in his native America. Tragically, Ken starved to death eleven years ago because of psychosis. He was in Israel playing with the Jerusalem Symphony at the time, and I hadn't seen him for some time before that. Ken's lifeline was his trumpet, which he picked up at the age of ten and never put down until he died. For me, grief is easier when I'm involved in the end of a loved one's life. The pain of this loss remains acute. His absence is a constant presence, as if he's the other half of me. His death, I believe, is a result of the trauma and neglect that occurs in families with severe mental illness, and his story could so easily be mine, except that for whatever reasons, I persist where he could not.

It wasn't only Ken who suffered from a mental illness. I can only diagnose my relatives in retrospect, with knowledge I have now but didn't have back then. I was told my mother had manic depression, but I think it was more likely schizoaffective disorder of the bipolar type. She abused me directly (emotionally), and I was often on the receiving end of her delusions and hallucinations. I think Ken mostly suffered from neglect, from having a mother who wasn't equipped to care for children and a home, so I truly believe that neither of us learned how to care for ourselves. Fortunately, I had many years of therapy and 14 years of Jungian analysis, which greatly helped me overcome dissociative disorder, which often occurs in abused children. I have severe anxiety, post-traumatic stress disorder (PTSD), yada-yada, and was finally diagnosed with bipolar disorder at age 47 following my father's death. He was the glue that held the family together, and I'm certain that it's because of my relationship with him that I'm something of a survivor. There was also alcoholism and Asperger syndrome, and I don't think that heredity and environment can be separated, at least in my case.

I'm going on about this because you seem like a person who truly cares, and you understand that relationships—especially those involving mental illness—are fraught with complications.

I may yet try to record my thoughts about this fascinating and troubling condition. It would be so much better for all of us if we could openly share our struggles in the same way people with cancer or heart disease are encouraged to do.

Several weeks passed, and then on 18 May 2020 I wrote, "Hi Amy, I'm just following up with you to hear how life is treating you in general during the pandemic. I trust that you and all your colleagues at the store have escaped the virus, and that shoppers are taking good care to avoid passing on the virus? Take good care!"

There was no reply from Amy. Then on July 12, 2020, I emailed her again to encourage her to submit something for the anthology. She replied the next day.

July 13, 2020

It's so good of you to remember me. I'm conflicted about writing about my bipolar experience, mostly because right now it wouldn't be a positive piece. There are days when I give myself credit for simply being able to work and be independent, with little or no support from anyone else. Then there are times, especially lately, when I so hate my situation and wish I could have employment that was fulfilling and provided an income that was enough to keep me out of debt. My creativity apparently thrives only in a manic state, which is an awful thing. At other times I have no urge to write, draw, or play the piano; and when I do attempt to play, just to see how it feels, there's none of the spontaneity or joy that used to come out of nowhere. This has always made me wonder if my talent stands apart from the illness, or if it is merely a symptom. As I don't know anyone personally who has bipolar disorder, I'm left to ponder these things on my own.

July 14, 2020

Not willing to give up on including at least a taste of Amy's story, I wrote back the next day.

"Thanks so much for your prompt response. I gave it some thought and realized that we have had several quite detailed emails back and forth that could—if you agree—form the basis of a contribution from you. Anyone reading the email thread will get excellent insight into some key issues that living with bipolar raises: loss of creative drive, employment concerns, stigma, isolation, heredity issues, triggers ...

"We can always use a pseudonym for you if you prefer. I do hope you'll feel comfortable having your ideas and insights included in the anthology in this way."

July 14, 2020

She replied the same day.

On a day that finds me without the energy or will even to do laundry, maybe I'll feel better if I at least contribute to your anthology. Then my day spent staring at the lake could be redeemed.

There's no need for me to be anonymous. If anything, I feel I must be twice as good at my job to make up for what may be perceived as weaknesses, and my authenticity is something I consider to be a strength. I trust you to edit as you need to, and I will look forward to reading the stories you've gathered from other people with similar experiences.

Thank you again for your interest and for helping me to feel useful, even in a small way.

Amy Cox

I was born near Cleveland, Ohio, the second of three children, and have lived in the area for over six decades. I studied music in college but have mostly worked in unrelated fields. I was finally diagnosed with bipolar disorder at age 47. My days off find me immersed in reading long biographies and spending as much time as possible near beautiful Lake Erie, wandering through our many state and national parks. I love to drive far (and fast), as my car is the only place where I can control the environment and surround myself with the music that I love.

The HeART of Bipolar Disorder

Ellie Gainey

It's hard for me to say exactly when I first became aware of having bipolar disorder. I'm 23 now, and as far back in my childhood as I can remember, I was hyper-aware that there's something wrong with or different about me. I mean literally, from my earliest childhood.

My mom has bipolar I, so I grew up around it. But she has never taken treatment.

I witnessed all her mood swings firsthand. Often, it was depression: a sink full of dirty dishes, a mountain of laundry in the garage, a steady hum of television bleeding through the cracks of her bedroom floor. Mostly, a tired mom who picked herself up long enough to go grocery shopping and say hello when I returned home. Rarer was her mania: productive and sleepless nights, laughter between friends, a dire need to create. The smell of bleach hitting me when I walked through the front door.

For most of my life while I lived with her, she did not hold down a job. She raised us on her disability checks. My dad was in the picture only until I turned two. He hasn't paid child support one single time. I have no recollection of him, and I've never even had a conversation with him. My grandparents helped look after my brother and me, and they also supplemented financially when my mom could not manage.

Diagnosis

I remember when I was about eleven, I saved up and bought a laptop, and one of the very first things I searched for was "bipolar disorder" on WebMD. They had a checklist of common symptoms, and I ran off to show my mom: "Look, look; I have all of these symptoms!" But she just pushed that aside and reassured me that I wasn't sick; I'd be fine; not to worry. I guess she didn't want to even contemplate that I might have the same disorder as her.

So, for many years our family was in denial...

Then, when I was 18, I was formally diagnosed with bipolar II. I was in a crippling depression which caused panic attacks, crying fits, combative behaviour, and lack of empathy.

Ironically, even though I had self-diagnosed years before, I refused at that time to accept the bipolar diagnosis. Now it was *me* in denial. My family still was, too.

I refused to take any meds. I was constantly filling my time with work, plans, adventures. Anything to keep my mind off my emotions. I was as volatile as I was successful. I graduated with a 3.7 GPA and honours. I also found myself in traumatic situations due to my lack of emotional and mental insight. I did go for some therapy, however, but therapy has been ineffective for me thus far.

Starting (and stopping) medication

Two years ago, when I was 21, I had an art studio, a job, friends, a car, and I was living in a nice house. I had everything going for me. I was still getting by with no bipolar medications and was still able to work. But depression was a problem.

I was working in a deli at the time. Suddenly one day, standing behind the counter during a quiet moment when there were no customers in the store, a strange and insistent thought came into my head. It was: "I want to kill myself." Immediately, another thought came: "That doesn't make any sense."

The thought of suicide crept up on me. I remember a feeling of deep loneliness. Or distance. Remoteness. I couldn't grasp reality. I felt like an alien in my own skin.

I knew without a doubt that this was serious, so I told my boss I needed to leave, and I drove myself to the hospital immediately. I was not kept overnight: they gave me an Ativan and sent me home, saying I could come back if necessary.

Soon after, they ended up prescribing lamotrigine (Lamictal). I'm still on that—luckily, with no bad side effects.

I stopped taking my meds twice. First, it was soon after I started the meds when the honeymoon phase peaked. I guess I thought maybe I didn't need the meds after all. Like, maybe I didn't really have bipolar or perhaps I was cured. Well, I got deeply depressed. So, I went back on the meds, and moved to Santa Cruz for college.

The second time I stopped the meds was in 2020 when quarantine for COVID-19 started, because my insurance from school was suspended due to the pandemic. Again, I went into the worst depression. At one point I called a friend and he reminded me of the importance of taking my meds. So once again, I restarted the meds, and I was able to continue my career in art (I worked on a mural at home). I feel much better now.

Mood swings

I'd say I've had about an equal number of hypomanic and depressive episodes so far. About ten of each.

In hypomania, I could go for two nights a week with no sleep whatsoever. I felt happy, productive, grateful. Work was good. I taught myself how to use the Adobe Illustrator program. I studied Spanish. I was running six miles a day. But it wasn't all rosy: I had anxiety attacks several times a day.

In depression, everything was on the table. Everything in my life was affected: I couldn't work, couldn't maintain any social relationships, couldn't even hold a conversation.

This last depression during lockdown for the pandemic, I couldn't even get out of bed. I would sleep all day, from 7 a.m. to 6 p.m., then stay awake from 6 p.m. to 7 a.m. This lasted about six weeks, until I got my meds again. I couldn't accomplish anything the whole time.

I've been at rock bottom a few times, and it's difficult to climb back up and look down. But it's a tremendous feeling, and I'm *so* proud of myself for doing that. And I know there are so many of us who have been there.

I guess I never acted on that suicidal impulse when I was 21 because I knew my life was valuable. How did I know this? My mom really loves me; and I know I am here to help make this planet a better place. For example, I want to destigmatize mental illness through my art. Bipolar allows me to be the artist I am. Art has always been a safe place for me to express myself. I love to paint oil portraits, so for my senior exit solo show, I plan to paint about eight to ten portraits showing people with mental illness as they'd like to be represented.

Conclusion

Some people ask me why I'm so open about my disorder. Keeping things to myself, under wraps, has never done me any good. Just think, if I hadn't spoken up at the deli and gone for help immediately, I might be dead by now. If I can help anybody find the right resources, walk away, not die by suicide, and find their happiness, that is worth everything to me. I would go through all the pain I've been through again if I could help someone else.

I'm proud of myself but speaking out about this also makes me want to cry. It's been a lot to go through. I'm really happy to be here; to be alive. Going public like this may affect me badly one day (e.g., when applying for a job), but I think it's vital. I have to do what's right. I hope I can inspire more people to speak up for people with mental illnesses.

As an artist, I'd like to end with some of my art. I painted this oil, acrylics and inks piece at Mendenhall Studios in Eureka, California. The diptych paintings are full colour; however, they have been converted to black and white for this book. These are the first canvases I had ever built for myself, and they were larger than life (8x6 feet). In 2018, I was experiencing both hypomania and depression simultaneously and as a result, I gave myself total creative freedom. Typically, I work in a rational and realistic approach; this is my first and only piece that came directly from my heart. I titled the piece *Adrift.*

Ellie Gainey's 2018 diptych paintings titled Adrift, created during a bipolar episode.

Editor's note: Please see youtube.com/watch?v=Pgi8LRakoHQ for a 5-minute video clip, Social Distancing Episode 02: Ellie's Story–Painting a Picture of Mental Health featuring Ellie talking about her experience dealing with suicidal thoughts.

Ellie Gainey

I was born in Sacramento, California in 1996. I have an associate degree in Fine Art and am currently completing undergrad studies in Art and the History of Art and Visual Culture. I live in Roseville, California where I work as a full-time visual artist with an emphasis on murals. I was diagnosed with bipolar disorder five years ago, at age 18, but I believe I've had the disorder since early childhood.

Learning to Live with My Bipolar Identity

Bruce Saunders

Editor's note: Bruce's wife, Laurel Saunders, has written about her experiences as a family member in part 2 of this book, in a piece titled "Living in the Shadow: A Family Perspective." You may want to read that account immediately after this one.

I'm surprised in a way to be writing this at age 70. Several times along the way, I've felt hopeless, "unhelpable," desperate. But looking back, I've had a charmed life in many ways. I live with bipolar.

Family history

My mom battled with severe anxiety and depression all her life. I learned much later that when I was a boy, she threatened to jump off a waterfall when our family was on a camping vacation. But she was never able to speak openly about her struggles. She made my dad promise never to talk about her mental health issues, electroconvulsive therapy, and so on. This was a sacred trust between them, and Dad had to carry this burden in silence all his life. Only decades later, when my mom developed Alzheimer's and had a stroke, Dad opened up to me about what he had been through with Mum all those years. It was cathartic for both of us to release some of the old stuff that had never been dealt with at the time.

As a result of this silence, my only sibling, Lynne, and I never learned about mental illness. No books, no information, no discussion. So later, when both of us experienced mental health issues ourselves, we were ill-prepared. We didn't know our family history, and like most people, probably just hoped things would resolve on their own.

Lynne was diagnosed with bipolar disorder when she was 23 and I was 21. She had married at age 22, having met her husband while studying nursing at the University of Victoria. After she experienced a couple of episodes of depression and some bipolar tendencies, she was treated with lithium, but the medication didn't agree with her. Her life became somewhat erratic, and she left her unsupportive husband. At one point, she needed a place to stay, so I invited her to come and live with me in my small cabin, but I was soon to be married and there really wasn't space for us all. As the wedding date approached, she went to a motel and took a fatal overdose.

Back in those days, we didn't have any idea how to support Lynne. Her eventual suicide seemed almost inevitable. We thought, "That was her fate." Only much later did I learn that it might have all turned out differently, that she could have been better supported and had access to appropriate resources. Now I deeply regret that we were unable to help her at the time.

Diagnosis and early treatment

I plugged along for many years after Lynne died—dealing with some depression and a feeling of maladjustment—before I hit the wall myself. There were many nights I was exhausted and sleepless, tormented by doubts and foreboding.

Despite all my advantages—a stable family life with a loving wife and two young sons, a comfortable home, and a job I enjoyed—finally the depressions became overwhelming, and I was eventually hospitalized at age 39 after a suicide attempt. They put me on a strong course of antidepressants, and as so often happens when the underlying condition is bipolar, not unipolar depression, that flipped me into hypomania. Suddenly, I had more energy and physical stamina than ever, and was bursting with bright, creative ideas—or so they seemed to me at the time! I remember rushing home to bake and ice a birthday cake for one of the people on the ward and wanting to arrange a battery of computers (a novel concept in 1989) for my poet ward mates. My poor wife couldn't understand my sudden transformation from suicidal depression to this uncharacteristic ball of energy, virtually overnight.

Only then, I was able to look back and see that I had lived for many years with a subtle pattern of depressions interspersed with occasional higher moods.

In other words, bipolar disorder.

And so, I was eventually diagnosed in 1989. Given my symptoms and my sister's bipolar diagnosis and suicide, I might have been diagnosed sooner.

Lithium was (and is) the gold standard mood stabilizer, but—as with my sister—it didn't work well for me. It took down the hypomania but left me flat much of the time. It was hard to find an equilibrium.

Mood swings

Depression comes in cycles, and for me, it's usually triggered by frustrating situations: forgetfulness, feeling inadequate and incompetent, or lost in a muddle. If my garden's growing well and I didn't leave my gloves behind, if things go as planned or better, that's a good day.

Depression involves pulling back from the world, not wanting to make plans or contact people. Who would want to hang out with me when I have nothing to say? Depression is really boring, negatively introspective.

Depression is also very hard to head off. It just feels like old business settling in. All the negative stuff feels normal to me… From that perspective, it seems like when I'm "up," I'm fooling myself. The true me is the depressed me. Anxieties, forgetfulness, incompetent actions, negative thoughts, and cogitations—all these just roost on me; burden me.

I don't get hypomanic much at all. When my mood does cycle up, maybe I'll send out more emails, or plan more elaborate events. My "to do" list grows. There's a sense of busy-ness and less time for sleep. I often feel expansive and have an awareness that I'm being what my wife, Laurel, calls "zippy": I think faster, move faster, am more creative. I become a bit less patient with others... (I don't like the term "zippy" myself. I prefer "overactive"!)

The pull to suicide

It has been well-documented by experts and researchers that suicide is a common risk for people struggling with bipolar and even more of a risk if someone you know has died by suicide.

My first encounter with suicide was way back with Ian, my good friend from high school. I got a call out of the blue: he had died by suicide as his brother had several years before. It was a real gut punch that just didn't go away. We had had plans to travel together after our summer jobs that followed our first year at university.

I know from my own and others' experience that suicidal thinking can be infectious. You see that things calm down after the initial shock and drama. And you think that at least the person is out of their psychic agony. An example like that can implant itself as an option, and haunt you in times of distress, even many years later.

Four years after Ian's suicide, I lost my sister Lynn to suicide. She was probably affected by Ian's death, too.

And yes; I've been there myself. In my late thirties, just before I was diagnosed with bipolar, I had been struggling with depression for a long time and was eventually hospitalized after a suicide attempt. I was just so frustrated with my poor memory. I got tied up in knots all the time. Or I'd lose something, misplace my clippers, forget names and details. I just felt so incompetent. And the more frustrated I'd get, the more depressed I'd get, and the dafter I'd become—until all I was doing was ruminating and cogitating.

This vicious cycle still happens. Then, when I get all my ducks in a row again, my mind is clearer, I start to feel empowered again, I feel more competent, and I function quite "normally"—in many ways, I'm "high functioning".

At the time of that first suicide attempt, I was in a day-program learning life skills and in group therapy. It wasn't working. I was really struggling with my memory and depression. One day, I just walked out at midday, got in my car, and tried to kill myself. I spent four weeks in the hospital after that.

Four years later, at age 43, I made a second near-fatal suicide attempt. At the time, I'd had a serious physical health crisis that resulted in ileostomy surgery and kidney failure, among other things. I was off my mood stabilizing meds and had spiraled into a severe depression. It was pure chance that Laurel discovered me before I died. It was a very close call. There followed another spell—about four weeks again, I think—in the psych hospital. To protect my compromised kidneys, they decided not to restart lithium and instead put me on Tegretol (carbamazepine)—an anticonvulsant often used in bipolar control—and, again, over the years, various antidepressants. Those medications worked much better for me.

Unlike my first hospital stay, this time there was a bridging program with home visits upon discharge. Laurel liked that, as we both had the support we needed to get me back into a healthy recovery.

You know, it's strange. I'm not as frightened about death so much since my suicide attempts. I know that many people are fearful of death, but I feel a bit more accepting of it. I've come so close—by choice, however confounded by depression I was at the time.

Recently, at age 68, I retired and experienced another deep depression. It lasted on and off for about nine months, and finally

I was hospitalized again. They got me off some anti-anxiety and sleep meds that were in fact depressing me more. My antidepressant was changed and olanzapine (one of the atypical antipsychotics being used to treat bipolar these days) was added. In other words, they switched up my meds. Although I didn't make a suicide attempt during that episode, suicide was still a strong drive. Even now, after everything I've been through, I'm still vulnerable: the pull to suicide still hangs over me in my low moments.

I have a suicide prevention plan that I developed with a therapist. You know, phone this person; call 911; whatever. But that all operates at the level of intellect, and suicidal ideation operates much deeper than that. At the level of emotion. Psychic agony. I just fall back into a groove. It's a learned response to negative events. I start going down the same well-worn road. I know that route; I've been there a hundred times before in my mind. The old patterns of negative thinking just sweep me along. I need to develop positive ways of thinking to counteract this, I suppose.

My family's reactions to my suicide attempts

My wife is a truly generous person; we tough it out together. After the two suicide attempts, it's really a miracle that she stayed with me. It was a horrible thing I did to her. I mean, that I would choose the option of dying and leaving her alone, with two boys to raise. After my second attempt, I thought surely she might kick me out and I'd be joining the homeless people under the bridge. We each did some counselling, both as a couple and individually.

When I made my first suicide attempt, our boys were still very young (Daniel was nine and Paul only five), so we didn't tell them the full story. "Dad is in hospital for a while, trying some new medications."

But four years later, when I made my second attempt, we told Daniel (then aged 12) the truth while I was still in hospital. It was very hard for him to hear.

We didn't feel we should burden young Paul with the full story as I was getting back on my feet again, so I waited about seven months to tell him the full story. I took him (then aged nine) for a walk and told him the full reason I'd been in hospital. His immediate reaction was: "But why didn't you tell me before?" He really wanted to feel part of the inner core, the trusted family circle.

At some point, we also told both boys that that had been my second attempt. They needed to know.

In a later conversation about the fact that I have bipolar disorder, Laurel and I were trying to put a positive spin on things: adversity makes a family stronger, more sensitive, closer, more accepting of others. Paul, then aged ten, said, "Then families that *don't* have mental illness aren't as lucky as us!" We smiled and said maybe things are a little more complicated than that. But I've often remembered the purity of that innocent response. In many ways, it *has* been good for our family that we've had to deal with mental health issues.

Recovery

While still an inpatient after my second suicide attempt, I had an idea for a project which I called Movie Monday. I select, obtain, and promote movies, and screen them weekly in the hospital auditorium. Patients, family members, staff, and people from the public attend. Within a few months after discharge, we held our first screening.

The events are funded by donation and are open to all but especially geared to be inclusive of folks who have experienced mental illnesses. We often discuss the movie afterwards. Many of the films have some link to mental illness and other life challenges. Sometimes it's just about sharing some well-chosen entertainment. I also feature artwork in the lobby, or invite people to share videos, photos, etc. This event is still going on (with a break for the COVID-19 pandemic) with great consistency. This project has been a consuming interest of mine all these years.

That's 26 years of *Movie Mondays* and counting!

So, I quickly progressed from patient to service-provider to educator and mental health activist. I still worked a full-time garden maintenance business; some projects I looked after for 38 years. A nice combination of very physical (gardening) and creative (*Movie Mondays*) activities.

Early on, I decided to be open about my personal mental health struggles—after all, our 100-seat theatre is located in our aging psych hospital. I guess you could say I "came out" as a person with bipolar. I had accepted my diagnosis as part of my identity. A key part, to be honest. I accept that I'm a member of the bipolar club.

Given my mom's refusal to speak openly about her mental health issues, she was—understandably, I suppose—not particularly supportive of my "being out" about my own issues. She was just kind of quiet about it. That generation preferred to keep stuff like this under wraps. But my dad became one of my biggest boosters. I chose to break the silence about my own mental illness, in the hopes that this might help others who were struggling. On a good day, I'm proud to be doing as well as I am and to demonstrate this to my community.

Interestingly, my psychiatrist warned me against being too open about my diagnosis. He was concerned that it might affect my ability to get a job in the future. But I was running my own gardening business, and I was doing well. Keeping busy. Running *Movie Monday*. Being relied upon by others. My openness about my condition had actually opened doors for me and I was determined to demonstrate that for my community. So I ignored his caution.

But I can see where he was coming from. If you are, for instance, a teacher, or in some position where stereotypes about mental illness might work against you, you might want to think twice about going public about your diagnosis. But within your personal circle of family and friends, it's so empowering and helpful to have support, so I'd really recommend "being out about it" as much as is practical. Every case should be considered on its own merits.

Current mental health

I still have occasional mood swings even now, at age 70. And I have a lot of psychological issues from a life lived with this condition. My mood can change with little warning, so I have trouble planning ahead with confidence. I struggle with insecurities, negative thinking, and lifelong memory deficits. (I can't memorize new things, and my poor memory—which has plagued me ever since I was a young boy—is hugely frustrating.)

I'll say this: living with bipolar can be tiring. It's caused me to struggle a lot in my life.

As mentioned, lithium didn't work well for me. I am now quite well-controlled—but not 100% free of mood swings—on a cocktail of four different meds. There's no perfect medication, it seems. Everyone will have to find what works for them. It takes a collaborative relationship with your doctor, and it takes time. That's why they call us patients!

Bipolar and creativity

I'm intrigued by the creative drive that's a defining characteristic of my personality, and in the connection between bipolar disorder and creativity. Creativity drives many people with bipolar. Just consider some of the famous artists, musicians, writers, performers, inventors, and others who had what was then called manic depressive illness. Sometimes I'm proud to be part of the bipolar community!

It seems to me that there's something unique in the bipolar spirit that pushes many of us to reach beyond our natural abilities to achieve an imagined goal. In my own life, I've often either been scrambling to keep up with my creative schemes or recovering from chasing them too hard. We feed off the energy and satisfaction that creativity gives back. But sometimes it has a cost. At least in our family, now we can all recognize what the dynamic is.

Speaking of creativity, I'd like to pay tribute to my late artist friend who also lived with bipolar disorder, Bob Choma (Robert Bogdan Choma). From 1993 to 2018, I collected photographs and footage about him and his work. What a character! And what unique talent! He embodied that creative drive, the bipolar spirit. I produced a documentary titled *Chomavision* that documents Bob's extraordinarily creative and unpredictable bipolar life interwoven with storylines from my own experience. Making this video was a huge challenge—an exhausting, but very creative process—and the final product is something I'm very proud of. Bob lived to attend the premiere of an early version of *Chomavision* at *Movie Monday* with his wife, Phyllis, and he said that was the best night of his life, receiving public recognition for his life's work as an artist. (The painting below, part of which is reproduced on the cover of this book, is by Bob and is one of many featured in the video.)

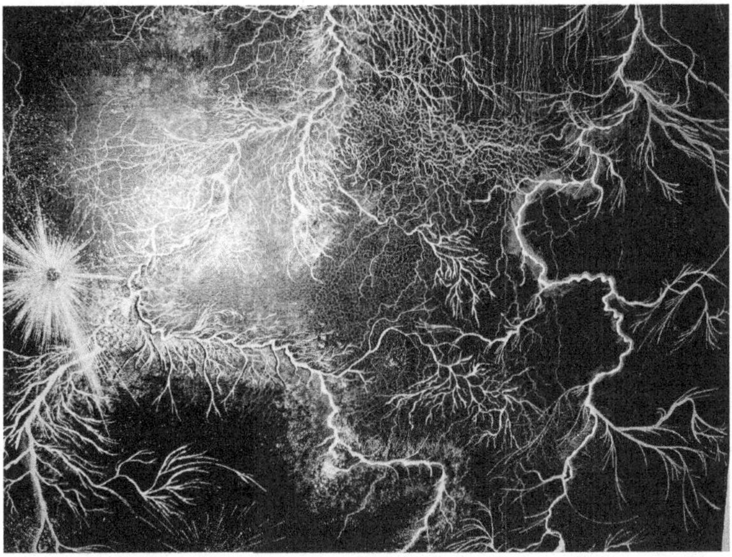

Reproduction of a painting by my late bipolar friend, visionary artist Robert Bogdan Choma. The left side is painted in red, and the right is blue (see this book's front cover).

Conclusion

Looking back, I know I've been lucky. I wasn't ever incapacitated for long. Although my illness almost ended my life twice, it has not been as severe as many people experience. I have a supportive life partner who stuck by me through some hard times, two wonderful children, a comfortable home, and I was able to maintain my business throughout until I retired at age 68. Even now, at 70, I am physically active and socially engaged. No doubt, things could have been much worse.

I've had my scrapes, and my family has had its challenges. But my bipolar identity is out there where we can work on it together—in an open manner. I know my late Dad would be proud of that!

Bruce Saunders

I was born in 1950 in Victoria, British Columbia, and studied Fine Arts at the University of Victoria. I live in Victoria with my wife, Laurel, and we have two adult sons, Daniel and Paul. I was diagnosed with bipolar disorder at age 39, but had struggled with anxiety since childhood, and depression since my mid-twenties. I retired at age 68 from my landscape maintenance gardening business, and now volunteer actively in the local community. Please visit vimeo.com/250067468 to view the 80-minute *Chomavision* documentary I made about my late bipolar friend, Bob Choma.

My Bipolar Reality

Jayne Warren

I am preparing to run away. I have never been able to live anywhere but here or travel anywhere abroad since I became sick. Doctors have perfected the science to cure me. I want to read an adventure novel that matches this high. Instead, I wake in a snap of time. Everything vanishes: the dream, my peace, my dashed hope for any kind of future ...

Walking down the hall to my bathroom I realize I could walk outside into the rain and just keep going. My cell phone would ring eventually, but who would find me? My hair is so long and wet I could drink from it. I would sleep in the woods by the highway, my dreams buffeted by the sound of cars speeding past. Eventually I would flag one down and tell him: "Take me anywhere but here." What will I do when the agitation arises again, and I am un-medicated and, in the end, un-free once more? I will find where I am and call home. I will climb into bed and sleep. I will sleep it all away. [My journal, May 19, 2018]

My mental illness leaves reality fractured, fragmented into what is real and present and what is in my mind. More confusing still is the fact that what my mind creates is a convincing reality. It even controls time. Seconds hang immobile as I am caught in a daydream, the daydreams like movies becoming more and more frequent around the time my medication wears off. In the half-hour on either side of my nighttime or morning doses I feel emotion more acutely. I imagine confrontations, things that are heated and grave.

A mental health staff person at my first psychiatric commitment gave me this advice: intrusive thoughts are like pop-up ads on a computer: if I keep my hand on the mouse ready to cancel them, I will be okay. But intrusive thoughts can come all day every day, my mind continually wondering what would happen *if. What if?* At some early point I realized these thoughts, these urges, would be there forever.

I recently argued with a person over semantics—whether one should be referred to as a person with disabilities or a disabled person. They said it is an argument of personhood: to put the disability before the person (as in "a bipolar patient" rather than "a patient with bipolar") strips them of their identity. But both are who I am. It's a Venn diagram: in one circle is personhood, in the other my disability. My identity lies somewhere in between.

I struggled for many years trying to form an identity apart from my bipolar. I finally found I could not. I can go 12 hours on medications before I feel it, my disease. I have to take something eventually or I lose myself completely. This is something that has happened three times in the past ten years.

I have been diagnosed with depression, anxiety, post-traumatic stress disorder (PTSD), and intrusive thoughts. I disassociate. I have attention deficit hyperactivity disorder (ADHD). I have bipolar disorder. I have been told mine is a severe and complex case.

I don't have the disorder people see in the media. I am rarely manic or even on a high. I mostly cycle between depressive and mixed states. In a mixed state I feel agitated, my thoughts going a million *times* a minute. I hate myself. I want to die. I think about dying. Mixed states are the most dangerous place to be in because with the mix of depressive thoughts and manic action one is more likely to do something irreparably damaging to oneself.

Editor's note: "Mixed episodes" are characterized by mania and depression occurring either at the same time or in rapid succession, with no recovery period in between. Mania with mixed features (also known as "dysphoric mania" where dysphoric means the opposite of euphoric) usually presents with extreme irritability, agitation, racing thoughts and speech, and hyperactivity. People experiencing mixed states are at higher risk for self-harm, suicide, or violence against others, and may need emergency care.

I have committed myself to a psychiatric ward three times for my own safety, mostly because I feared what I might do to myself. They always ask, "Do you have a plan?" And I do, I have twelve bottles of medication upstairs. It would be all too easy to take it all. I was locked up for ten, seventeen, finally twenty-eight days.

At my last stay, I didn't leave the ward for one whole month except for two supervised outings with my mother. My belongings were locked up in the "Sharps Closet." I could check things out only with privileges. "The Sharps Closet" was necessary because some people on the wards are actively suicidal. They try to hang themselves with anything they can get their hands on—belts, shoelaces, headphone cords. They break the plastic cutlery to cut themselves. They use nail clippers to cut their skin.

I am a stranger to a world outside of wards and self-harm and suicidality. Even now, two years out, I sometimes wake up not right. A piece of the puzzle is just barely askew, but I cannot find which one it is or figure out how to put it back correctly. It's strange not being able to identify my own emotion, but stranger still when that emotion scares me.

Over the years, on the advice of my doctors, I have begun to track my moods. For every mood there are signs—footprints in the undergrowth, fur rubbed against a tree—signs that show me where it is leading and then, maybe then, I can stop it, head off sadness before it becomes depression; happiness before it becomes mania.

But no matter how much I track emotions or keep my hand on the proverbial mouse, this is not a temporary state of being. Given the nature of my disorder I will always have a high rate of failure and recurrence. I can never heal myself. I can only treat the symptoms, the real damage is somewhere deep inside: the crossed synapses, the damaged neurons, the altered chemicals. I have seen MRIs of brains like mine. Whatever it is that is happening inside cannot be fixed.

I cannot say that I will never find myself on a ward again or need to change medications or have to explain my life story to another psychiatrist. I have tried to process that I will always be sick. Nobody calls those of us with mental illnesses survivors like those with cancer. Nobody congratulates me on having made it this long. Still, I have made it this long, from when I was younger and my mood swings and rash decision-making were attributed to being a teenager, or through three rounds of ECT, and dozens of medication changes.

In the end, mental illness is about taking things day to day. If I look too far ahead, I lose sight of where I am now. And I have lost myself on this journey too many times to let it happen again.

Jayne Warren

I was born in 1989 in Massachusetts. I studied Latin American studies and Spanish at Smith College but could not complete my studies due to my disorder. I was diagnosed with bipolar disorder at age 19 during my first hospitalization. I am on disability but continue to write. Prior to Smith College I studied at Walnut Hill School for the Arts, class of 2008, where I majored in writing. I plan to publish my memoir of autobiographical essays soon. I live in Norwood, MA, with my mother. clippings.me/users/jaynecw

After the Treatment of Last Resort

Natasha Tracy

In 2009, I had been under psychiatric treatment for bipolar disorder for 11 years, but treatment had only been what I would consider to be successful for a handful of those years. I'd taken mood stabilizers, antipsychotics, anticonvulsants, benzodiazepines, and antidepressants, among others. I had been to countless therapy appointments. I had even had a vagal nerve stimulation device surgically implanted to help me feel normal again. Unfortunately, for years, these things hadn't been working. After I had consulted many psychiatrists, it was clear that medicine had almost nothing left to offer me.

It was time for the treatment of last resort.

Had you asked me about electroconvulsive therapy (ECT, or "shock therapy") in January of 2009, I would have said this: ECT is utterly barbaric and the fact that it goes on to this day is appalling and terrifying. I would never, ever, let someone fry my brain. I am not sticking my finger in a light socket and praying. I would rather die.

But September of 2009 saw me undergo my first ECT treatment.

Desperate people do things they never would have considered before getting into an interminably painful situation, and I was the picture of desperation. I had been battling a depressive episode for years. The medication I took effectively controlled the hypomania, but the depression slipped by with nary a nick. Depression was slippery and writhing and evil, and it was out to kill me. Every day. Every day it tried to kill me. Every day I tried to resist. Every day was getting harder.

I researched ECT, at first out of curiosity. The stories ranged from miraculous to living nightmare. The treatment seemed like someone would flip a switch, toss a die, and whatever happened, happened. But then I started looking at the stats. And the stats on ECT to treat depression were surprisingly favourable. There were undoubtedly horror stories out there and on the internet a light is sometimes shone brightly on them, but clinically the evidence was weighted heavily in favour of the patient. At the time, the number being bandied about was 80: up to 80 percent of people with depression who were treated with ECT saw positive results.

And so I pinned my hopes on a number. I just kept thinking, "80." Because, honestly, the treatment itself is rather insane. It's designed to induce a tiny seizure—something that is avoided in almost any other context. And yet it's the goal here. People often call ECT a "reboot of the brain." This is a ridiculously inaccurate metaphor. It's more like hitting the side of a TV set and hoping that will clear up the static across the screen. It could work. Or it could land your TV on the floor. You just don't know until you do it.

The day of my first ECT treatment I was terrified. I tried to screw a brave face onto my head for the friend who accompanied me to my appointment. When we got to the hospital, we were told the ECT room was in the basement. "Yeah, just follow the flickering lights and screams," I thought.

When we got to the waiting room my desperation found company. The people there waiting for treatment were wearing pain on every inch of their beings. But those are the people who end up there: people in pain with no better options. ECT is often the treatment of last resort.

When it was my turn to go into the treatment room, my friend accompanied me. The doctor showed me around a little bit and my friend sat in a chair while I was prepped. Part of me thought I was going to die. Part of me was sure I would never wake up from this brain scrambling. But I kept saying "I'm going to be fine" to my friend, over and over. I didn't want her to worry. Unfortunately, my tears betrayed my true feelings by soaking my cheeks. I became almost hysterical.

Modern electroconvulsive therapy is done under general anaesthetic. There are no screams because the people are asleep. It takes but a few minutes to complete the treatment and be moved into the recovery area.

I woke up from the anaesthesia in physical pain. That is something no one tells you will happen. According to the doctors, there may be "some discomfort" after the procedure. For me this wasn't right. For me, there was pain. My whole jaw hurt so much I could not move it to make sound and tell the nurse I was awake. Then I looked down and saw it: I was locked to the gurney. This was a terrifying surprise.

There are reasons for both things. The jaw pain happened because the electricity which ran through my brain, was close to my jaw, making my jaw clench inhumanly against the protective bite block they'd inserted into my mouth. And the lock was there for my protection. The staff don't want you tumbling off your gurney or trying to walk off while still partially under anaesthesia. These things make sense now. It's unfortunate that no one bothered to explain them to me ahead of time.

Eventually, through much pain, I did manage to signal the nurse and she ended up giving me multiple rounds of pain medication. And after an undue amount of time, I was allowed to leave the recovery area and go into the next room.

I had nine ECT treatments in all. Each one got less acutely painful and, despite being terrified, I felt cared for. The staff did their jobs well. And even though that time was characterized by pain, suffering, and cognitive issues, I do remember something in particular: I remember Fruit Loops.

After I left the recovery area, the next thing to do was eat breakfast. I wasn't allowed to eat before the procedure so they had me eat there, where I could remain under observation afterward. In that breakfast room, they had Fruit Loops. Now, I had never eaten Fruit Loops before. As a child, I wasn't allowed to eat them and as an adult, I didn't allow myself to eat them either. But here's the thing: Fruit Loops taste good.

So, I said to myself, "If I'm going to get electrocuted three times a week, then I'm eating Fruit Loops, damnit!"

But unfortunately, Fruit Loops were not enough to distract from this overwhelming fact: I was not getting better. And not only were there no positive effects from the ECT treatment, there were many negative effects. I was in constant pain and sleeping all the time from having the general anaesthesia, but considerably worse than that were the cognitive side effects. I was experiencing amnesia, which they had warned me about, and I was prepared for. But I was also experiencing symptoms like not recognizing my own neighbourhood, not remembering how certain things came to be in my apartment, and a general confusion and fuzziness that kept getting worse.

With ECT, results tend to be fairly rapid. Sometimes they happen after only one treatment, but after nine, some improvement should definitely be evident. So, I had a choice: I could opt for a form of ECT that was stronger and would likely have even more cognitive side effects, or I could stop.

Because I was terrified about what was happening to my brain, I stopped.

Put succinctly, the last-ditch effort of science and medicine hadn't worked in my case. All the pain turned out not to be worth it for me. I was truly beyond help and hope.

I muddled through the next little while. My life was a mess-ridden tangle at that point, and I was triaging every moment:

rampant mental illness has a way of requiring that. In a few months, a new psychiatrist would confirm that I was beyond help by refusing to treat me. Her exact words were, "You've tried every treatment and they've all failed. What's the point in you having a doctor?"

It was after that exchange that I truly broke. I shattered into a million pieces on the floor of my kitchen one day. I knew that if I couldn't get a doctor, then I couldn't get help. If I couldn't get help, then I couldn't get better. And if I couldn't get better, then what was the point? The depression was winning. Maybe it had won. I considered that maybe nothing existed after the treatment of last resort.

It was then that I tried to take my own life. My suicide attempt was doomed by fate, and probably some tiny part of me that still wanted to live, despite everything; some tiny, stubborn part of me that the depression hadn't destroyed.

When I came to from my attempt, I realized something: that the doctor who had denied me treatment was wrong. I needed help. I needed a doctor who could see past the failures; a doctor who knew about something beyond the treatment of last resort.

Through good fortune, a doctor who used to see me agreed to see me again. He didn't have to. He wasn't even accepting new patients at the time. The system had said I was broken; that I couldn't be fixed. But he agreed to treat me anyway. And to this day, when I think of that kindness, I want to cry. If it weren't for that doctor, there truly wouldn't have been anything past the treatment of last resort.

At my first appointment, he said, "I want you to take this little blue pill."

I said, "I've tried that little blue pill and it didn't work."

He said, "I know, but you haven't tried it in this combination of medications before."

I sighed heavily, and merely to appease him said, "Fine, I'll take your little blue pill."

And within about two weeks, a miracle happened: I started to feel better. I started to feel better in a way that I hadn't felt in about a decade.

It was right around then that I found out about a friend's pregnancy. She was a lovely person, as was her husband, and I thought they would make great parents. And, sitting across the dinner table from her, as she talked about getting swollen ankles and using an app to track her pregnancy's progress, I remember feeling happy for her. Happy! That was a word that hadn't crossed my brain with any sincerity in many years. But I was genuinely happy for her. I could feel the warmth and light that true happiness brings. I had forgotten about that. I had forgotten how happiness felt. It was a sweet breath of air after years of anguished strangulation. I wanted to cry—but for the first time in a decade, it was from joy and love and happiness and not from despair.

Unfortunately, that little blue pill lost its miraculous touch very quickly. Within a handful of months, the depression clawed its way back into my brain. The pain and suffering and agony all returned with gusto.

But I wasn't exactly back to where I'd started. No amount of depression and pain could take away the lesson I'd learned. I learned that medical miracles happen and, in fact, if I kept trying—even after everyone else had given up—one could happen to me. I found out that my brain could be in a good place. I found out that all my little neurotransmitters could fire properly. I found out that, despite forgetting what happiness feels like, happiness could visit me anyway.

And with all my heart and all my head, I still believe it can happen again.

Natasha Tracy

I was born in British Columbia (BC) in 1978, and still live here. I studied computer science at the University of Victoria, BC, achieving a Bachelor of Computer Science in 2002. I was diagnosed with bipolar disorder in 1998, after many years of undiagnosed and untreated mood-related symptoms. I am an award-winning mental health thought leader, speaker, consultant, and author of the book, *Lost Marbles: Insight into My Life with Depression & Bipolar*. I bring high-quality and trusted information on bipolar disorder to the public while engaging with the mental health community. My blog, *Bipolar Burble*, has appeared on top 10 lists for a decade and my blog, *Breaking Bipolar* at HealthyPlace, has won back-to-back Web Health Awards. I also received the Didi Hirsch Erasing the Stigma Leadership Award in 2014.
NatashaTracy.com

Holding On by My Fingertips

Janet L. Stanley, MA

It was a beautiful day, driving over the pass, filled with possibilities as I contemplated where I would drive my car off the cliff to kill myself. That was April 2017. At that moment, I believed killing myself was the answer. The thoughts, "Kill yourself; end your life; your life is worthless; just do it; stop being a chicken and kill yourself" swirled around and around in my head and had led me to that moment. All the while, the desire to end my life strengthened.

And then a sudden realization: I had Maia, my beautiful lab, with me and I couldn't end her life; I simply couldn't.

I called my dear friend Candace, and with her love and support I eventually found my way home that day. Candace called my wife, Kris, alerting her that something was terribly wrong. And yet, when I returned home, I couldn't bring myself to tell Kris what I had been experiencing for months. I just couldn't find the words.

The following day, I asked Candace to meet me for tea. It was there I found the words and the courage to tell her what I had been living through for months. All the disturbing details. How I had been spiraling downward into a very black hole and the speed was accelerating. I said I wondered how far into the abyss my psyche could sink before I could no longer see the light to bring myself back. I explained how I felt I was holding on with my fingertips and my fingers were beginning to slip little by little as I tried desperately not to let go. I willed myself to tighten my grip and no matter how hard I tried, I kept falling further into the depths of despair, having no idea where to turn or who to turn to.

I said the downward spiral felt as though I was tumbling out of control into a barren land where hope no longer existed. Where joy and happiness were merely fleeting ideas and where black clouds followed me wherever I went. And I knew something was different. There was a part of my psyche that was demanding to be heard. There was something wrong with my brain and I needed help.

We drove to my home and there, with Candace's help, I finally told Kris everything. I sat on our couch fighting back the thoughts in my head that I continued to hear over and over: that my life was worthless, I didn't deserve to live, I should have the courage to just kill myself, get it over with—thoughts I couldn't control. At times I found myself hitting my head with my fists, crying: "There's something wrong with my brain; there's something wrong with my brain."

Kris listened to me quietly. I had warned her that this was very difficult for me to talk about, so she was prepared for heavy news. She was deeply concerned and very supportive. She and Candace agreed to support each other as they both provided a loving and safe environment to protect me from myself.

My history with depression and mood swings

Before I go any further, it is important for you to know I have been living with depression and mood swings most of my life. Of course, I couldn't have identified it as such as an adolescent, however, looking back it is clear this has been part of my life since I can remember. Alcohol and pot became my best friends helping me negotiate the tumult that had become my life.

In 1996, at age 42, I was finally diagnosed with depression and began taking an antidepressant. Yes, it helped somewhat and yet for years, I continued to experience times where I would feel "manic." I used that word to explain to others what I felt during periods that were far different than my depression. (I later learned it was "hypomania.") Even though I continued therapy for years, none of my therapists ever addressed these "episodes" that I was becoming more aware of as they were becoming more prevalent.

In 2005, I had a mental and emotional breakdown. All I could tell my primary care physician was I wanted to run away. I didn't know who I was running from or where I was running to. I just wanted to run away. I was eventually placed on permanent disability and yet, not one of my providers explored these hypomanic episodes that were becoming more pronounced. There were times when I would begin working in my garden at 7:30 in the morning and my wife would come out around 7:30 in the evening, put her arms around me and gently tell me it was time for me to come in. At times, it was nearly impossible for me to "see" what was happening. These hypomanic episodes were becoming more and more the norm.

Seeking help

Two days after the crisis while driving over the pass, Kris helped me seek professional help. It was a fiasco. We phoned therapists and psychiatrists, reaching out for help but none was offered. We were direct and told them I was suicidal and yet, nothing. Earlier that day, I had sent an email to my primary care physician and hadn't heard back from her which was very unusual. We ended up in a community counselling centre which was pathetic. At this point, I felt completely helpless and defeated. I was continuing to receive messages that it really was time to end my life. I had made two separate suicide plans and had the means to carry out both.

Then my phone rang. It was my physician. She hadn't been working that day. Her assistant had read the email and phoned her. She asked me where I was and where Kris was. I told her Kris was sitting next to me. She told me to go to the emergency room (ER) immediately. She would call ahead to let them know I was suicidal, and they would see me immediately. When I arrived, I told them who I was and, sure enough, they took us directly to the ER Psychiatric Unit.

It was in that Psych Unit where hope began to find its way back into my life. An ER Hospitalist came in. He was compassionate and caring and truly interested in learning about what I had been experiencing. I felt heard. He brought some light into a very bleak time in my life. He left the room for a few minutes. Upon his return, he let us know the hospital psychiatrist would soon be in and assured us that the psychiatrist would provide us the support, care and concern I deserved, and we needed as a family.

Getting a bipolar diagnosis

When the psychiatrist arrived, she asked me to tell her everything. And I did. She asked me questions about not only my depression, but about the episodes with mood swings. I told her of days and weeks when I would feel as though I was the Ever-Ready Bunny: going and going and going, unable to stop. When I finally did stop, I would feel depression knocking on my door and the absolute exhaustion that followed my busy-busy, "high" episodes.

She asked me if I had ever heard of hypomania. I had not. She went on to explain it was part of the bipolar spectrum, an elevated mood with excessive energy, grandiose thinking, rapid speech, flight of ideas, decreased need for sleep, and so on. She then said that I, as someone living with both depression and hypomania, had what is called bipolar II.

At last: a diagnosis that made sense of both my depressions and other mood swings!

We talked for quite some time. She went on to say she felt she could help me. She acknowledged that lithium had a reputation for its toxicity yet, at very low doses, the psychiatric community was beginning once again to see its benefits, if prescribed responsibly. She went on to disclose that she herself took 150 mg per day and had never experienced any negative side effects. She asked if I would be willing to try 150 mg per day of lithium along with increasing my Wellbutrin from 300 mg per day to 450 mg per day. I agreed. Yes, I was apprehensive. And yet, I knew if I truly wanted to live, I needed to trust her. And so, I did.

She then asked if I felt I needed to be admitted into the psychiatric ward or did I feel able to go home? With both Kris and Candace at my side, I felt that going home would be doable.

> *The psychiatrist encouraged me to read a book entitled* Bipolar, Not So Much *by Chris Aiken, MD, and James Phelps, MD. I read about my life in the pages of that book: about how long I had suffered unnecessarily, and how there is hope for the many of us who live with a mental illness. I strongly encourage others living with a mental illness on the bipolar spectrum—and their loved ones—to read that book.*

Kris and Candace, with my approval, took all my medications and put them away where I wouldn't have access. They knew I was still fragile, and that having those medications easily accessible wasn't in my best interest. I agreed. They didn't leave me alone. One of them was always with me until we all felt the newly prescribed medications were doing what they were intended to do.

Recovery

I don't want to leave the impression I no longer cycle through hypomanic and depressive episodes. I do. However, they are fewer. Most often, I can identify when I'm experiencing hypomania and I let Kris know. It's a commitment I made to her. I no longer feel the need to hide when my moods are cycling. I'm not always aware and there are times when Kris will gently let me know what she is observing. We are in this together. I know my mental illness impacts her life and I want to help minimize that impact.

As long as I do what I know I need to do to stay stable (exercise, yoga, garden, pursue my spiritual path, and—of course—take my meds daily), I'd say I can function at about a seven or eight out of ten, and for that I am truly grateful.

As for suicidal thoughts… I won't say I never have them. But they're much more fleeting than before I was treated. And not nearly so insistent. A few hours to a day or two and they're gone. I talk openly about it with Kris and Candace. I have promised them I'll be honest and forthright with them. It's reassuring for me to have made this agreement with them.

Fighting the stigma

Once I felt stable and strong enough, I began telling my family and friends what I had gone through. I was determined to help de-stigmatize mental illness. I remembered the years I had suffered by not being diagnosed correctly and I wanted to help raise awareness. And I knew that there was nothing to be ashamed or embarrassed about. I was born with a chemical imbalance. There isn't anything I did or didn't do that caused my mental illness.

I believe it is imperative for those of us living with a mental illness, and our loved ones, to speak openly about how the illness impacts the lives of all of us. To help deconstruct the stigma and to do away with the arbitrary social constructs currently assigned to those living with a mental illness. We are your parents, children, caregivers, grandparents, physicians, teachers, healers—we are part of your families and communities. We aren't "crazy" and to say so is disrespectful and demonstrates a lack of understanding and compassion. It minimizes the reality of our lives and of those we love. It marginalizes us and places us in the category of "Other"—not quite worthy of being treated with the same dignity and consideration as those not relegated to this category.

Conclusion

Living with bipolar has been a gift in many respects. It has taught me a great deal about myself I'm not sure would have been revealed without the disorder. And it has provided me with a platform to share about my lived experience with mental illness in an open and honest way. I hope my story will touch at least one person's life as a result.

Maybe that life is yours?

Janet L. Stanley

I was born in Montana in 1954 and was raised in California. For my undergraduate degree, I studied Communications and Women's Studies at San Diego State University and my interdisciplinary graduate degree was in Women's Studies, Sociology and Anthropology at San Jose State University. I retired from working in the non-profit sector and am now a spiritual healer, mentor, and shamanic practitioner. I live with my wife, Kris, in Grants Pass, Oregon, where I am an avid gardener and hiker with a passion for cooking.
shamaniccrone@gmail.com

It's Hard to See the Light

Wayfarer*

** Editor's note: This author used a pen name to protect his privacy, particularly at work. He was diagnosed with bipolar disorder in 2019 in his early fifties. When I started corresponding with him, I thought that some of his early reflections would be of great interest to readers going through a similar experience and urged him to write for this anthology. However, the combination of persistent bipolar depression and the stress of the COVID-19 pandemic during the first part of 2020 ultimately made this too difficult for him. These excerpts from our email correspondence will hopefully provide a glance into the reality of a newly diagnosed, middle-aged man. He died tragically, shortly before this book was published.*

October 17, 2019

Dear Merryl,

I just ordered your memoir, *Mad Like Me: Travels in Bipolar Country*. I look forward to reading it. A friend brought it to my attention.

I was diagnosed with bipolar disorder (in my case, bipolar II) this year in my fifties, a year after the death of my father. Before that, apart from a depression in my twenties, I was doing fine and got a couple of degrees from MIT and McGill University.

Your journey will also be of interest to my wife and family (I have three children); and will no doubt provide hope as I go through the iterative process of trying a host of different medications to see which ones work for me.

Same day

On the same day, I replied, "Yes, please be very patient as your doctors try to find the perfect combination of medications and dosages for your body/brain. In my case, as I explain in my memoir, it took quite some time and two psychiatric hospitalizations before they finally got it right. But I have now had almost a decade entirely episode-free. So, there is hope for all!

"As for your wife and family members, yes, I've been told by many readers that my book really helped them to "get into the shoes" of their affected loved one, to understand them, and to treat them with the human respect and dignity they deserve—even when they're acting totally irrationally in mania, and so on.

"I'm currently compiling short essays for a bipolar anthology. If you're interested in learning more about that, please let me know and I'll send you the Writers' Guidelines. Your reflections on being diagnosed so recently would be a wonderful addition to the book."

October 18, 2019

Thank you for the email. I am hoping a sustainable solution can be found for my condition soon. I have read many medical studies and journals on the action of various drugs to better understand what we (with my psychiatrist) are trying to achieve. Mental health care here in Africa lags substantially behind that of more developed countries and some of the latest medicines that I am now taking aren't even available here—I had to get them from Canada. I'd be happy to write a short essay for the anthology. I am not out of the woods yet and the situation is fluid, but some reflections—even in such a difficult time—may be of use to others.

Same day

On the same day, I sent a note of encouragement along with the Writers' Guidelines for this anthology. There followed a few months with no contact between us.

January 18, 2020

"I hope you are doing well, and learning to cope with your bipolar disorder?

"In October, you expressed interest in contributing to the bipolar anthology. I do hope you are still interested in submitting a piece? If so, I very much look forward to receiving your submission sometime in the coming months."

February 3, 2020

Thank you for your recent email and your kind wishes. Apologies for the delay in responding to you; hope you and yours are well.

I am still struggling with finding the right antidepressant (the antipsychotic having been established) as nearly all medications are too activating or have terrible side effects. The way things are going, it's currently hard to see light at the end of the tunnel, so I am not sure what sort of a story I can put together for the anthology, unless my fortunes change.

Same day

"Thanks so much for writing: I know it takes enormous energy and headspace. I'm so sorry to hear that you are still struggling to find a combination of medications that will work for you. Every case is so individual... Please keep your hopes up. As I always say, 'Bipolar is a beast. We have to learn to tame it. But tame it, we will!'

"For your possible contribution to the anthology, I remember how foggy and inept I used to feel in the early days. So I've taken the liberty of giving you a list of writing prompts below, just to stimulate your thinking. If any of them don't appeal to you, just skip over to the next... Please take them as suggestions, only.

1. *I am .... years old and trained as a .... [if relevant].*
2. *I work for [.... organization, if relevant] as a .....*
3. *I am single/married/divorced etc. and have .... children [if relevant].*

4. *At the age of .... [which symptoms initially caused concern; and which led you to seek help]?*
5. *Did anything trigger your disorder, do you think (e.g., extreme stress, death of a loved one, etc.)?*
6. *Who did you consult for help, and what was the initial diagnosis? (Has that diagnosis been revised since then?)*
7. *How did you react to the diagnosis?*
8. *How did your family, friends, and colleagues react? (Did you tell colleagues, or try to hide your illness? Why?)*
9. *How do you feel about your diagnosis now?*
10. *Is your disorder well controlled at present? If not, what symptoms are you experiencing? How is this affecting your family and work life?*
11. *What advice would you give to someone who is getting a psychiatric diagnosis right now? Why?*
12. *What have you learned about yourself and those around you since you were first diagnosed?*
13. *Anything else you can add or feel moved to share."*

The COVID-19 pandemic hit North America in March 2020, so again, several months passed with no contact between us.

July 12, 2020

"I do hope you are feeling at least a bit better than when we last corresponded in February. And that the pandemic hasn't adversely affected you or your family.

"I'm just writing now to ask how you are doing, and to hear if there's any chance of you writing something for the anthology? I do hope you'll be able to participate!"

August 12, 2020

Thank you for the kind email and apologies for the delayed response—it's a full month later that I now write. I am doing a bit better, but still no mood stabilizing medication has been found that helps—it's essentially the depression that isn't lifting. I have no mania and most antidepressants they have tried on me are too activating, although an old antidepressant that is negatively affecting my memory does get rid of my anxiety.

About writing something for the anthology, I must pass for now—my apologies, I am not at a stage that I can look back and write clearly about this. I mostly try to put bipolar disorder out of my mind.

Same day

On the same day, I expressed my understanding and suggested that—if he was comfortable with the idea—we could simply edit and publish our email correspondence. I asked his opinion about a title for the piece. He immediately consented on condition that he could use a pen name and suggested "It's hard to see the light" as a title.

After I sent a query about his biography and the draft of his piece for review, he thanked me and sent me this.

August 20, 2020

My biggest worry now is for my children who may carry the gene for bipolar disorder. That's the last thing in the world I would want for them. Not sure if the gene is enough for someone to develop bipolar or whether a trigger/trauma is also part of the equation (i.e., genetic and environmental drivers). Do any of your children show signs or symptoms of bipolar?

Same day

I replied the same day, "No; so far, so good: my biological kids (aged 27, 29, and 32) are not showing any signs of bipolar. (Yet!) I keep warning them to live more balanced lives, get good sleep, and to build mental resilience through meditation, and so on, but ... they still think they're invincible.

"I'm not sure how old your kids are, but when they're old enough, the best thing you could do is to talk frankly to them about your experiences with bipolar. (Many families still seem to try to sweep it under the rug.) There is nothing for us to be ashamed of, and I find that speaking openly about it helps others to do so too. At least then your kids can take steps to protect themselves as far as possible: live in balance; consciously protect their possibly fragile brains; recognize and cope pro-actively and effectively with triggers as they emerge; etc.

"Here is an extract from my notes about bipolar. Hope there's something in there to reassure you—especially the last line, since you were in your fifties when bipolar emerged in your life!" (Please see textbox.)

Bipolar disorder is more likely to affect the children of parents who have the disorder. When one parent has bipolar, the risk to each child is 15–30%. When both parents have bipolar, the risk increases to 50–75% (National Institute of Mental Health).

Many individuals with bipolar disorder have relatives with other mood, anxiety, and psychotic disorders (such as depression or schizophrenia). These disorders may run in families in part because they share some genetic risk factors with bipolar disorder.

So, the bottom line is that if you have bipolar, you were likely born with the predisposition for this disorder, and for many, a stressful life event and/or upbringing can trigger the onset of the illness. (What is stressful to one person may not be stressful to another.)

More than two-thirds of people with bipolar disorder have at least one close relative with the illness or with unipolar major depression, indicating that the disease has a heritable component (National Institute of Mental Health).

The younger a person is when bipolar emerges, the more likely there is to be a genetic component (Mood Disorders Society of Canada).

Same day

Many thanks for that, Merryl. My mother has bipolar; being from the Middle East and with all the cultural stigmas attached to mental illness, she never sought help (and she put the family through the wringer) until after some 20 years of constant encouragement starting when she was 50, she agreed to get help at age 69. She still doesn't accept that there is anything wrong with her.

With me, there was childhood trauma followed by enormous stress as a young man when I became the sole breadwinner for my family for some years. All this then triggered a depression that seemed unipolar at the time.

I agree that when my children are old enough, I should talk to them. I do think that preparing them for a healthy, balanced life without undue pressures and hopefully minimal traumas might spare them. I was always an over-achiever and perfectionist and that created a lot of mental pressure.

Same day again

"My goodness: with your family history, it seems to me you're lucky to have lasted till age 51 before bipolar showed its full face... But the great news is that—after an awful period of transition while the doctors tinker with various meds

and doses and combinations, and while you learn to rigorously apply self-care strategies—recovery is possible. And may you be the one to break the cycle of silence in your family!

"Would it be okay if we add extracts from these last two emails to your piece for the anthology?"

Same day again

I was thinking the same—yes, please do include this.

Wayfarer (a pen name) was born in the Middle East, moved with his family to Africa as a child, and studied in the USA and Canada. He lived with his wife and children in Africa where he worked for an international organization. He died tragically in 2021.

How Can I Have a Positive Future Now?

Maggie Taylor*

** Editor's note: This South African author has chosen to use a pen name, and to anonymize all names and places in this piece to protect her child and others.*

I would like to share my story with you in the hope that others may learn from it and take bipolar disorder more seriously than I initially did. Let mine be a cautionary tale: no one is safe from bipolar; no one is "above" it; and everyone is at risk of losing everything to it.

Like I did.

My early years as a lawyer

Let me back up. I was admitted as an attorney in South Africa in the late 2000s. At age 26, I opened my own law firm, Taylor Attorneys, in Johannesburg. At the beginning of that year, my long-term personal relationship of seven years came to heartbreaking, gut-wrenching end. Jack moved out of our home and left me alone. I was devastated.

Looking back now, I think his decision to leave me had a lot to do with my emerging and undiagnosed bipolar. I think the living situation with me just became untenable for him.

After Jack left me, I started seeing a psychologist, Michelle, once a week to help me cope.

The only thing I really had in my life at this time was my law firm, so I threw myself into it and it became my entire world. I was determined to make it a success and to become a dominant player in the legal fraternity.

To cheer me up after Jack left, a close school friend of mine who had attended law school with me, Linda, would insist that I spend weekends with her away from Johannesburg, either in Pretoria or on a game farm in the bush nearby. For a whole year while I was single, I spent most weekends with Linda. We'd often go together to watch rugby matches at the stadium in Pretoria.

Hypomania and hypersexuality

One weekend at the stadium, after the game, a group of young men in a box above us shouted down and threw something onto the stands to get our attention. We looked up, smiled, and chatted to them, and next thing, they invited us up to their box. This is where I met a guy called David. We began drinking in the box, one thing led to another, and he and I ended up in a passionate embrace which later led to us having sex right there on the stadium field. This seems unbelievable to me now: it was not at all typical behaviour for me. I just became a different person in hypomania.

Linda and some of the guys from David's group exchanged cellphone numbers. The following weekend, David contacted me. He was at a bachelor's party and wanted to see me. Before I could think twice, I jumped in my car and drove all alone at night—keep in mind, this is in South Africa, where the crime rate is sky-high—to a place that was unfamiliar to me and to a man I did not know. I reached David safely and he and I ended up having sex in my car until the sun rose.

When I told my psychologist about my recent conduct with David and how much fun I was having, she raised the bipolar flag and referred me to a psychiatrist. I wasn't informed enough about bipolar and in my mind an attorney just seriously could *not* have a mental illness. I mean, how could an attorney practise law with a mental illness?

That first hypomanic episode gradually wound down, and my risky behaviour slowed down substantially. However, I continued to see David. It even went so far that I met his entire immediate family and stayed at their farm on occasion. Until his father banned me from the farm. The reason I was given was that he didn't like me and didn't think I was right for his son. Be that as it may, David and I continued to see each other until I fell pregnant with his child. Initially, when I told him I was pregnant, he was interested in being a part of my child's life until I insisted that he tell his family. The last civil phone call we had was when he said that he had told his family, and they decided to have nothing to do with me or my child. David was not interested in ever marrying me and he didn't want to be part of a "broken home." He said he would step in only if something should happen to me and none of my family members would take care of my child. A father of last resort! It has now been almost ten years and he has not been a part of our child's life at all.

Life as a single mom

After giving birth to my daughter, Georgina, I really tried to pull myself together and the risky behaviour ceased. From what I can recall, life continued in a normal fashion for a single mom with a newborn. I hired a full-time nanny and threw myself back into legal work. Completely to the detriment of my daughter and myself.

There were a couple of small incidents from the time Georgina was born to the time I really started destroying my life when Georgina was about two years old. I won't delve into them here. It is too painful for me, and a mother should know better.

When Georgina was about a year old, I moved from my smallholding in Heidelberg to a house I purchased in Johannesburg. I also moved my law firm into the same house. I thought it would make things easier to have the law firm at home and raise a baby. I was wrong!

The turbulent "John years"

Soon after moving, I started a romantic relationship with another attorney from Johannesburg, John.

This relationship was volatile from start to finish. So much so that at one point I had John arrested, and the whole abusive matter landed up on the front page of the local Johannesburg newspaper.

My house was right next door to John's, so we were neighbours, lovers, and colleagues in the legal fraternity. I truly was not thinking!

Nevertheless, even after that whole ordeal of being in the newspapers, we still kissed and made up. John went on to propose and I said yes. Even as I write this today, I shake my head and think, what on earth were you thinking! But I wasn't thinking, I was just acting, following emotion, and trying to live out this fantasy I had created in my head.

I won't elaborate further on my relationship with John: I will just say it was one helluva rollercoaster ride. It officially ended after about a year, but John never really left my life during the following two years: he was continually toying with my emotions. He also raised the fact that he thought I had bipolar and said if I sought treatment we could reconcile. At this point I went to a psychiatrist, who within about ten minutes diagnosed me with bipolar. I purchased the medication prescribed and started taking the meds but, in my heart, I still didn't believe that I could possibly have a mental disorder. As I'd done in the "David days" when my psychologist had first mentioned bipolar to me, I rejected the diagnosis with my simplistic refrain: "How could an attorney possibly practise law with a mental illness?"

John and I never reconciled. I finally got it into my head that I needed to cut him out of my life and keep him away from me. I thought that if I moved a woman by the name of Joanna into my house, John would stay away from me because he hated her.

Cocaine

Joanna moved in with her four children from three different fathers. It wasn't long before she was running my life. She resigned from her job and started working for me as my office manager. Again, I don't know what was happening in my head here. But it gets worse. Much worse. Joanna introduced me to cocaine. I became an addict. I used the drug to push myself harder than ever, to work longer hours and sleep less. The drug served its purpose and I worked like a machine, but I would then crash into great depressions for a week at a time.

Through all of this I was still trying to look after my child and run a law firm.

One morning I woke up and had a moment of clarity. I phoned my mother and told her what was going on. She told me to drive home to Kimberley at once. My father drove to Johannesburg and evicted Joanna from my home, law firm and life. Litigation between Joanna and me followed, which obviously did not help my mental state.

In retaliation, Joanna contacted the advocates that I had worked with from the Johannesburg Bar and advised them of my cocaine addiction. I started receiving phone calls from a senior advocate, who happened to be my neighbour on the other side, asking where I was and when I would be home. To save face and attempt to dispel Joanna's accusations to the Johannesburg Bar, I moved back to Johannesburg.

By myself, I tried to pull my life together and break my addiction, but it wasn't working. I just replaced cocaine with benzodiazepines, or alcohol, or both together. One week, I'd be super happy, then one week I'd be in bed, not able to get up to see to Georgina. It was awful. I saw another psychologist and had myself admitted to a rehab centre in Johannesburg. I didn't stay in rehab for the recommended 21 days because I thought I was fine after ten days. I was also not honest with myself or with my doctors and therapists.

My personal assistant and employees in my law firm took care of Georgina for me during this time.

Things from here just got incredibly worse. My head was fuzzy, spinning with thoughts, just racing. I would use drugs to try and stop the noise in my head and attempt to find some clarity. It never worked. One of my friends told me that I had lost all elocution in my speech: I was apparently babbling and slurring incoherently. How much of this was hypomania and how much was cocaine related, I honestly don't know.

"How could an attorney possibly practise law with a mental illness?" Indeed.

Forgery, fraud, and jail

The following year, a man approached me to do his legal work, which included holding large sums of money in my trust account for him. A specific amount of R750,000 (about US $50,000) was placed in the trust for the purchase of a specific immovable property. As I write this, I have many times replayed what was going through my head. I cannot believe I did what I did, thinking it was perfectly awesome! I misappropriated those trust funds. I used this money to run my law firm because I just couldn't work. (I never used the money for personal expenses as far as I can remember.) All my professional staff had left me, with good reason I can see now. I was alone, with a lot of energy one moment and absolutely none the next. There were times when I couldn't even read, write, or focus.

But again… "How could an attorney practise law with a mental illness?"

I dreamt up an elaborate plan to have a modern all-women leading law firm with state-of-the-art offices in the middle of the city. I leased high-end office premises, bought expensive furniture, and hired interior designers to completely style, decorate and furnish the office space for me. All funded with money I simply took from my trust account. I organized an elaborate cocktail party to open the offices that we hadn't even moved into yet. I took a lot of benzodiazepines to try hold myself together and quiet my mind, but instead I managed to space myself out badly. I simply was not with the program. I arrived late for the party I was supposedly hosting.

The week after the party, I decided I needed more money to keep my dream alive and funded. So, I forged bank statements and income statements to prove to lending agencies that I would qualify for huge loans. I thought that my forgery work was excellent, and nobody would ever be the wiser. In a state of utter euphoria, I approached several lending agencies and went to work getting money. This came to a grinding halt when the bank discovered the fraud and had me arrested. I spent the weekend in jail. There was not enough evidence at the time to prosecute me, so on the Monday morning at the court jail cells, I was released without even attending a bail hearing.

Fortunately, my parents always stepped in and looked after my daughter. I thought I was invincible. Not even the arrest brought me back to earth. I wasn't wrong, they were. I was an attorney, and I would show them. I would show the whole world!

Talk about grandiose thinking!

The man whose money I'd stolen to fund my unrealistic dream demanded his money and eventually brought an application against me ordering me to pay him or to prove that I had paid him. I forged a proof of payment, once again thinking no one would be the wiser. I carried on as if nothing was wrong. The Law Society then launched an investigation into me and my trust account. I ignored them and their notices too, insisting that I was right, above the law, and who did they think they were?

Escape to Cape Town

It was December and I went home for Christmas. I can still remember the way my father looked at me, as if I had completely lost it. After just two days, I went back to Johannesburg. I don't know if I had a moment of clarity, but I knew everything was wrong and I had absolutely no money. I packed Georgina into my car with my cat and all the assets I might be able to pawn. I geographically escaped to Cape Town, a city where I'd lived as a child. I pawned some stuff, booked into a B&B and enrolled Georgina in the very same pre-primary I had once attended. I could feel my body and mind were battling, so I used wine to suppress my pain and enable me to function.

A fight, a rescue, another fight, another escape, another rescue

Fortunately, the tracking system on my car was still being paid by my father's business, so he managed to track me. My mother arrived at the B&B and after a fight where I screamed, yelled, and shouted at her, blaming her for everything, I finally calmed down and got into the car with her and drove home to Kimberley. (My father's accountant lives in Cape Town and he took my car.)

On arriving in Kimberley, I enrolled Georgina in school and tried desperately to pull myself together. I just couldn't. Everything had fallen apart, I had broken the law and evaded it. I continued using alcohol to try and make myself feel better. Then one Friday afternoon, I had too much to drink and had another huge fight with my mother. She lost it and gave me a black eye. My father called the police and we all ended up in the police station. The police were not inclined to get involved in a family dispute and advised that neither of us should press charges.

That night, I took Georgina to a local B&B and the next day, I bought tickets and put the two of us on a bus to Durban. When I ran out of money there, I contacted a friend who has an undergraduate degree in psychology. I guess she could tell that I was in a really bad way. She flew to Durban and drove us to her home in Nelspruit.

Rehab and acceptance of my bipolar diagnosis

With my friend's assistance and support, I went into Healing Waters Rehabilitation Centre for three weeks. Georgina stayed with her during this time. This is where I finally accepted my diagnosis: bipolar II.

It made me feel like an absolute failure.

Then, on top of that, while at Healing Waters, the Law Society launched an application to strike me off as an attorney.

I was totally humiliated, and astonished that I had let things get so bad that I might lose the right to practice law.

On leaving Healing Waters after my first twenty-one days, my father collected Georgina and me in Nelspruit and took us back to Kimberley with him. But I still wasn't alright. I had gone through withdrawals while in rehab and my head was much clearer, but now guilt about what I had done hit me hard. I was clearly no longer invincible. I was still feeling hopeless. So I decided to go back to Healing Waters for another ten days.

On finally leaving rehab, I attempted to oppose the application to have me struck off as an attorney but was unsuccessful. The court granted the strike off application. My father gave me the R750,000 so I could pay back the money I had stolen. Criminal charges for the theft of R750,000 were pressed against me, and the police initially pursued the charges but that died down and I haven't heard anything from them for three years. It is still possible that the police may pursue criminal charges, so that's still hanging over me.

Starting a new life after rehab

After coming out of rehab, I isolated myself for an entire year. I moved in with my parents and stayed at home just looking after Georgina. The following year, I started assisting my father in his business, working half-days. Another year later, I managed to slowly start integrating myself back into society. I am now the most balanced I think I have ever been in my life. I work a half-day, take care of my daughter in the afternoons, volunteer at her school, am the class mommy for her grade, serve on the parent-teacher association, and the parents voted me onto the school's Board of Governors. I have started piano lessons, am cycling and entering family races with Georgina, and I registered with the University of South Africa (UNISA) to do a Bachelor's in Archaeology and Anthropology by distance education. We attend church and I am gradually becoming an active member there. I have made several good friends and have two very close friends that I have confided in about my bipolar disorder and cocaine addiction.

I have been clean and stable for almost three years now. My bipolar medication is working. I am absolutely petrified to ever go back to that state of being where I conducted myself in a manner that is so utterly foreign to me.

Looking forward

There are times when I wonder about what I am doing with my life now and in the future. The newspaper in Johannesburg published articles regarding all my unlawful conduct, bipolar and strike off. So now I tend to avoid ever going to Johannesburg. The articles are also all over the internet. The damaging aspects of my story are public knowledge, and the negative narrative has been written, published, and widely disseminated. When I think about future employment or what I'm going to do, I stop myself because how can I have a positive future when the whole world knows what I did. Nobody will ever trust me, and I have been found guilty in the public eye. I have no options! I need to change the narrative; I am just not sure how to do it.

I want to move forward; I am ready now. The question is: how?

I assure you I am not inherently a bad person: I just did some really bad stuff before I was diagnosed and before I finally accepted my diagnosis. I don't want my past to define me but at present it is defining me. Generally, people just do not understand that for that period in my life I was crazy. Nothing I did was calculated, and I never, never meant to hurt anybody. I lost everything: my law firm, my identity as an up-and-coming professional, and every relationship—both personal and professional—that I had. Not one person wanted anything to do with me, and I don't blame them. Except my parents who have bailed me out again and again over the years.

I just really want to build a solid, meaningful life for my daughter and me. Georgina has been diagnosed with learning difficulties and developmental delays, so I have become well versed in those issues too.

What I have written here is just a brief overview. I could go deeper and flesh out my story but then I will be writing for days. It's not pleasant for me to re-live those years of my desperate, disordered life. I only hope that my story will help readers of this anthology in some way. It's a cautionary tale, as I said at the start.

Epilogue, one year later

I love my life now more than I have ever loved my life. Currently, I am not on bipolar medication, but I am stable. I have been clean and sober for the past four years.

I am still working half-days for my dad, doing his company's legal compliance. I am not studying now, so I can put more of my energy into living a balanced life. I have purchased a home for Georgina and me in Kimberley. We are currently renovating it and hope to move in within a few months.

Georgina is now doing extremely well in school and her extra-curricular activities. She is thriving, in fact! With the assistance of speech therapy and occupational therapy, it seems that we have bridged all the earlier developmental delays she once had.

I too am thriving. I have never been as settled and happy as I am now. As mentioned, I was voted by the parent body at Georgina's school onto the Board of Governors for a term of two years. Just last night, which was to be my last meeting on that Board, the Board of Directors asked me to serve another two-year term. After all I've been through, it feels good to be recognized and appreciated, and to know that I can make a positive contribution to my community once again.

For the first time in a very long time, I am excited about life and my future.

I am South African. I was born in the early 1980s and studied law in the early 2000s. I was first diagnosed with bipolar in my early thirties, and again two years later, but was in denial for several years and refused to take medication for the disorder. Instead, I self-medicated with cocaine, benzodiazepines, and alcohol. I finally accepted my diagnosis five years after I was first diagnosed and am currently stable and rebuilding my shattered life together with my young child and the support of my parents.

PART 2

Reflections by Family Members

… in which children, siblings, partners, ex-partners, parents, and a volunteer reflect on their relationships with the people in their lives who have bipolar disorder.

You Can't Fix It

Gina Roitman

I was 14 when I started to experience stomach cramps on a regular basis. When it got bad enough, I went to see our family doctor, Morris Solomon, MD, who had known me since I was two, just after we arrived as refugees from Europe in 1949. I liked Dr. Solomon; he looked like the singer Frankie Laine and had an ashtray full of cigarette butts in defiance of the sign that hung next to his medical degrees: "Smoking is Harmful to Your Health."

My parents were Holocaust survivors, and I was the miracle born to a 35-year-old woman who had been told she could never have children again because her womb was "floating" in her pelvic cavity after giving birth to a baby under unspeakable circumstances in 1943. She and her first husband had escaped to Soviet Poland at the outbreak of the Second World War and were then summarily put on a train heading east toward Siberia. They were dropped off in Uzbekistan. Life there was very hard. My mother said that in summer the mosquitos were the size of bats and in winter you could easily lose your toes to the cold. Within a year, her husband died of malaria and sometime after, her three-year-old son, my older brother, died of starvation. My mother told me how she finally found a man with a cart to carry the tiny coffin to a burial spot, but the earth was rocky and hard. The sound of the stones as they covered the casket haunted her dreams forever. And eventually, my reality. Repeated frequently, without any prompting, these stories were tattooed onto my memory.

My mother had been the fourth of six daughters in a poor family living in Chrzanow, Poland, about 35 miles due west of Krakow. Her father was a bookbinder, her mother a homemaker. And each daughter had a gift, an attribute. She claimed she was the practical one, the only one to survive the war. She would lament the unfairness of it all and sometimes bemoan her role as the last of her family to survive.

"Why me?" she would cry. "I was not the prettiest, not the smartest, not the most talented. I was not the one who married well."

When friends found her, close to the end of the war, my mother was days away from death by starvation. They nursed her back to life.

My parents met in a displaced persons' camp in Germany, married (because life must go on), and after having me, were accepted as immigrants to Canada. One of the first things they did upon settling in Montreal was to join an organization called the Hebrew Protective Association, which provided two main services to members: guaranteed burial plots and access to a family doctor (which, before the advent of social medicine in Canada, was an essential). This brought me to Dr. Solomon with my complaint about stomach pains.

After a perfunctory examination, Dr. Solomon handed me a three-ring binder with one word on the cover: "Study."

"I want you to read the stories in there and when you're finished, we can talk." And he shooed me off to the waiting room.

An hour later, I returned to his office and handed the binder back to him.

"So," he said, not looking at me directly. "What do you think?"

"I guess they're all stories about kids with parents who were in The War, and mostly about their parents' stories." (The word *Holocaust* had not yet come into the common lexicon. We just called it *The War*.)

"Anything sound familiar?" Dr. Solomon asked, now examining me across the expanse of his desk.

"Yeah, sure, a couple of stories." I shifted uncomfortably under his scrutiny but also at the effort he made to put me at ease by smiling.

"Anything in particular?" he pressed.

I had not wanted to assume anything so had kept my answer deliberately vague, but the good doctor was looking at me with a tilted head and a clear question in his eyes. I finally responded. "Yes, the story about the woman who was a manic depressive."

"Who *is* a manic depressive," he corrected.

"So, what's a manic depressive?" I asked.

And with his finger in the air, Dr. Solomon drew a sharp line of ups and downs, a ridge of mountains and valleys. "Their moods are extreme, going high and low like this."

Then he continued, "You know how you don't know who you're supposed to be when your mother walks in the door at night … her daughter, her mother, her sister, her servant, or you? The way she can be full of energy sometimes, but then has to lie down and doesn't move for hours? How she screams at you for the smallest thing or insists that you be a grown-up but will then chastise you for being too independent?"

I sat dumbfounded. How did Dr. Solomon know all these things about my life? Had he been following me around?

"I'm sure she was not always like this but … The War, you know," he added, looking down at his desk, not at me.

> *Thinking about it now, my mother's disorder is unlikely to have been an issue before the war, since she was able to marry and have a child. Mind you, even if she had shown symptoms back then, there would have been no one to diagnose her, and no adequate treatment. The extreme stresses she endured during the war could easily have triggered bipolar disorder. I'm so grateful that Dr. Solomon took notice and made the diagnosis.*

Then, Dr. Solomon got very serious. "Your stomach aches are the beginning of a real problem if you don't take care of it soon. But there is no medicine I can give you. Getting better will rest in your hands. And this is what I want you to know. You are a clever girl and mature beyond your years. You must understand that what's wrong with your mother cannot be fixed. She lost two families before you came along. No matter what you do, you cannot fix her life. And you cannot make her happier, so you must do what's right for *you*. You are good and kind and smart. You know the difference between right and wrong. You must take care of yourself. Always do what's right for you. As long as you don't intentionally hurt anyone, you will be fine."

It is the best advice I have ever received. My stomach pains disappeared shortly thereafter because I understood that what my mother was experiencing—although it affected me, sometimes greatly—was not about me. It was about her. And, like Dr. Solomon said, I couldn't fix it. But I could understand that she needed me. In me resided all the souls she had lost: her mother, her sisters, and her close friends living half a world away. I was her interpreter, her sounding board, and her whipping boy. She could call me the worst names, accuse me of not loving her as much as I loved my father, and rail at my stubbornness for insisting on being who I wanted to be. But at the end of the day, I was the one to curl her hair or rub her sore, calloused feet. At the end of the day, she knew I would always love her.

Years after her death, I wrote this:

Photo finish

Static   earnest   sepia faces
trapped on dog-eared paper
strange landscapes   drained of colour
each photo a story
a picture book for a small child   alone with her mother

me and my mother
she is feeding me stories
piece by piece
photo by photo
stories mixed with sobs
told in fierce whispers
gagging words stuck in the throat

I feel the spoon clank against clamped milk teeth

is this my zeydeh   where is my zeydeh

silence lives in the eyes of these strangers
more tragic than any imprisoned princess
threatened by a fire-breathing dragon
my whole family in cinders and inhaled
before the dragon was slain
before I was born

but after the photos
here I am

Gina Roitman

I am a Montreal-based writer and the author of *Tell Me a Story, Tell Me the Truth*, linked short stories, and *Midway to China and Beyond*, a biography. My work has aired on CBC Radio and appeared in several anthologies: *The New Spice Box* and *Wherever I Find Myself.* My poetry has been featured in *carte-blanche*, *Poetica*, and most recently, *Montreal Serai*. Over the past five years, I have led memoir workshops in both Washington, DC, and Montreal. And in 2013, with producer-director Jane Hawtin, I co-wrote and was the subject of the award-winning documentary film, *My Mother, the Nazi Midwife and Me*. I recently completed my first novel, *Don't Ask*. GinaRoitman.com

My Bipolar Mother

Tami Hammond-Collins

Editor's note: Tami is my daughter; she was in her late teens in 2008 when I was diagnosed with bipolar disorder, and she has accompanied me on every step of my journey to recovery. In these poems, she recalls the early years when bipolar first derailed my life—and swept up our entire family in its wake.

Only her body is here

Hello, Mom …?
My whisper from her bedroom doorway
gets sucked into the vacuum of black stillness.
She's not here.

Her body is here, but she is gone.
Is this what death is like:
to see her skeletal form lying there in bed, but to know she is not present?

I want to shake her lifeless limp frame,
to shout: Where have you gone?! Come back now, I need you!
But I know she won't hear me.
And I know her absence is neither her fault nor her choosing.

So I wait here in the doorway, standing guard
over her body until her mind is released
from the echo chamber it's trapped in.
I'll be the beacon that beckons her home,
showing her it's safe to return.

I know she'll return.

And I know she'll leave again.

The many faces of bipolar

I brace myself at the sound:
the stairs creak as she climbs.
Who will she be when she reaches my door?
Which version of Mother will she be today?

Will it be Dragon Mother?
With wide, flashing, maniacal eyes
and vicious, cutting tongue
that spits hateful words in piercing jolts
that manipulates, blames, and punishes
gleefully attacking, merciless.

Will it be Carnival Mother?
Who jitters with delight and exhausting curiosity

and marvels at beauty only she can see—
each spectacular sight
a vision gifted to her alone
each one so excruciatingly magical it brings her to tears.
Vibrant swirls of elated emotion
spill out of her in undulating melodies
and paint her world in such an exquisite rainbow of dancing colours
you can only step back and stare in awe and envy.

Will it be Child Mother?
With anxious frown and needy, desperate expression
who clings to every bannister and wall and countertop
for reassurance that reality won't shift and give way beneath her.
Terrified
because the fall is too crushing and violent.
But she is condemned to walk on shaky ground
and no place is safe for her.

Will it be Paper-Doll Mother?
Who obediently goes through the motions
A cardboard cut-out with a blank stare.
There, but only just.
A shrunken shell, bled dry of all colour
melting into the monotonous background.
A discarded plastic bag
swept along by air currents.
An old helium balloon
deflated, drained of opinion or interest
detached, out of touch, aphasic, vapid
incapable of even pretending to care about me.

Or will it be Phantom Mother?
Who glides silently past my door, empty-eyed,
in a wintry trance
A ghost on her way to her tomb-bed
where she will lie motionless in darkness
for an eternity of days or weeks
unable to speak or even sleep.
Hollowed.
Gone.
Yet her absent-presence is so heavy
I cannot even breathe under its ghastly weight.

Tami Hammond-Collins

I was born in Montreal in 1991. In 2008, in my last year of high school, my mother, Merryl Hammond (the editor of this anthology), was diagnosed with rapid cycling bipolar I. I studied history and communications at Dawson College in Montreal, Quebec and editing at Simon Fraser University in Burnaby, British Columbia. In 2017, I started working as an editing and digital marketing consultant. I live in Montreal with my partner and two cats. In my spare time, I enjoy painting, travelling, and studying meditation and consciousness.

I Forced Myself to Smile

Lara Beaulieu*

** This French-Canadian contributor is using a pen name to protect her mother's privacy.*

I grew up in a family with both my parents and my younger brother. We were close, back then. When I was a kid, my dad worked nearby, so he'd come home for lunches together, and dinners, too.

My mom stayed at home. She used to have a busy career, in the public eye, before we were born. Actually, that was quite unusual for a woman back then. I now wonder if she ever resented just being at home with us.

Mom always had a lot of anxiety and depression. Dad never spoke to us about it, but my brother and I felt there may be something going on with her. But we just got the feeling that we shouldn't talk about it, shouldn't dig too deep.

From a very young age, maybe seven or eight, I never knew how she would be when I came home from school. I would force myself to smile. I remember getting cramps in my cheeks from smiling. I was just trying to make sure she knew that she didn't need to worry about me: "I'm okay, Mom!" I also tried to make sure my brother wasn't too worried about my mother's moodiness.

Later on, as teenagers, we would get such intense reactions from her. I remember she was once super-mad and shouting at my dad in front of us. And I would fight with her. For example, about her cooking, which I didn't like. I remember one time she burst into tears in front of me because she couldn't buy me a pair of pants that I liked. I tried to console her: "It's okay, Mom. I don't really need them."

When I got older, she would hang up the phone on me if we disagreed about something, or she would let me down at the last minute when we had planned to do something together.

A few times over the years, she "went away" for a while. Looking back, I assume she was hospitalized at the time. Again, this was never spoken about openly. I guess my poor dad just tried to protect us by keeping everything to himself.

My mom's diagnosis

Finally, when I was 25, my mom was hospitalized for a few weeks, and we were told she has bipolar II. They put her on lithium. I think she's quite well-controlled now. But she told me about a few things she did during hypomania, like going to a music store and wildly dancing like a performer on stage. And one time, she left the house in her pajamas and just walked away. Dad had to bring her back home.

But for her, depression is more common. She just shuts down, there's no communication, and we don't even hear about it because Dad covers for her.

My dad is very accepting of her diagnosis, and the limitations it places on their lives together. He always wants to help. He read up a lot about bipolar disorder, to educate himself; he reached out to support groups; even took some classes about cognitive behavioural therapy.

I think my mom had some therapy, but as far as I know my dad never did.

When they got married, they were both very active Christians. They would pray together every day, and so on. But after my mom's illness, she couldn't pray anymore. My dad said, "I never expected to pray *less* in order to take better care of my wife." But he understood that she simply couldn't focus to pray like she used to.

I wasn't close to my brother during this time; he was off with his buddies, experimenting with drugs, and so on. So I don't know how he reacted to Mom's diagnosis. When we got older and eventually married, we became closer again. During the pandemic lockdown in the spring of 2020, he experienced a big depression. That really worried me. With our family history, we both have to be vigilant.

The long shadow of bipolar

I myself had an episode of depression in the mid-2000s. The doctor called it "adaptation trouble." (I'm translating that from the French; maybe that's "situational depression"?) My grandfather died and my boyfriend at the time just left me. I ended up taking meds for three years until I married and became pregnant.

Of course, when I had that depressive episode, I was very concerned that it might be the start of bipolar for me. I think I'm quite alert to that possibility and would definitely reach out for help at once. My husband is also cautious and would help me to seek treatment if necessary.

> I saw three different therapists during my depressive episode. The last one taught me to ask myself these questions.
>
> For anxiety:
>
> 1. What can go wrong?
> 2. How likely (give a percentage) is it that this will actually occur?
> 3. If it were to occur, what's the worst that could happen?

And for depression:

1. What did I do wrong?
2. What is the impact of it?
3. How can I fix it?

I've found these questions so helpful, and I'm teaching them to my young kids already.

Right now, my husband and I are concerned about one of our kids who shows some signs of anxiety and depression. He also has issues with concentration (attention deficit disorder) and sleep-disordered breathing (a form of sleep apnea). He's currently working with an occupational therapist; we'll see if he needs psychotherapy in the future.

"Absent" mother

My mom still suffers from a lot of anxiety. For example, grocery shopping is stressful because there are so many people. (Of course, the COVID-19 pandemic has worsened the anxiety for her.)

Years ago, when I was getting married over in Europe, her anxiety became a huge issue. She's super-afraid to fly, hates the idea of leaving her home, and definitely didn't want to meet all my husband's relatives for the first time. So, at first, she refused to come to our wedding. But my dad finally convinced her that she really needed to be there. They got some anti-anxiety medications for her, but either she took too many, or they reacted with her lithium, or something, because she really wasn't "present" at the wedding at all. Even now, I look at the photos and she's just staring off into space or turning her head and looking blankly at a wall.

Maybe we shouldn't have insisted that she come, after all? If we could have discussed her disorder more openly with her, maybe we would have understood her better.

These days, Mom and I have quite a good relationship, but for sure, there is a real distance between us. She is quite cut off from my family. I am now so scared to get no for an answer that I don't really ask anymore. We talk on the phone sometimes, but we don't meet much. So we each stay on our own side of the invisible fence. I have a feeling that without social contacts now, during the pandemic, she might feel isolated and it could negatively affect her mental health.

As for my dad, he always has his projects. I am sad that they have recently decided to keep so much to themselves and not see us, but at the same time, I understand their concern with COVID-19. My dad spends time on Zoom with my kids, so that's wonderful.

Protecting my own mental health

Protecting my hours of sleep is the main strategy I use to stay mentally well. If ever I feel stressed out or anxious, I just go to bed earlier than usual.

I also find things I like to do, and then I do them! Read a book; listen to a webinar; buy fresh raspberries and eat them all by myself! In other words, I do conscious self-care activities that bring me pleasure. I'm not great about exercising, but I do ride my bike to work whenever I can.

My advice to others

If you yourself have bipolar disorder, I urge you to learn more about it; talk to people; and research it. My mom was too prejudiced to do this; the stigma around mental illness was too great. (I think that's a generational problem, too; hopefully it's getting better these days.) You need all the knowledge you can get to cope with your disorder. And obviously, reach out to professionals as soon as you sense that something is "off."

If you are the child of a parent with bipolar, expect a lot of unusual—even startling—behaviours. Try to open the lines of communication within your family. The pretending and denial are so painful; open communication is a gift. Please remember, it's not your responsibility; it's not in your hands. The adults have to take charge. Oh, and don't do what I did: don't false-smile so much that your cheeks get cramps!

If your spouse has bipolar, also talk openly and discuss the disorder and how it affects them. That way, you can better understand them and learn to support them in the most effective ways.

Conclusion

Working on my contribution to this anthology has made me reflect more deeply on my mom's behaviour and my reactions to her as a person with bipolar disorder. I realize now that a lot of what she lives with—her anxiety about changing her routines, her angry outbursts, her unpredictable behaviour, her emotional numbing, her fear of travelling—is very "normal" for a person with bipolar. I hadn't realized that before because we don't talk openly about her disorder in our family. Even now, after all these years. (That's why I'm using a pen name here, to protect their privacy. If it were up to me alone, I wouldn't give in to the stigma!)

Writing this has also made me realize that I'm a big girl now. It's time to give my seven-year-old self with the fake-smile and aching cheeks a warm, maternal hug, and reassure her that it's not *her* job to take care of her mom. (Thank goodness, Dad stayed around to look after Mom! She's so lucky to have his acceptance and support.)

Maybe one day, I'll be brave enough to have an honest, adult-to-adult conversation with my mom about all the ways her disorder affected my brother and me when we were growing up. Not to lay blame; not to seek sympathy. Just to open the lines of communication that have been so blocked off by the stigma of her mental illness.

If people like me don't try to bring down the fences, who will?

I was born in 1980 and grew up in a small farming village outside Montreal, Quebec. I attended high school in a nearby town and graduated from Laval University in Quebec City. I own a professional practice in the Montreal area and live with my husband and young family.

Living in the Shadow of Love

Barbara G. Jacobson, LCSW

The psychic I visited on that cold November morning said, "Your sister was destined to die young." I believed her, mostly because—like so many who die too soon—Betty had lived an intense life.

And here I was, at 70, still trying to make sense of my life in relation to hers. With a psychic. Her comforting words were well-intentioned but didn't really help much. My years of on-and-off therapy helped to reveal some truths to the complicated story that continues to be disturbing. I understand myself better now and know that my issues are mostly related to survivor guilt.

The biggest question, and the one only I can answer, is whether I knew enough at the time to put the pieces of the puzzle together. The sudden, painful loss of my only sibling has marked my life and caused so much suffering in the family. The overarching dilemma has been the inability to know for sure if it could have been avoided. Why was I, at 22, oblivious to the impending catastrophe? Even though I know that her bipolar disorder was the ultimate culprit, I still struggle to accept that she had to die from it.

Could I have saved her from herself? It's unlikely. And yet the idea persists, at times still dominating my thoughts. My sister had bipolar I, the more aggressive form of bipolar disorder. If it had been cancer, it would have been called Stage 4 that became metastatic. Despite this, her bipolar was only treated sporadically, when it erupted into a full-blown episode. And unlike cancer, there was no chemotherapy, no surgery that could excise it. It was like a mystery, and I was an inexperienced detective.

Betty's youth and marriage

Betty was the artistic one, the temperamental teenager. She was also fun loving, and a risk taker, unlike her much younger little sister—me—the shy one. While I loved to read, she rode horses and won ribbons. Unfortunately, she didn't have much time to develop an identity, because she met her husband at age 13, while riding in the woods behind our home. He was hunting squirrels. They quickly began a relationship. I would sneak around to watch them lying on the couch kissing, while I hid behind a chair in the living room.

My parents weren't happy about this early, intimate relationship. They tried to intervene, setting limits, and trying to slow things down. That just added a forbidden quality to Betty's romance. When she was just 15, and I was nine, my father sold his business and we moved to California. Betty was heartbroken and miserable. After a year, we moved back—partly because she was so despondent—and her relationship with her first love continued. At 18, she became pregnant. She quit college and got married in a quiet evening church service, wearing her high school graduation dress.

Bipolar disorder

When the baby—a son—was born, Betty decided to go to work full-time. Her husband was in graduate school, and she seemed a bit overwhelmed with motherhood. What nobody thought to diagnose—possible postpartum depression—soon morphed into a full-blown psychotic breakdown. This confused and totally upset everyone. She threw her wedding band down an incinerator shaft, walked in traffic up Wall Street in Lower Manhattan, and was hospitalized.

Shock treatments—routinely used back then in the 1960s—brought her back in touch with reality, but they also ruined her short-term memory and defeated her spirit. She settled for life as a housewife and moved with her husband as he completed his PhD, paid off his debts, and built his career. They had a second child—another son—and in Oklahoma she had another manic episode during her husband's military service, followed by a depression. They ultimately moved to Houston, Texas, for him to take a job in aerospace.

This move turned out to be a recipe for disaster. Living in Houston in 1970 was hard on her in many ways. She was cooped up in a conservative, cookie-cutter community in a development filled with brown split-level homes in hot, dusty Texas. She tried to befriend people with whom she had nothing in common, except a husband, a house, and children. She was still recuperating from her last bipolar episode and decided she wanted a third child, so she got pregnant again and gave birth to a daughter.

Over time, our whole family became overwhelmed and confused by her; we didn't understand her illness. Our parents made numerous trips to Texas, and flew her back to New York several times, both with and without the children. I visited often, and although we were close, it was frightening and frustrating to watch the repetitive process of sickness and hospitalizations without progress or stability. It hurt to see how she struggled with the burden of this illness lurking around every corner of her life. I read as much as I could about bipolar disorder, but unlike with physical illnesses there were lots of conflicting theories, and there didn't seem to be a standard treatment.

At some point, Betty stopped communicating with me, and I hardly noticed, being busy with a summer job and a boyfriend. I sent her a perfunctory gift for her birthday. It was a half-slip, a common piece of lingerie, serviceable but basically meaningless. I didn't hear from her, which was a bit strange, although I thought about her, and wondered how she was doing. I may have felt "no news is good news," and yet the emotional distance was unusual for us. We had been close all our lives, and so simpatico, like good friends who catch up and get comfortable as soon as they get together. I severely underestimated what her illness was doing to her.

She had had another "nervous breakdown," as it was called back then, and was hospitalized again. At a more modern treatment centre this time, she was able to have family visits. The centre seemed to listen to our concerns but didn't have much to offer beyond advice to get more help with the children. A sitter was hired—a woman who judged Betty for not being able to cope on her own as a mother. My parents and I tried to visit often from New York. Betty's psychiatrist prescribed chlorpromazine (Thorazine), known to be a chemical straitjacket. She did not have access to a therapist.

A friend she met while in treatment had made many suicide attempts. I met him when I visited her in the hospital. He had scars all up and down his arms, like the railroad tracks of a heroin addict. I was afraid he might take advantage of Betty's vulnerability, but it didn't occur to me she might continue to be in contact with him after her discharge. I believe her judgement began to be impaired, whether from the medications, or the repeated bipolar episodes and their impact on her brain. Maybe she just needed a friend, someone who understood her suffering. I have often wondered: Could he have contributed to her death?

Marital stress, suicide, and its aftermath

After experiencing several psychotic episodes over ten years, each of which resulted in her being hospitalized, given shock treatments and multiple mind-numbing drugs, Betty couldn't take it anymore. She also had achieved the goal of having a daughter. She may have been disillusioned in her marriage, but she had been sticking with it.

However, as it turned out, she and her husband had been having more serious marital issues, and they were discussing divorce.

His burden was hardly recognized, even when it became clear he was not able to bear it. He didn't reach out either, until he was absolutely desperate. Couple therapy didn't happen.

To solve the problem, Betty's husband asked my parents to move Betty and the children to New York. I think she knew there was a discussion happening and may have felt caught between her husband and parents with no clear path to freedom. Especially since she had no career and could not support herself, even with child support. In the 1970s, divorce was still a major source of shame, on top of which was humiliation from the mental disorder that had stolen her sense of self.

On that fatal day, with tragedy just around the corner, Betty and our mother had what Mom would recall as a normal, innocent phone conversation around noontime.

And then …

Betty left no note. She had made no previous attempts. She simply went ahead and did it. Died by suicide. I'm pretty sure she didn't really want to die, but she just couldn't see any other choice at the time.

Just a few hours after Betty's phone conversation with our mother, our grandmother, who was over at Mom's home at the time, got the call from Betty's husband, who explained what had happened. Their eight-year-old son had discovered Betty's body when he came home from school. How devastating for him.

I was at work when it all happened. My boss called me in to say I needed to go home at once. He didn't tell me why at the time, I guess to protect me from breaking down on public transit. When I got home and heard the awful news, I was in shock, utterly speechless. I remember that my closest friend came over to be with me immediately.

Just around then, the phone rang, and that same male friend of Betty's from the hospital in Texas—the one who had attempted suicide many times—called to talk to me. I'd always mistrusted him and figured he might have been part of a suicide pact with Betty, or at least that she'd presumably been talking to him about her intentions. Why else would he be phoning me? I was too overwhelmed, and just told him I couldn't talk …

My parents were also in total shock, of course. And my poor grandmother said she wished she herself had died rather than Betty.

Betty's body was flown to New York, and she was buried in the churchyard where she had been married not ten years earlier. I was just 22 at the time. Her children were two, five, and eight.

After the funeral, we all went into our respective corners to grieve. My parents were inconsolable. I couldn't help them. And I had to come to terms with the fact that I had lost my lifelong companion. I was now an only child.

For years, I unjustly blamed Betty's husband for my sister's death.

He remarried almost immediately, thus providing the children with a mother figure. I did and still do have a relationship with my nephews and niece, but it's complicated and contact is limited because they all live in different cities now.

I think I stopped growing and maturing after the shock. I became frozen in time. I ended up marrying the wrong guy. It took me five years or so to find my feet. After that I was confused about my direction in life and was depressed for a long time, until I remarried and had my children. At times I was fearful that I might have bipolar disorder myself. When I described my symptoms, I noticed the diagnosis seemed to be dependent upon the doctor I consulted. I believe my depression was caused by my ongoing grief over Betty's bipolar disorder and subsequent suicide.

In my attempts to reconcile and make sense of what happened, I always come back to one thing: "What would Betty say or do?" I trusted her implicitly. She was so much more than my only, very close sibling. Because of the six-year age gap between us, she was almost like a second mother to me when I was young. I remember before I got married for the first time, she asked me if I really loved my boyfriend. I guess she could tell that he wasn't right for me.

I have missed her so much, all these years. I especially wish I could have spoken to her about the experience of raising my children. That would have been wonderful to share with her. And for them to have had a wonderful aunt like her, of course, would have been fabulous.

People have asked to what extent her disorder and subsequent suicide might have influenced my choice of profession as a social worker. Absolutely! She started having bipolar episodes when she was 19 and when I was a young teen. So, I became intrigued, studied psychology in college and then became a social worker. I have always worked in the helping professions, and though psychiatric hospitals are not easy places to work, most of the time I felt I was able to connect with and understand the patients.

Conclusion

I think the seriousness of Betty's illness went unseen by a fragmented and incomplete health system that did not consider her hormonal difficulties after giving birth. Nor did the health system try to see the ongoing nature of her illness. Stigma, shame, and ignorance prevented the family from being more resourceful. Our mother did discover a research study at Columbia University and tried to interest Betty in it, but by that point Betty was skeptical about medications (the study was using lithium, a lifesaving drug that was not yet widely available like it is now). There was also no thorough evaluation of contributing factors; for example, the disconnect within her new community in Texas. A talk therapist might have helped enormously.

Now, forty years later, there are better drugs, but still it seems the hormonal connection has not trickled down much from research into practice. The stigma of being in therapy has lessened, and most hospitalizations include an aftercare plan.

My focus on the circumstances of Betty's life and death is an effort to understand what might have been done differently. Was it possible to have seen that coming? Did her children have to lose their young mother at such an early age? There have been many generational consequences, including divorces, and prison for one of my nephews. Even though we all loved Betty, we didn't realize what we were up against, and we weren't paying close enough attention. In the end, the scourge of bipolar disorder etched away at her brain, one devastating episode at a time, and finally it took her from us.

It didn't have to happen.

If I could suggest one thing to people reading this, it would be to recognize that bipolar disorder changes people, weakening them and making them doubt themselves. Keep helping them consult doctors until they find the right one: one with compassion and sincere interest in pursuing the best possible treatment. If you have a strong relationship with someone who has bipolar, try to build them up and stay in close contact, making sure they know you love them.

Barbara G. Jacobson

I was born in Staten Island, New York, in 1949. I studied at City University of New York and am a licensed clinical social worker. I have worked in psychiatric hospitals over the years—including the former Women's Medical College as head of the Department of Social Work, and as an instructor in the Department of Psychiatry. I am currently in private practice in Valley Forge, Pennsylvania. I am married and have two grown children and one new grandson. I am an avid reader and enjoy gardening, cooking, and painting with acrylics.

In the Storm and the Sunshine

Catharine McKenty

Editor's note: In early 2020 when I got to know about her, Catharine McKenty was 89 years old, living in a seniors' residence in Montreal. In 2019, she had published her memoir, Riding the Elephant: Survival and Love with a Bipolar Partner. *Her late husband, Neil McKenty—who had bipolar disorder—had published his memoir,* The Inside Story: Journey of a Former Jesuit Priest and Talk Show Host towards Self-Discovery *in 1997. Neil died fifteen years later in 2012, aged 87.*

Catharine and Neil's 40-year marriage was unusual in two major regards, besides the fact that he had bipolar disorder. First, Neil had spent 26 years with the Jesuits. He left the priesthood after six months in an alcohol rehabilitation centre, about three years before he and Catharine married. (Neil's father had also been an alcoholic.) Second, Catharine was 41 and Neil was 47 when they married, and this was the first marriage for both.

Catharine and I worked together for her contribution, with me asking her questions by phone. Several drafts later, and with the help of her assistant Jeri Pitzel, Catharine gave her approval.

The contribution that follows is a summary of our extended conversation, with Catharine's words in normal text, and mine offset in italics. We tried to keep returning to the essential question: What might a reader of this anthology be most interested in to help them "live alongside" (Catharine's phrase) and support a partner who has bipolar disorder?

Our early days

Catharine, although you and Neil were both mature in years when you married, Neil—as a former priest—had absolutely no prior experience of being in a healthy, committed relationship. And maybe he never had a good role model either, given that his father was alcoholic. Would it be fair to say he had a whole lot to learn about being a good husband?

[Laughs.] Oh yes, I think that's very fair to say!

And moreover, you both had his bipolar disorder to contend with as well. When did you first become aware that Neil had bipolar?

You know, I can't exactly recall. It's so strange that Neil himself never once used that term to refer to himself—not in conversation, and not in his memoir, The Inside Story. He wrote very frankly about the suicidal depressions he suffered over the years, but not about bipolar disorder as such.

When you got married, were you aware that Neil had a mental illness of some kind?

No. No, I didn't. Neil had told me that he'd been in an alcohol rehabilitation centre for six months. But he'd not had a drink in three years by the time we met, so I wasn't worried about that. But then, about eighteen months after we married, a priest visited us and brought Neil's medical records from his time with the Jesuits. It was only then that I learned that he'd been in a Jesuit mental hospital in Detroit for three weeks after a bout of suicidal depression back when he was in his early thirties. I can tell you, those medical records scared the hell out of me. I wondered what on earth I had gotten myself into!

Were you upset that Neil had never confided in you about that psychiatric hospitalization?

Not really. I think he just buried that whole experience: it was part of his former life, and he didn't see that it had any bearing on his current life—our life together.

Did you discuss Neil's medical records with any of your friends or family members at the time?

Oh no, no. Not at all. You see, back in those days, no one ever spoke openly about mental illness. It was such a taboo subject. The tradition in my Irish family, going back to the time of the Great Famine, was one of going through trouble in silence. If you talked to anyone, it was to God. And you know, I didn't realize it at the time, but there was a considerable psychic cost to me for all the efforts involved in keeping up a kind of front about what was really going on in our home. My friends didn't know how to talk about it either; they knew we needed support, but they just didn't know how to offer it.

My own feelings were so bottled up. I was so distracted by my own thoughts I couldn't even focus on everyday things around me. Even the label "mental illness" wasn't known! People didn't have the words or vocabulary to start a supportive conversation! I didn't have the language, either.

That's such a key point. You can't ask for support if you don't have the language to articulate your needs. Hopefully, things are getting better these days!

In your memoir, you mention that your aunt wrote to you, about eight years into your marriage, and said: "Your relationship is unfolding in the storm and the sunshine." It certainly seems that she knew something about the ups and downs of your marriage. Had you ever confided in her?

Ah! I remember that letter very well. That's a perfect description of a bipolar marriage, isn't it! "In the storm and the sunshine." It does seem that she was aware that something was a bit different about my marriage. But no, I never confided in her—or anyone else, for that matter. As I said, it was all taboo, back then.

Was Neil already on meds when you got married?

No, I don't think he was. He only started taking medications later when our family doctor referred Neil to Dr. Pablo Cervantes from the Mood Disorders Clinic at the Montreal General Hospital.

Can you remember why Neil was referred to a psychiatrist at that time?

No, I can't remember now. But possibly it was done at his request since years before he had seen a psychiatrist when he was with the Jesuits.

I gather from Neil's memoir that in his case, severe—often suicidal—depression was his major concern. But can you think back to the first time you became aware that there might be something a bit different or troubling about Neil's behaviour; that he might have a mental illness of some kind?

It didn't occur to me at first that it might be an illness; I thought it was just part of his personality ... It was only when I saw those medical records that I became aware. And then later when our doctor referred him to the Mood Disorders Clinic, of course.

You know, I was just so focused on living alongside Neil as a *person* that all the technical details about bipolar passed me by. I never separated him from the bipolar. It was just who he was. In my mind, I was living alongside Neil, not living with "a bipolar spouse." I connected deeply with him as a person, just as he was.

That's amazing. It sounds so accepting; so mature. But at the same time, I wonder whether it might have been useful for you as a spouse if you'd been helped to learn more about the disorder. Maybe you could then have separated Neil—as in "stable Neil" or "mentally healthy Neil"—from his disorder (regardless of whether it was manifesting as a depressive or hypomanic episode). As in, "This is not Neil being irrationally irritable with me; it's just his hypomania. I must ask him if he's taking his medications correctly." What do you think?

Oh yes, that would have been enormously helpful! If only Neil and I had had access to the kinds of books published today, to educate ourselves about bipolar. I would have better understood his symptoms like extreme impatience, irritability, hurrying, and so on. That's why I'm so thrilled to be contributing to this anthology; to share something of my experiences.

Yes. You can help other spouses in bipolar marriages gain a better understanding and feel that they're part of a network of spouses, all learning to live with the challenges of a bipolar marriage.

Earlier, you said you thought Neil's symptoms were "just part of his personality." Can you elaborate on that a bit?

Well, Neil could get extremely angry and irritable at times. He'd often snap or snarl at me. And he had that almost obsessive need to control. Later, he became aware of that. Perhaps it was because his father was an alcoholic: they say that children of alcoholics often try to control their environment, to ensure some predictability, some certainty in their lives.

But I keep thinking how people just didn't talk about any of this. And that's why I felt so strongly about publishing my own story in *Riding the Elephant*. I really want to bring hope to people who are dealing with this right now. Hope is so important! And love and forgiveness. I want everyone reading this to cling to those things: hope and love and forgiveness.

Forgiveness?

Yes. I had to learn to forgive Neil for some of his difficult behaviours (like being controlling, or irritable, or angry, as I said), and also to forgive myself for my own anger that occasionally erupted in reaction to Neil's. At the most profound depths of my being, I experienced the power of love and forgiveness. Living alongside someone who is deeply wounded required a degree of patience I did not know I possessed.

As I matured in the relationship, I learned to look for the positives in Neil, and in myself, and in everyone else, too. Ignore the negatives! Focus on the positives. That was a crucial insight for me.

One of my friends whose husband was alcoholic used to say, "We do the best we can!" That's such a comforting thought: all we can do is our best with the strength and resources we have at the time. Don't be hard on yourself if you slip up occasionally. Just pick yourself up and try again!

Some spouses blame themselves in difficult situations. For example, they may think, "If only I hadn't done so-and-so!" or "Why did I do such-and-such to set him off again?" Did you ever blame yourself for Neil's outbursts of anger or irritability?

No, I never really felt at fault. I just tried to stay positive, come what may.

Neil's hypomanic episodes

In your memoir, you use some wonderful phrases to describe Neil in hypomania: "a magnificent Irish racehorse ... hooves flying ... galloping to the finish line"; "a thunderstorm of energy"; and "joyous energy." I'm sure many readers will relate to these vivid descriptions! Can you tell us whether you tried to calm or soothe him when he was in this state, and if so, how?

As long as Neil's excess energy was focused or channelled into something positive and creative (in his case, his radio show, researching for and writing books, being politically engaged during the Quebec referendum, etc.), everything was okay. I was enormously happy and supportive of him during those times.

That might be a key insight for readers to consider: what creative projects could I encourage my bipolar spouse or family member to do during (mild) hypomania?

I gather it was during hypomania that Neil's controlling behaviours got worse. In your memoir, you mention his frequent attempts to control you, his authoritarianism, dictatorial tendencies, and verbal blow-ups and outbursts. Did you ever find some of his behaviours oppressive?

Oppressive? Oh yes! That's a very good word for it. And I can tell you, I didn't like it one bit. Sometimes I felt embarrassed in front of other people when Neil erupted at me, and I sometimes boiled over with anger myself and lost control. For example, there was one time I swept all the dishes off the table in a rage. But I learned that any explosion of anger on my part was physically damaging to Neil. The sound and the vibration of my anger went right into his body. Even though for me it felt like a relief.

One of the hardest things for me was coping with Neil's need to control me: he often didn't want me to go out and leave him alone; or if I was a few minutes late to the front door when we were going out together, he'd snark at me. This would then ruffle my feathers … And he never wanted me to be away longer than about four days. He always demanded to know when I'd be back from a trip to visit my family, and so on. And I often found him to be arrogant and irritable.

Did his irritability last long, or pass quite quickly?

It passed quickly, thank goodness. I became aware that if I could just hold steady through the outbursts, they would pass. And thankfully, in between the outbursts, there'd be wonderful breakthroughs. For example, we'd take pleasant drives together, or go dancing, or try new restaurants, etc.). These were moments of pure sunlight and enjoyment!

His irritability and anger would disappear during his depressions. Also, there was no irritability during his and our writing projects. That was such a relief. And I always had such enormous admiration for him: he truly was an extraordinary man. So I was able to focus on that, not on the negatives.

Also, Neil was very supportive of me as I grew into new endeavours. For example, I loved my work with the meditation centre and organizing international meditation conferences, and researching with Neil for books we co-wrote, and so on.

Just to be clear: Neil was sometimes oppressive, controlling, and irritable, and at other times he was supportive of you—one might even say empowering?

Yes, that's right. I'd say so. And those two types of behaviours didn't go together. When he was irritable, he wasn't supportive, and so on.

And were these different behaviours mood-related?

Yes. Oh yes.

I see. It must be really difficult for a spouse because—as I know from my own experience as a person with bipolar—one can never predict or know with any certainty which mood will dominate, when, or for how long. The disorder is utterly unpredictable—at least until they find the correct combination of medications, and the correct doses of each.

Absolutely. It could be so frustrating: there were happy times, then times when he was critical and aggressive, pressuring, and so deeply depressed.

And a partner can never know in advance how long an episode will last, so they can't pace themselves.

Yes, exactly!

That's a huge part of the problem for both the person with the disorder, and their family members, friends, and colleagues: the cruel unpredictability of each bipolar episode, and of the overall frequency and severity of the episodes over time.

How did you cope with all the stress of Neil's irritability and oppressive behaviour? What anger management strategies did you use?

One of the strategies I invented was what I called the "Sumo wrestler technique." When I felt tension building up in my body, especially my biceps, I would go down the cellar stairs, pose like a Sumo wrestler, and punch the air repeatedly until all my negative energy dissipated!

I love it! Any other tips for readers?

Just leave the room when you feel your anger building up! A short walk round the block is often all you need. Any form of exercise is excellent. And I always tried to do something for myself; have an outlet for my own energy and interests. Learning meditation was vital for both me and for Neil. Oh, and I can't recommend this highly enough: please find a support group where you can speak openly, and make friends who understand what you're going through, and where you can laugh!

Laugh?

Oh yes! I developed an inordinate capacity for laughter, much to the irritation of Neil, who would often growl, "What are you laughing at?" I just think that laughter and joy are at the very heart of life, of the universe!

Returning to Neil's need to control, did you ever find him abusive?

No, not at all. I didn't ever consider it to be an abusive marriage. In fact, I felt he had a protective instinct that kept him from ever directing the full force of his anger toward me. Even when he was controlling or arrogant or irritable. Of course, the person closest usually takes the brunt of the anger and frustration.

If someone reading this is considering separating from or divorcing their bipolar spouse, I'd urge them to go for counselling first. I went for counselling in the early years of my marriage, and it was a real godsend. It helped save my sanity! It was so wonderful to have someone to talk to.

We should emphasize, however, that if a reader does have an abusive partner—bipolar or not—that's not safe. So please take steps to protect yourself and your children, and then seek counselling.

Neil's depressive episodes

People who have no lived experience of depression, or have not lived with someone experiencing it, often don't fully understand its depths. They think it's like having "the blues." What would you want these people to know?

Oh no! In Neil's case, this was definitely not just a matter of feeling down or blue. The "blues" are normal feelings that eventually pass. Depression is something else entirely. Neil could hardly find words to describe the state of total blackness and utter hopelessness that took over his life; no effort of will could lift him up. He found himself in a tunnel with no light at the end. The emotional turbulence he had struggled with all his life, with whatever means came to hand, went totally out of control.

> *Neil dedicated his memoir to you, saying that without your love and support he "should not have survived." From his own account, he experienced at least six suicide events (threats, thoughts, plans, and attempts). What was it like for you to live with a man who seriously considered suicide so many times?*

It was gut-wrenching to see this man, who had been so alive and curious about every subject under the sun, no longer able to respond to anything. It was absolutely awful. Neil was unwilling or unable to be cheered up, or be distracted … I was aware it was beyond his control. And beyond my control, too, of course. But that didn't make it any easier. During his first depression, I found myself almost numb with disbelief about what was happening. I only learned later that he had what is called treatment-resistant depression.

Once I emerged from the initial stage of shock, I went on the warpath. For the next month or so, I used every weapon I could think of to defeat the depression. Like a civilian throwing rocks to slow the relentless advance of an armoured tank, I tried aromatherapy, music, tasty foods, and changing all the lightbulbs to natural light. I tried every reason to get us out the door, into the sunlight and onto a bus where there would be people and changing scenery. These efforts made very little dent in the depression, but they did help me maintain my own balance, at least.

There was such a dark energy in our home at those times. I was frightened by it, terrified in fact. I feared that I might be sucked down into the same vortex with Neil and be paralyzed with him. My whole home was being attacked by this dark energy. I knew instinctively that I must not allow the darkness to enter my own soul. If I allowed self-pity, anger, or fear to overwhelm me, I would be engulfed by the darkness.

I was living in an emotional war zone.

Sometimes, I just had to get out of there, even though I hated to leave Neil alone in that state. I had to try to keep my spirits up and stay busy with my own activities.

During depression, Neil's relationships were not good. So I had to find ways to deal with all that. The counselling I got helped. Sometimes I just had to leave the room.

Fortunately, I was comforted by a series of positive inner images, dreams, and spiritual guides that kept me going. For example, snippets from inspiring speeches, verses from the Bible, even things I saw in movies. I imagined an epic *Star Wars* standoff with Luke Skywalker bravely going to face Darth Vader. We were in a cosmic, life-or-death battle. I had a clear image, once, that we were both surrounded by a cloud of light and love and would continue to be—regardless of Neil's choices. That was such a help.

And through it all, I learned that we all have untapped capacities deep inside us; we can cope with a lot more than we initially imagined.

> *That's amazing that you were able to take something positive from the experience. What other advice would you give to readers who are living with a deeply depressed or even suicidal family member?*

Keep busy! Do things that nourish you as a person: a hobby, an outlet of some sort, a creative project. I had a dream in which a friend said to me, "You're becoming ill, and everyone can see it." Of course, we can't take care of others if we fall ill ourselves. So I joined Al-Anon—that's a support group for the family members of alcoholics and people attending Alcoholics Anonymous (AA). I had been bottling up all my emotions for so long. Oh, what a relief it was to be with friends in Al-Anon! I tell you, we'd laugh our fool heads off! It was such an emotional relief for me.

Needless to say, Neil didn't want me to leave him alone at home when I went to meetings, or to do anything without his control or permission, really. But Al-Anon saved me. I felt total frustration and powerlessness in the face of Neil's disorder. In Al-Anon, those people were also powerless over the alcohol that their spouses abused, so we had that in common.

But if Al-Anon is not for you, I'd advise readers to go to any support group. These days, there are groups specially for the families of people with bipolar. This is crucial, because family and friends in everyday life can often be quite ignorant or tactless about the topic of mental illness. And they simply don't have the same insight and life experience as you.

Did you ever fear that he would go through with a suicide threat?

Oh yes! It was terrifying to listen to all those suicide scenarios that he described in great detail. I don't know how I coped.

Thank goodness I was given that image of Luke Skywalker. I often didn't want to leave Neil alone in the house, not knowing what I'd find when I came back.

I never imagined or visualized his suicide. I was protected from that, thank goodness. But I also knew that there was nothing more I could do to protect him. In the end, it was his choice.

You know, Neil ultimately saw depression as a spiritual journey. I think that's why he never died by suicide. Being alongside Neil was a major part of my own spiritual journey. I had to draw on strengths I didn't know I possessed. As I said, we're so often disconnected from our own strengths.

Even through the most difficult times, I sensed that Neil was reaching out to a power greater than himself. I am profoundly moved when I re-read his memoir of a life journey that took him to the depths of suffering and near despair, and through those depths to a spiritual experience that continues to encourage and inspire others.

But even so, by the end of Neil's two-year depression, I was so physically and emotionally exhausted, I was losing a grip on this world. I honestly thought, maybe this is enough for one lifetime. I felt that I might give up and just blow away peacefully through the paper-thin veil that separates this world from the next.

Of course, Neil wasn't aware at the time how profoundly his depression was affecting me.

Catharine, that sounds really heavy. May I ask, were you ever suicidal yourself?

Oh no. Not at all. But certainly, sometimes Neil's low mood would cause a semi-depressive state in me.

Did you lose your appetite, and maybe lose weight during this time?

Absolutely! I lost 20 pounds during the two years of Neil's final depression. And friends felt that Neil aged about 20 years during those two years.

Was that the time Neil wrote the suicide note?

Yes. One morning, Neil told me he was plunging down into depression worse than ever. After breakfast, I told him I would call at 5 p.m., then put on my coat and left the house as if led by some inexplicable force. It was an effort to put one foot in front of the other down the path to the car. I went to the meditation centre where I just shook with terror until 4 p.m. when suddenly I sensed that everything would be alright. Back home, Neil had written a suicide note and gone down to the metro station, fully intending to jump in front of a metro car.

After watching half a dozen trains go by, he walked home, tore up the suicide note, called a young friend, and arranged to have dinner with him. Over dinner, Neil told his friend, in a desperate voice, "I just want to be real." It was as if the self-loathing of a whole lifetime needed to come out. He'd always felt he was never good enough. His friend said Neil should ask for help from a man named Jim. As it turned out, Jim, an AA buddy, became a major part of our lives. In Neil's memoir, he says that Jim "would guide me on a new journey and save my life."

Were you ever envious of Neil's dependence on and close relationship with Jim?

Oh no, not at all. It was a huge relief for me to have someone else to help with Neil, so that I wasn't carrying that load alone. People need to not feel solely responsible in these circumstances. It's too much.

What survival strategies would you recommend to a reader who is living with a depressed or even suicidal partner? How can they protect their own mental and physical health?

1. Join a support group!
2. Take up any healthy physical activity (exercising, walking in the fresh air, dancing, etc.).
3. Do things you enjoy.
4. Find ways to express yourself—a creative outlet of some kind. I wrote my first book, for example.

Living with a bipolar partner

Compared to your friends' and family members' marriages, what would you say was the biggest difference in your own bipolar marriage?

You know, I was so occupied just coping, I never had time to look around at other marriages! But I will say this: Neil was such a high achiever, so unusually gifted. I was just so proud of him! We were a really good team. I absolutely loved working with him on our various projects.

If you had to choose, would you prefer to live with Neil in hypomania or in depression, and why?

[With absolutely no hesitation.] Oh, hypomania, for sure. The depressions were so very dangerous for him.

Now, every marriage involves sacrifice and compromise. But I think you were willing to sacrifice a huge amount for Neil.

I don't think of it as sacrifice. As I said, I was simply living alongside him.

Fair enough. But would you be comfortable with the term "compromise"?

Yes, "compromise" is fine.

And would you say you had to compromise more than spouses with non-bipolar partners?

I daresay. I would do virtually anything to keep the peace!

A bit of "walking on eggshells" around him sometimes?

Oh yes, certainly.

And does the term "bend over backwards" fit with your experience?

Yes! More than other spouses have to do, I'm sure of that.

> *You've already mentioned four key survival strategies for a partner living with a depressed or suicidal person—join a support group, do healthy physical activities, do things you enjoy, and express yourself creatively. Looking back over your long and very eventful marriage, is there any other advice or encouragement you'd give to the spouse of a person with bipolar?*

I think the absolute key to surviving and being loving in a bipolar marriage is joining a support group like Al-Anon, a church group, or maybe best of all, a bipolar support group. Find people to talk to who will understand what you're going through; you need outside support. Honestly, I can't say enough about that! That's what I didn't do in the early days: I went unsupported for about 20 years except for my counsellor. Oh, and get counselling for yourself, if you can.

For me, it's been a healing process, a journey, to face the challenge of forgiving, paying attention to my own needs, learning to accept, and to love—even when it's not easy. Pay attention to your own strengths and the strengths of others, and those strengths will grow. Don't blame yourself or others. This changes your perspective. As I said, a positive attitude to life is key.

Don't forget the power of gratitude! A friend of ours recommends thinking of four things every night to be grateful for.

I grew from learning to deal with my own anger, the source of which was Neil's irritability.

Also, I needed to learn to like myself! Then you're not as hard on yourself, or on others.

Always remember the power of the human spirit. I was so inspired by people like Helen Keller and my own grandmother and my strong-willed mother.

Most important, I had a profound sense that I could listen to an inner wisdom. We all have a capacity to listen to the inner heart of the universe. That allowed me to live alongside Neil all those years.

That's great advice. And I'd also like to add: Please don't blame your bipolar partner. Remember that it's their disorder saying and doing strange things, not them!

Is there anything else you'd like to add before we end?

I just want to share hope! Looking back, I can see that caring for Neil made me more compassionate toward myself, and Neil, and others. I hope that something in the story of my forty-year bipolar marriage will be of use to readers. Just remember to take special care of yourself as well as your bipolar spouse.

I feel so privileged to be a part of this anthology project. I wish I had had the kind of information and support that your book will provide when I was going through it all alongside Neil, the darling man!

Yes. Especially when things seem overwhelming or at their darkest, right?

Oh yes! Just do the best you can, and, as I said earlier, please cling to hope and love and forgiveness. Cling desperately! Cling for dear life!

Catharine laughs long and with great delight at the phrase "for dear life" in this context.

[Also laughing.] And don't forget laughter, I guess!

[Continues laughing.] Oh yes, absolutely!

Catharine McKenty

I was born in 1930 in Toronto, Ontario and grew up on a farm just outside of the city. I studied English at Victoria College, University of Toronto, spent four years in reconciliation work in post-War Europe, and did a stint as a researcher for *PACE* magazine in the 1960s. My late husband, author and broadcaster Neil McKenty, and I lived in Montreal. Together, we wrote two best-selling books and initiated charitable activities. Sandwiched between our many accomplishments were Neil's mood swings, suicidal depression, and my desperate attempts to cope. My other books include *Polly of Bridgewater Farm: An Unknown Irish Story* and my memoir, *Riding the Elephant: Survival and Love with a Bipolar Partner.*

amazon.com/dp/1611533465/

[Editor's note: Catharine passed away in Montreal in January 2021.]

Living in the Shadow: A Family Perspective

Laurel Saunders

Editor's note: Laurel is the wife of Bruce Saunders, who shared his story in part 1 in a piece titled Learning to Live with My Bipolar Identity.

I was born in Victoria, British Columbia, Canada in 1950 and I have an identical twin sister. Our mother was quite anxious and worried, but intelligent and social. Our father was in the Navy, quiet and reserved but very funny.

Before I retired in 2014, I worked first as an elementary school teacher, and then, for 22 years, as an Augmentative Communication Assistant in the Victoria School District.

My husband Bruce and I met through my best friend while I was at university. I remember he showed me how to use a camera. And we kept in touch after I graduated and left Victoria to teach in the Cariboo. We went together for about a year and got serious when I was teaching in Parksville. We've now been married for 46 years and have two adult sons, both of whom are doing well in the world.

I loved Bruce's parents and was close to them both. But they were different in many ways from my family. They highly valued physical work and practical skills, whereas my mother, in particular, loved to read and encouraged my sister and me to go to university. I was vaguely aware of Bruce's mother's mental health challenges, but back in those days people didn't talk about such things, and I didn't know much about mental illness anyway. Later, I became very involved in her care when she was living in a long-term care facility.

Bruce's sister Lynne died by suicide just two weeks before our wedding, when she was just a young woman in her twenties. I didn't know her very well because first she had been away and then I had been away while Bruce and I were dating, but I liked her. I remember Bruce's father talking about Lynne's "manic depression"—probably when Bruce's mother wasn't around—but I had hardly even heard of the condition at that point and found the diagnosis rather alarming.

Before we were married, Lynne stayed at Bruce's cabin in View Royal while I was teaching in Parksville. She had recently separated from her husband and needed a place to stay. It was a very small cabin with only one bedroom, and I do remember being a little worried that she would still be living with Bruce after we were married. I regret now that I didn't make more of an effort to assure her that she was welcome to stay on.

When I heard about her death, I was very shocked and distressed, and my principal in Parksville gave me some time off to go to Victoria to be with Bruce's family. I also remember the principal saying, "We'll just say that she'd been sick and won't mention suicide." Naturally, Bruce and his parents were very upset by Lynne's death, but I remember that Bruce's mother insisted that our wedding should go ahead as planned. She said she wanted something happy to look forward to.

Mood swings and suicide attempts

About six years later, around the time of our first son's birth, I became aware that Bruce was experiencing depressive episodes and mood swings. Living with his moods could be hard, especially for me as a new mother. His depression was the prevalent mood. He especially got down every winter when he wasn't busy with his gardening work. Nevertheless, he was always a very involved dad—a great dad, really.

When he was 39, Bruce attempted suicide for the first time. He was supposed to be participating in a day program at the psychiatric hospital at the time, so I was surprised when I came home and found his car in the driveway. He was distraught and said that we needed to go to the hospital at once. I had no idea why. Once we got there, he told the psychiatrist that he'd just attempted suicide. That was the first I heard about it all and I started to cry. I was devastated that I hadn't realized how much emotional pain he was in.

After that suicide attempt, Bruce was hospitalized, and they put him on a strong antidepressant which provoked a hypomanic episode. He switched, almost overnight, from suicidal depression to a fired-up ball of energy. In a very short space of time, he was trying to run the whole psych hospital! I thought he'd be worrying about the boys and me and how we were getting along without him. But instead, he was calling the maintenance staff at the hospital to get some defunct parking meters moved and lobbying the dietician to get peanut butter added to the breakfast menu. One day, he even gathered up some of the other guys on the ward, called a taxi and took them out to a movie, strictly against the rules. And when he came home on a pass, he spent all his time baking an elaborate birthday cake for one of his fellow patients. I was confused and alarmed and quite angry. Of course, I was glad he was feeling better, but I felt he was doing all these other things rather than working on his own recovery. I kept expecting the hospital to call me in to help me deal with Bruce's illness and give me updates on his condition, but the only time they met with me they just asked me some questions about his family history.

Four years later, Bruce needed emergency bowel surgery and was in hospital during a long recovery after that. He finally returned home, and just a few months later, he made his second suicide attempt. I was on my way to a conference in Vancouver and I came home to pack. That's when I discovered Bruce, lying unconscious on the floor. I remember running outside to shout for our neighbour who is a nurse. Luckily, she was home and rushed over. Someone else called for an ambulance that took Bruce away. Meanwhile, I had to wait for our youngest son to get home so I could tell him that Dad had to go back in the hospital, so he needed to go to my mum's, who lived only a block away. My therapist helped me a lot to deal with this trauma.

I kept Bruce's first suicide attempt a secret from our sons because they were so young at the time, and even from my own friends. I just told people that he was depressed and had to go into hospital to have his medication adjusted. After his second suicide attempt, our older son and I visited him in hospital and Bruce and I together told him what had happened, but we didn't tell our younger son at the time. He was quite upset about that later and felt that we had been keeping secrets from him.

After that hospitalization, Bruce was put into a bridging program. It was a pilot project, and a wonderful psychiatric nurse came to do home visits, with follow-up for the family. It was the first time anyone in the system seemed at all concerned about me and the boys. It really helped us navigate the system. It should be a no-brainer that family members are an integral part of the team to help patients recover.

Coping with life in the shadow of mental illness

There's no question that living with a spouse who has bipolar disorder is hard. For years, when Bruce was depressed, I kept thinking that I just needed to say or do the right thing and he would start feeling better, and when he was manic, or "zippy" as I call it, I felt like the world's dullest person because I didn't always want to have company over or drop in to visit people that I didn't even know.

Bruce is very sweet when he's on his way either down or up, but in his extreme moods, not so much. When he's zippy, he tends to look outward a lot, away from the family. He gets very busy and wakes up early in the morning to get started on whatever he's excited about at the time. It often makes me feel a bit lonely—he becomes very self-contained, focused on his own projects, not really part of the family. He wants to socialize a lot. I find all this rather challenging.

And when he's down, he needs a lot of support. I watch over him, monitor when he may need outside help or intervention, and try to get him out of the house for walks, and so on. He turns to me much more when he's down, which can get exhausting after a while.

We have had rocky patches over the years. We had conflict when our sons were young because we had different parenting styles. Bruce felt I was too easy on the boys, and I felt he was too critical of them and wanted them to be more like him. I must admit I did occasionally daydream about leaving him back then, but not seriously. Now that our sons are adults and it's just the two of us at home, our relationship is much better, and Bruce is very close to both our sons.

One thing that helped us a lot as a family was *Movie Monday*. Bruce got really involved in setting up this film program at the hospital where he had just been a patient after his second suicide attempt. To be honest, I was rather resentful at first because again it seemed like he was spending time doing that instead of working on healing our family, but it ended up being a very good thing for all of us. When our sons were at home, it was something we did as a family. The boys and I helped by working in the concession selling popcorn and snacks, and we swept up the theatre afterwards. Most important of all, *Movie Monday* has given Bruce an activity and project to focus on over the years, so he doesn't get as depressed. Also, because of this project, Bruce decided to be "out" about his mental illness and his struggles with suicide, and this was very freeing for all of us.

As well, when Bruce had a depressive episode, I realized that I had a lot to bring to the partnership. Besides reassuring him and listening to him, I realized I could take on the mundane tasks, like paying bills, that he found so frustrating with his memory problems. This didn't come naturally to me because my father was a bookkeeper and had always done all the business tasks in our family. But I found I could learn how to do it.

It's not at all that I'm the "well" one, and he's the "sick" one in our relationship. I've had struggles with anxiety over the years. Certainly, Bruce's mental illness has been difficult, but it has also made him a kind, compassionate man who has given me a lot of support over the years when I've needed it.

About two years ago, Bruce had another very severe depression and ended up in hospital again. Although he didn't specifically mention suicide at the time, I asked him directly, "Are you thinking about suicide?" He said, "I'm thinking about it, but I don't have a specific plan." That was a real wake-up call for us all, that after so many decades without the spectre of suicide in our lives, it could reappear and upend everything we've built up together.

Over the years, I've concluded that no one can prevent another person from taking their own life if they're really determined. During Bruce's suicidal episodes, I tried everything—encouraging him to get therapy and go to his peer support group, reminding him to take his meds, taking him out for walks, and hours and hours of talking. In the end, nothing I said or did made any difference. He began to get better when new medications lifted his mood enough for his high intelligence to start overriding the punishing inner voice that was telling him he was stupid and not good enough and everyone would be better off without him.

I have a wonderful therapist who I've been seeing for over 30 years. She's helped me so much through Bruce's mental health crises and all my big and small challenges over the years. I strongly recommend counselling for spouses who need to look after themselves before they can support their suicidal or even just depressed family member.

I've learned through therapy that Bruce's mood problems are not my fault. And I've learned to take care of myself first. If I don't take care of myself, who will? Remember what they say on a plane: Put your own oxygen mask on first before you try to help someone else.

Laurel Saunders

I was born in Victoria, British Columbia, in 1950, and live there now with my husband, Bruce. We married in 1974, about 15 years before he was diagnosed with bipolar disorder. We have two adult sons. I received my Bachelor of Education from the University of Victoria and worked first as an elementary school teacher, and then, for 22 years, as an Augmentative Communication Assistant in the Victoria School District. I retired in 2014.

Staying Together, Living Apart

Olivia Innes*

** This is a pen name and all her family members have been anonymized as well.*

Unfortunately, I am no stranger to mental illness and addiction. I have a history of depression—mainly Seasonal Affective Disorder (SAD)—dating back to my late teens. Luckily, I easily found effective treatment, and by my mid-twenties had learned how to cope very well. Initially, I took an antidepressant in the winter months, but in my thirties, I started experiencing premenstrual syndrome (PMS), so my doctor suggested I take the meds year-round. Even now, about 20 years later, I still take my meds. I guess you could say I understand the value of prescribed meds—when taken as prescribed.

I add that caution because my first husband—whom I'll call Chris—suffered from depression and ended up abusing both alcohol and prescription meds to self-medicate. We had two kids together, and by the time we finally divorced I had lived with Chris for almost 20 years and he had frequently been in a depressed and later an addicted state. At that time, I promised myself I'd never live like that again.

Even now, more than ten years later, Chris barely has any relationship with our children, who are now young adults. My younger child, who also suffers from depression and anxiety, doesn't want anything to do with Chris, but my older child is concerned their dad is in such poor physical health that he may die soon.

My second marriage

Enter Andrew, my second husband. When we first got involved about ten years ago, I knew that I was definitely not looking for another partner who had mental health issues. Famous last words, as it turned out!

Andrew was a smart, creative, funny, kind person whose emotional intelligence and apparent stability greatly appealed to me. He was very supportive of my children, and I felt the two of us were able to model a healthy relationship, which was important to me because my children hadn't seen that between their dad and me. Andrew had three children—younger than my own—from his first marriage, and months into our relationship I learned their previous family situation was complex. His ex-wife had substance abuse issues and was physically and emotionally abusive to him and their kids. I could tell the kids hungered for female attention and I am a nurturer, so I gladly took on the role of stepmother. For many years, things were very good.

I noticed from the beginning of our relationship that Andrew had occasional outbursts of anger, road rage, and the like. His reactions seemed like overreactions and concerned me, but the behaviour was infrequent, so I justified it to myself as "stress" or "testosterone-driven male behaviour."

About 18 months into our relationship, his mood changed markedly for the worse for several months. I thought I recognized clinical depression, so I suggested he consider treatment and was pleased that he agreed. Andrew found a therapist and a psychiatrist, and was put on meds. Unfortunately, he had strange side effects from the different antidepressants he tried, and the whole experience was a frustrating struggle. He stuck with the therapist and medication, even though no antidepressant worked well for him. He continued to experience milder periods of depression for the next few years.

Stress builds

More recently, his oldest child, Blake, showed us distressing video evidence of their mom abusing the younger kids. Andrew was able to get emergency custody, and the kids lived with us full-time for almost a year, flourishing emotionally and academically. But then their mom was given limited access to the kids, and Blake, susceptible to her manipulation, began to misbehave. He had a history of lying, stealing, and engaging in malicious behaviour with both a biological sibling and my younger child. Shortly after Thanksgiving that year, I confronted Blake about a lie and other troubling behaviour that Andrew and I had observed. Blake responded very disrespectfully to me in front of Andrew. I fully expected Andrew to back me up, but he didn't, and I felt betrayed by him in that moment. Much to my regret, I snapped and lost my temper with Blake. My behaviour was an isolated but very hurtful experience for both Blake and Andrew. I apologized to them soon after, but Blake was not receptive and stopped staying with us, returning to his mom's house.

A few months later, we learned that Blake had recanted the evidence of his mom abusing the younger kids, and she regained shared custody. This was all very upsetting for Andrew and me, and for the younger kids. It was awful to think of them returning to an environment that was at best neglectful, and at worst emotionally and physically abusive. I had apologized to Andrew several times about the incident with Blake, but I sensed he was unable to forgive me.

Andrew had begun the slide into what became a very deep depression, and on top of that, the COVID-19 pandemic hit. His job didn't allow him to work from home, but mine did, so I supervised the schooling of Andrew's younger kids when they were with us. Andrew withdrew more and more from family life. When he was home, he mostly sat and looked at content on his phone, barely communicating with us unless he was angry, which was increasingly often. The younger kids were withdrawn and troubled after their mom regained custody. I was struggling to hold things together without much participation from Andrew, my partner and best friend.

By midsummer, Andrew was having frequent outbursts of rage over the smallest things: the placement of garbage cans, how a car had been parked, and incorrect packing for a trip, for example. Sometimes he remarked that people were doing these things deliberately to upset him, which struck me as a bit paranoid. Andrew's kids and my younger child were often the focus of these outbursts. When I mentioned this unacceptable conduct to Andrew, he would say he was having a hard time and then shut down. He never apologized to any of us for his behaviour: it seemed we were all expected to simply accept it. It felt like such a double standard to me: any time he felt upset, he could blow off steam any way he liked; but when I cracked that one single time with Blake, it was unforgivable. Clearly Andrew held me to a higher standard than he held himself. The previously close relationship between the two of us was gone and it felt like he didn't love me anymore. I began to wonder if he actually had stopped loving me.

Throughout this time, Andrew became increasingly fixated on all kinds of negative financial and behaviour issues concerning his ex. It was exhausting listening to him go on and on about the same old wounds and injustices that we couldn't do anything to change. I found myself tuning out and answering him abruptly, saying things like, "Why can't you just let this go?"

I knew he was in therapy, and I saw him take his antidepressant every day throughout this time, so I assumed he was receiving the treatment he needed to get through a highly stressful period. I tried to be patient. But the worse and more hurtful Andrew's behaviour became, the more I suggested and finally demanded he try other approaches to put a brake on the relentless negativity and anger.

Remember, after living with my ex-husband's mental health and addiction issues for nearly 20 years, I had promised myself I'd never again live in a similar situation. Yet here I was, back on that same awful treadmill again. I didn't want to abandon Andrew or especially the younger kids, who were still living with us half the time in a generally calm environment with established routines. I felt like the current Andrew was unrecognizable compared to the person I thought I knew. I wondered how we had gotten to this state and often blamed myself. I didn't know what to do, and my own experience with depression wasn't helping me help him at all.

His suicidal crisis

One evening in mid-October, Andrew came back from therapy and—out of left field—calmly accused me of emotionally abusing his children. My mind reeled as I tried to make sense of his accusation. I was not in the habit of lashing out or losing control. Had the one incident with Blake nearly a year before reminded him of his ex-wife's abusive behaviour? If so, why bring it up now? And what about his own behaviour? In fact, Andrew often yelled and snapped at his children (and mine), so I thought he might be projecting, and said so. I was stunned and deeply hurt by his words.

Here is an excerpt from my journal, written after this incident:

> *He sat down and calmly asked if I wanted to talk. I thought the talk would be about our relationship and his emotional withdrawal and what he planned to do to help himself and us as a couple, and the kids. But no, he implied I am routinely verbally abusive to his children. It was unbelievable.*
>
> *The whole conversation seemed and felt insane. This is the same man who barks at his children half the time, the man who just a few days ago had a rage incident at his ex's house in front of the kids! I was so*

angry it was difficult to speak. I reminded him again that we have all borne the brunt of his anger, especially recently, and that he had now crossed a line with me.

I asked him to go stay with his father; he packed a bag and left.

Andrew didn't argue; he just packed a few things, and—without my knowledge—took the handgun safe with a gun in it, too.

About an hour later, his youngest child texted me: "I'm worried about Dad; do you know where he is? He just called me, crying, and said goodbye."

I was stunned, and if I'm honest, angry, too. *Are you* kidding *me?* I thought. I immediately tried to call and text Andrew, but he didn't pick up or respond.

After that, I think I was in shock, and a bit slow to respond. It took me a while to get truly scared. It was my youngest who stepped in and told me what to do. "Mom, you have to do something; he's going to kill himself! Hurry! Call the police!"

So I called the police, and they came to the house but they said they couldn't do anything unless I signed an order to have him involuntarily committed.

I tried calling and texting him again. No luck.

Then I called his sister, Anna. I badly needed to consult with someone about our options. Anna and I decided that we shouldn't pursue an involuntary commitment and further police involvement at that stage. Anna said she would also call and text Andrew after we hung up and would encourage him to come to her house.

By then, I felt desperate and sick to my stomach. I was consumed with regret and guilt that I had asked him to leave; it was now obvious Andrew was very ill and I had completely missed it.

Thank goodness, Andrew showed up at Anna's house at about midnight. She called me at once, and I then texted his youngest child to say their dad was safe. My youngest was taking good care of me this entire time.

I journaled again later the same night:

> *He is at Anna's house and he's OKAY. I'm so relieved, but I can't imagine us recovering from this. I don't see myself being able to trust him again, and he has hurt me a lot these last few months. I feel I've selectively overlooked things to believe ours has been a positive relationship. Maybe it was, once. All I see now, looming over all other aspects of his personality, is his anger.*

Andrew called me the next morning to let me know he had been suicidal the night before—he had held a gun to his head while sitting in his car. He was crying when he called, and was very hard to understand, saying over and over, "It's all my fault; what should I do now?"

I encouraged him to call his therapist to confirm he should go to the hospital, which he did. He called back to let me know Anna was taking him there. I asked if he wanted me to meet him at the hospital, but he said no. I felt like I was shirking my responsibility, but I was also very relieved.

I felt so grateful that Anna had stepped in. I really, really needed a break and I realized that I had to take care of myself now; the past few months and this suicidal crisis were just too much for me. I hadn't recognized the looming crisis. I saw Andrew's uncontrolled and irrational anger and I noticed how withdrawn he was, but he had continued working and doing volunteer work the entire time. I had no idea he was that deeply depressed and at risk for suicide.

In the hospital and getting a diagnosis

Because of the pandemic, each patient was only allowed a single support person to visit. Anna was that person initially, and when Andrew asked if I wanted to replace Anna, I said, "No, let's keep it like this. It's probably less stressful for both of us if it's Anna, and anyway, I need time to process everything."

To be honest, I was seriously re-assessing our entire relationship. This was *not* how I wanted to live my life! I had already spent too many years living with my mentally ill ex-husband, and I felt like the victim of incredibly bad luck. Or maybe I was just a bad "partner picker." I had a lot to think about and I needed time and peaceful space.

It was while Andrew was in hospital that they diagnosed him with bipolar II. So, what he needed more than an antidepressant was a mood stabilizer. (He's currently taking Lamictal and for him a new antidepressant, Zoloft, which initially caused some anxiety and headaches that went away after a few weeks.)

As it turned out, Andrew had been lying to both his therapist and me for about four months before his breakdown. He was pretending that everything was on track, but in fact he was having increasingly frequent suicidal thoughts during those months. And this, even though he had been taking antidepressants for about five years by then.

My initial reactions to his bipolar diagnosis were fear and despair. I hadn't read a lot about bipolar, and my only experience with it was through my paternal uncle, who was never treated and whose behaviour destroyed his family and multiple businesses. I imagined Andrew's condition would be very difficult to treat and that I, as his partner, could be looking at a relationship with a chronically unstable, fragile, potentially miserable, angry person for the rest of our lives.

After his release

When Andrew was due to be released after about a week in the hospital, his therapist encouraged him to move out of our home for a while if he could. Andrew's sister Anna encouraged him to stay at her house for as long as he needed, and he accepted.

What an overwhelming mix of emotions I experienced when Andrew shared this decision with me. On the one hand, I felt hugely relieved that I wouldn't be living with him during an undoubtedly difficult recovery, trying to step-parent the kids and simultaneously support and care for him. I dreaded the return of his relentless negativity and anger. On the other hand, I felt guilty about the relief I felt. What kind of partner doesn't want to nurture her very ill husband and play an involved role in his recovery? Complicating my feelings was that I felt undervalued and rejected as a long-suffering family caregiver, as if his therapist thought I was somehow a toxic influence in Andrew's life. I was really miffed! And I wondered, *What had Andrew been saying about me in there?*

We have been living separately ever since that time, for the last several months.

It's only now that Andrew is able to look back over his life and recognize the patterns of his bipolar behaviour. He thinks he's probably had it—undiagnosed and untreated—for three decades or so, since he was a young man in his twenties. I feel so sad for him that it wasn't diagnosed and treated years ago. I grieve the lost opportunities in his relationships with his children.

(And now that I think about it, he's not the only person in his family with a mental illness. His mother has several issues—too complicated for me to go into here—and one of his aunts was hospitalized for a mental illness; people in the family don't really speak about her diagnosis.)

Something else Andrew only recently disclosed is that this was his *third* suicide attempt. The first time was when he was young, before his first marriage; the second time was when his children were very young. I was shocked to hear this and asked him why he'd never told me about these previous attempts, and he said he had repressed them.

When we've spoken recently, he shared that what changed his mind that night was the thought that he "couldn't do this" to his children. I wonder if receiving several concerned phone calls and positive texts that night might also have reassured him that he's needed and loved? I don't think Anna's and my efforts to contact him did any harm either.

I realize now that Andrew has significantly damaged his relationship with my younger child. She was here the whole time and witnessed what I went through with Andrew and his children as well as experiencing her own difficulties with him. There's a significant rupture in their relationship. My daughter was like a cat trying to hide behind a bureau throughout it all; now she's out exploring freely all over the house since Andrew and his children no longer live here. I feel guilty that I subjected my child to this experience.

I journaled this after Andrew left the hospital, one week after suicidal crisis:

> *Andrew came to visit me at our home for the first time since he was discharged. We both cried. Neither of us knows what to expect. He'll be staying at Anna's house for some time. Again, I experienced that dichotomy of emotion: "Why was Andrew told not to live with me?" And "I am relieved he won't be here. It has been so peaceful."*

While Andrew was in the hospital, we talked on the phone each evening. He was fairly open about how he was feeling and what was going on with his treatment. After his discharge, I followed Andrew's lead regarding communication between us and this resulted in our speaking less frequently and then not at all. Our communication dwindled to periodic texting, and I was upset by what I perceived as Andrew distancing himself from me. I didn't know why he was doing it or what it meant.

About two weeks after his discharge, Andrew began Intensive Outpatient Therapy that lasted for several months. During this time, he experienced a wide range of emotions, including an angry, blaming phase that was very painful for me. For example, prior to Andrew's breakdown, I had spent time talking to a high school friend, Jim, who was coping with a serious physical illness and a painful divorce. Three or four weeks after leaving the hospital, Andrew angrily texted me that one of the reasons he never told me how much he was really struggling was because I had been more concerned about Jim than I was about him, and that I hadn't been there for him. *Not there for him?* I felt hurt and angry. From my perspective, I had very much been there not just for Andrew, but also for his kids, picking up the slack while Andrew was checked out emotionally and doing only the bare minimum of parenting.

Thanks to the support and leveling influence of my own therapist, I was able to text back that I was sorry he saw things that way and that I hoped we could discuss them when he felt better. I could tell that he was feeling abandoned by me. I was feeling rejected and abandoned by him, even wondering, *Maybe he wants to end our relationship?*

Six weeks after Andrew's suicidal crisis, I journaled this:

> *Sometimes I think he just needs more time to eventually recover himself, the Andrew I know. Other times I think he won't ever be able to return to himself. Mostly I remind myself there's really no way to know. I have grown in my ability to care for myself, be patient, and sit with uncertainty.*

Taking care of myself

I have had to learn—to really, really understand—that Andrew is recovering from a serious illness and cannot be there for me right now. I have to put my relationship needs on the backburner and focus on self-care. He's ill; and he's going through so many changes. His job right now is to get well; and my job is to give him the time that takes.

If I were to give advice to other partners or caretakers of people recovering from a serious mental illness, it would be this: Take care of yourself and don't expect anything from your partner right now.

I take care of myself by eating well, exercising daily by taking a vigorous walk or using my elliptical machine, and journaling. (You can tell a journal anything and it will never tell a soul!)

I've been in therapy on and off since my late teens, and I currently see my therapist every other week. I've been attending a weekly National Alliance on Mental Illness (NAMI) Family-to-Family program and a weekly Depression and Bipolar Support Alliance (DBSA) support group. Both NAMI and DBSA are free to participants, and NAMI's Family-to-Family program has been particularly helpful because it is part educational program, part support group. I came to understand that Andrew could not possibly support or even hear me because he was too ill. To remind myself of that and stay focused on supporting his recovery rather than on feeling hurt and blaming him, I bought myself a bracelet engraved with the word *LISTEN*. I look at it or touch it when I badly want to say something I know I will later regret, and that has been amazingly helpful and calming.

One thing I've struggled with is how much to disclose about Andrew's diagnosis, and to whom. For example, I told my mom, and she was fine with it. She's a pragmatic person who has some insight into bipolar because my paternal uncle had it. With others in my family, I just—I don't know—I don't want to be judged in any way. Especially since they all know what I went through with my first husband. So I haven't told a lot of my family.

I do have a strong network of friends and co-workers, and they've all been very supportive. I feel very fortunate to have these people in my life. My children, who are young adults, have also been loving and supportive.

I am grateful that Andrew is a very courageous, persistent, generous, and sincere person. That's why, after much soul-searching, I'm still committed to our relationship. I came to realize the similarities between him and my ex-husband are superficial.

Andrew is diligently complying with his treatment program and wants to do whatever it takes to get well. When he lied to me and his therapist earlier, it was because of an undiagnosed and improperly managed illness. I'm confident he'll find his way back, and this gives me hope.

I'm a nurturer, and a glass-half-full kind of person, and I believe Andrew is lucky to have me as a partner. I must continue working on learning when to step back, and not unknowingly disempower or emasculate him. I'm a planner and a doer who tends to "rescue" others. I'm still learning that though it is very hard to watch someone you love struggle and be in pain, it's very important to let them address their own problems because their struggle is self-empowering.

Conclusion

In the last few weeks, things changed dramatically. Andrew came over to tell me he's bought a little house where he's going to live and "work on" himself. He stayed for several hours; we sat next to each other on the couch, and even got in some cuddling. I felt close to him for the first time in a long time. At last.

Another journal entry nearly two months after Andrew's suicidal crisis:

> *Living separately has been very good for me. Andrew's negativity was always hard to live with and became unbearable. I hope his hard work in therapy allows him to become a less negative, less judgmental person—especially of himself—someone who can enjoy life more of the time.*

I am hopeful that we will stay together, living apart for now.

He clearly misses me. The other day he said his new place would make a good rental property, so it seems he's imagining a day when we'll live together again.

I was born in the late 1960s in Pennsylvania. I got a bachelor's degree and completed most of a master's before being offered the chance to establish a new department at work. I have two adult children from my first marriage and am stepmother to three teens from my second husband's previous marriage. My husband was recently diagnosed with bipolar disorder. I am a voracious reader and also enjoy needle arts, writing, and gardening. I live in Pennsylvania with my youngest child, and at the time of writing, my husband and I are living separately.

I Lost My Husband to Undiagnosed Bipolar

Isabelle Lipari

Bipolar hits a family the way a tornado hits a small town. You don't see it coming and when it hits, it throws everything up in the air, destroys families, and ruins lives. When the storm calms and leaves, you are left to pick up the pieces—what is left of them—to rebuild and heal. Sometimes you can and sometimes it's just too much.

I had a wonderful life, a beautiful family with three amazing children and an awesome husband, whom I'll call James. Together we had built a business, had a beautiful home in which our children were born, and which housed all our memories of them growing up. Our friends always said what a great couple we were and asked us how we did it, staying in love and keeping the passion alive even after 25 years of marriage.

That is, until the tornado hit. At first, it was only small storms, but they grew and grew and grew in intensity until I could no longer bear the thought of picking up the pieces yet again. The first one hit in 2004 and then they came and went until 2017, when James asked me to separate. Yes, you read that correctly: HE asked ME for the separation!

We were together for 32 years. About one year prior to our separation, at the age of 54, he was finally diagnosed with bipolar II, but his first symptoms had first appeared about 12 years earlier.

In between the storms, living with a person who has undiagnosed bipolar is like living in a pinball machine: The bipolar person is the pinball, and the caregiver tries to be all those pins, running constantly, trying to stop the ball from falling through the holes. I was on high alert and my own mental health suffered greatly. It takes energy and blind love to sustain this type of living situation. I knew, in the long run, it would also affect the kids. And it did, to different degrees and at different moments. I tried to protect them as much as I could. But that also takes its toll.

In hindsight, I strongly believe that certain external events triggered his illness. And then, denial and a sequence of errors from the medical system all contributed to him not facing and accepting his illness, and not getting proper help or medication.

Losing James and my close-knit family to bipolar disorder is the greatest loss and sadness in my life. I loved him unconditionally, just the way he was—with all the ups and downs. I knew he had bipolar about nine years before his formal diagnosis. I knew and I accepted it. I also knew we could have helped him; I knew we could have taken steps to control the depression and attenuate the hypomania. I knew and I had faith and I kept on trying, but nothing worked, not even love. They say love conquers all! Unfortunately for us, not this time, not for this situation. And that is something I will carry with me for the rest of my life.

Our early life together

To better understand how this illness can start and how it manifests, let me share some important facts about our lives.

James and I had a very passionate relationship. We met in our early twenties, and we hit it off right away. He was so very charming and funny. He was also vivacious, energetic, dynamic, and full of ideas. It was never, ever boring to be with him. Although he was very busy with work, we managed to see each other a lot. We spent whole weekends together. We had a hard time being apart: we were so connected, and we felt an immense magnetic force pulling us together. We each felt we had found our soulmate.

We moved in after only a year of dating.

The early days living together were very difficult. We both had strong personalities and we often fought. He was a workaholic, and this scared me. He worked so much that my family asked me if he was on cocaine or other drugs to be able to sustain such long working hours. He often worked around the clock without sleep and then would go home, shower, change and go back to work for another full day! It was crazy. I just thought he was young, full of energy and a workaholic. I was certain he wasn't doing drugs, so I reassured my family. I was in love and willing to make many compromises. Little did I know back then that his excess energy and lack of sleep were almost certainly signs of hypomania. Our love was so strong, though, that we got through all the conflicts.

A few years after our marriage, I got pregnant and was very tired, but he was always working. He would work through dinnertime and sometimes through the night. He would phone me from work, late already, saying he was coming home but he wouldn't, and I would wait for hours and hours. He often went out with his co-workers after work and came home at 1 a.m. or 2 a.m. I finally gave him an ultimatum. He would stop this behaviour, or I would leave. I gave him six months.

Unfortunately, I had a miscarriage, but it made us reconnect. It shocked him back into his "other" personality. He was very sensitive to my needs. He was back to normal, respectful, and loving—the way I knew he could be.

Our family life and James's checkered work history

An economic downturn combined with many bad business decisions (his impulsiveness and risk-taking habits were sure signs of bipolarity) led to our eventual bankruptcy. We lost 35 thousand dollars, all our savings at that time, back in 1991.

This was the first of many ups and downs in his work life. Over the years, he repeatedly tried to start an ad agency, changed business partners, started unrealistic projects, held different jobs, accumulated debts and, in the end, we lost most of our savings including our retirement savings. It was always up and down. But in between these highs and lows, there were rewarding periods when things went well, and we would be very happy.

After our bankruptcy, he was again hired by his first employer. We bought a house and had our first daughter, Julia, in 1992. Things were stabilizing at that time, and we were happy again.

However, two years later, I was diagnosed with malignant melanoma. I went into a depression and that put a lot of pressure on James. He was working very hard, and my state of mind was affecting him and his work.

I was in therapy and doing better and better each month. By the summer of 1996, I got pregnant with our second child, Sofia, and James and I started working together. He had more and more clients, and I was helping him with administrative tasks and client servicing.

The increased income enabled us to live better, and the lifestyle helped with his moods. But it also encouraged spending and we started disagreeing on certain expenses. This was very gradual: it worsened over years and years. But it certainly was another surefire sign of hypomania.

In 1997, our business was doing so well that we were able to hire a babysitter and work from home. Three years later, we had our baby boy, Maxime, and were so elated. This stability and family setting was allowing James to function really well. The next seven years were the best years of our family life and our relationship! We were so happy to work together, and we got along so well.

Triggering events

This is when two major triggers occurred. From 2003 to 2004, our business started to plummet. We lost our biggest client and started having major financial difficulties, but we kept hanging in because we thought that's what entrepreneurs do.

Then, in the fall of 2004, our neighbour had a heart attack and James went with our neighbour's daughter to do CPR on him. They did CPR for 19 minutes! Unsuccessfully. It was awful. After that, James was never the same. I always had the feeling that a part of him died that day too. He started to have symptoms of depression. I didn't know what to do. I recommended that he see a therapist, but he refused, saying he would be okay and that he could deal with this on his own: typical male behaviour and stigma at its best! The only other thing that I knew I could do was be there for him, support him, encourage him, and be patient and nurturing. And I was all that. I loved him so much! I would do anything. I would go to the moon for him.

I also told him I thought he was suffering from post-traumatic stress disorder (PTSD). But he denied that. In hindsight, I think this is when his bipolar disorder was triggered, because that is when some of his actions seemed hypomanic and some depressive.

In February 2005, he told me he didn't think he could continue with his life.

Mood swings

At this point, everything went haywire. The depression and hypomanic episodes started to increase in frequency and intensity. But I wasn't sure, and things weren't always clear-cut. At this point, he also started to drink, every night, sometimes a whole bottle of wine to himself.

He started becoming very impatient and aggressive. Bad moods almost took over his whole personality. He went back into business and a series of bad associations and poor business decisions made our financial situation worse. I also started a business of my own and that put more strain on our couple relationship and our finances. We had to cut our usual activities and outings. Slowly, our lifestyle started to change and that made him more depressed.

I had a hunch he had bipolar from about 2006 onwards, and began telling him about bipolar disorder around 2009, but he always denied it. I showed him descriptions of bipolar symptoms and even though he would admit he had many of the symptoms listed, he still denied having the disorder.

One summer, he drove us down the winding Cabot Trail Road at 45 km/hour when the signs say "10 km MAX." I still remember this vividly. Our three children were in the van. I was terrified but he was laughing hysterically. Hypomania!

By now, our beautiful loving family had started to deteriorate. By 2010, he was a completely different person—almost unrecognizable—but I didn't know what to do. I loved him so much and didn't want to criticize him or give up on him. I forgave his unacceptable behaviours and juggled it all so that it wouldn't have negative effects on the children's lives and their relationship with him. I was being the pins in the pinball machine, day in, day out.

In 2011, our daughter Julia was diagnosed with thyroid cancer and that affected James very much. He got severely depressed and aggressive. His negativity was directed more and more toward the children: he resented their presence and the financial burden they represented. There was a nasty incident in August 2012 where he got so upset with Sofia and Maxime for no apparent reason that I blew my top at him! I was fed up. I screamed at him, and he got mad and broke a kitchen cupboard door. The glass shattered onto the floor. The kids got scared and ran outside while we argued.

At that moment, I decided to take him to our family doctor. We saw the doctor in November 2012. This is how the conversation went that day—and all the other times that we consulted a heath professional.

Me: I think my husband has bipolar.

Doctor: Really? *[With a blank look on his face.]* What did he do? Did he empty your bank account? Was he promiscuous? Any psychotic behaviour? Did he try to commit suicide?

James: *[Just sits there, saying nothing, staring blankly.]*

Me: No, none of that. *[Thinking: I can't tell the doctor what James has done without criticizing him, bringing him down. I don't know what to say in front of James that would explain my hunch about bipolar. So, I shut up, don't say anything, and pray.]*

Doctor: Oh well then, I don't think that this is bipolar.

No further questioning, no evaluation, no questionnaire, no testing, no referral to a specialist, no individual interview with me or any of our children. None of that.

What I couldn't say at the time was that James had—for years—been risking our family and finances with too many unwise business associations, speculative deals, and bad ideas. And toxifying our household with his mood changes and aggressive behaviour. But I couldn't say any of that in front of him: I loved him too much and didn't want to make him feel bad. So I stayed silent.

Our doctor prescribed antidepressants and I was sent home with an unstable husband, to continue being the pins in the pinball machine.

Four years of hell

November 2012 (when we first consulted our family doctor) is the beginning of a sequence of events and medical mistakes that would catapult us into the next four years of hell.

- We had no follow-ups from our general practitioner (GP): James was prescribed an antidepressant but not told to come back in a few weeks or a month to evaluate his progress.
- Therapists would tell James he was not depressed and didn't need therapy. He was hypomanic when he consulted with therapists so of course they saw a very happy, confident, and energetic person.
- A mental health nurse decided James did not have bipolar disorder, even though she did not have the medical knowledge and power to make a diagnosis. She ignored our GP's eventual referral to a psychiatrist. Again, no follow-ups were recommended.

I was the one who had to call back our doctor's office and insist on getting a follow-up appointment. Things were getting worse at home, and I knew this environment was not at all healthy for our children.

Now, what the medical system doesn't understand and see as important is that while the patient and his family wait for a follow-up appointment, people must go on with their daily lives. And medical staff are obviously not there in the home, observing, on a daily basis. And that is what takes its toll: the daily consequences of living with a person with a mental illness and the lack of knowledge to deal with this in a proper manner.

More hypomania

Hypomania shows itself in many different forms. One such hypomanic episode happened in November 2013 when we were at a fundraiser James had helped organize. He was feeling expansive and overconfident. He put in a bid on all 30 items in the silent auction, with individual bids ranging from $75 to $375! I was dumbfounded when I went around the auction and realized what he had done. That same night during his thank you speech, he wished me a happy birthday in front of about 300 strangers. This gesture might be seen as sweet or touching, but in the moment, it was very awkward and out of place.

Another example of this happened in 2014 when I published a book about healthy habits. I asked James to order 500 copies from the printer he did business with. Without telling me, he ordered two thousand copies, which cost me over 11 thousand dollars. It took me six years to sell those, just to cover printing costs. Again, you might think he was just being supportive of my writing project, and had great faith in me, but it was a financial disaster.

Multiple diagnoses

In 2015, we finally got a neuropsychology evaluation that diagnosed James with obsessive-compulsive disorder (OCD), attention deficit hyperactivity disorder (ADHD), depression, anxiety, and a moderate risk of bipolar disorder. He filed the report in a drawer and did not follow up on any of its recommendations. Nine months later, we finally saw a psychiatrist who prescribed an ADHD medication. James took it for three weeks then stopped. He went into another depression. So we returned to our GP, who prescribed another antidepressant. This one sent him into a very dangerous and prolonged hypomanic episode. It lasted four months during which he would often stay out late at night, making weak excuses for never being home for dinner, and so on. I felt so helpless.

Then one night, after months of this, he told me he would take the 10 p.m. train home from work. When he didn't arrive by 10:30 I tried to call and text him, but he didn't answer. By 11:30 when Sofia got home, I told her that her father hadn't come home, and we decided to track his phone. We found that he was downtown in a bar (we later learned he was there with a woman he knew) and then the two of them went off to visit a friend of hers in a palliative care facility. So much for me expecting him home on the train!

I was beside myself. I just couldn't take it anymore. When he finally came in at 1:30 a.m., I told him to pack his things and leave our home.

That was my breaking point. Everything had become too much for me. I was slowly dying of psychological and emotional trauma.

That summer of 2016, he spent two months away from our home. I lost 15 pounds and had to stop working. He finally checked himself into a private medical clinic. Within 20 minutes of interviewing him, the doctor diagnosed bipolar II: twelve years after the initial symptoms had emerged!

A couple, a family, two careers, a lifetime of savings, three children—all affected by an undiagnosed and, therefore, untreated mental illness. No one listened to me. No one ever interviewed me. No one ever asked about our children, how they were, what was going on in our home with a mentally ill father.

He came back home after his diagnosis and we tried to reconnect, but he lacked the insight to realize what had happened over the course of those 12 years, how much I loved him, and how patient I had been. I wanted recognition; I wanted him to love me back; to tell me he was sorry he had not listened to me. I asked for couple's therapy, I asked for help myself because I was totally burnt out. None of these were helpful. Someone advised me to read a book about how to live with a difficult husband!

Separation

In May 2017, James had a major panic attack, so he checked himself in to a private clinic for ten days. One week after coming home, he told me we should separate. I was appalled but I agreed: I had no energy left, no will to fight anymore. On that day, in an instant, our 32-year relationship ended. We never spoke about it again.

And then, after the separation, it got even worse. He went into hypomania and totally dissociated himself from the kids. I think he was maybe over-medicated. My children could not relate to their dad. This is probably the saddest moment of all. I had hoped that he would finally see what was happening, that he was losing what was most important in life: his family, his wife, and his children. Him turning his back on us was the greatest betrayal I have ever felt.

To me, my marriage vows were sacred: *In sickness and in health.* I tried so hard to honour them. But in the end, it did not work, and the illness progressed and was made worse with added environmental stressors and the wrong medications during the last four years of our marriage.

Caregiver burnout and alienation

I suffered caregiver burnout, which caused depression, anxiety, and PTSD, resulting in severe insomnia. Recurrent nightmares started about three months after the separation and lasted for over two years. A lot of anger and frustration came out in the nightmares. They are still present today as I write this account, although less terrifying, less frequent, and have less impact on my emotional health.

I have no words to describe how this saga has affected us all and I still feel that all the health professionals involved contributed to the negative impact of this illness on our family. No one ever considered our children or me, and they still don't. Luckily, the love and bond I share with my kids helped us through this difficult time and has been our lifeline. My children were there for me when my life came crashing down. Our love has helped all of us continue and grow from this. Sadly today, Julia and Sofia do not speak to their dad anymore: it's too difficult and hurtful for them to see him so different and disconnected. Maxime still speaks to him, but very little.

As for me, I don't speak to James at all anymore. I am simply unable. Apart from all the hurt from before our separation, since then, he has only given me hardships about money and child support.

People ask if I could ever consider getting back together with James. I did at first. I thought he would surely realize what he had lost, but now it seems not. He's not the same person now. We don't recognize him. He's moved on with his life, and I don't like his new lifestyle. I have so much anger and deep feelings of betrayal. So, no, I don't think I would ever be able to reconcile.

Conclusion

Bipolar disorder is very complex and so different for each individual that it makes it very difficult to diagnose, but the sooner a diagnosis is made the better. A big part of the person's healing process will depend on their willingness to let go of the (hypo)manic part of their personality. This is the most difficult as the bipolar person thinks this "high" person is their true self.

The impacts on—and traumas suffered by—the bipolar person's loved ones are immeasurable and can last long after the person is effectively treated. Medical personnel should consider and take care of the family members as much as the patient.

I truly wish that people in the medical system would change their ways of dealing with mental illness so that others would not have to go through what my family went through.

Isabelle Lipari

I have a bachelor's degree in commerce, am a workplace health consultant, a personal trainer, and a wellness specialist. My life experiences prompted me to turn my career goals to the promotion of healthy lifestyles. I lost my mother when I was only eight years old, and then many other family members before I turned 15. My eldest daughter and I are both cancer survivors, and I have also helped family members with mental health issues. In 2014, I published my first book, *21 days to change your lifestyle habits* and in 2016 *Aveoactiv – exercise programs for office workers*. I am the proud mother of three young adults, to whom I transferred my passion for a healthy and balanced life; and I am caregiver to my father who has dementia.

My Son's Lost Youth

Shauna Michaels*

** This is a pen name and all names and relevant details in the piece have been anonymized as well.*

This story is about my much-loved son. I'll call him Jeremy. He's in his late twenties, single, handsome, intelligent, and funny. He was diagnosed with bipolar disorder in his teens—more of that later.

I have been trying to write this piece for a very long time but feeling stuck. I've been putting it off for a long time. Then this morning I woke up and realized why. As the parent of an adult child with severe mental illness, not a day goes by that I don't question what I could have done differently. So, writing about my experiences will of course tap into my own vulnerabilities. Ones that I may be hesitant or fearful to examine for very good reasons.

I am not sure where to start or what to say. My story is long. It is complicated. It is painful. And it brings great, great sorrow. I know I am grieving the opportunity as a parent to watch my son become the man he wants to be. The one he hoped to become, and the one I saw him becoming. He was robbed of the opportunity to grow into the person he could have been and was capable of becoming. This is deeply painful for both of us. If the services and supports had been there for him and me, things might have turned out differently.

Jeremy's childhood

My first marriage was an emotionally abusive one to—let's call my first husband John. I grew up in a family of abusers, so it's probably no surprise that I married one. It was not a safe marriage, and he and I had even talked about separating before I got pregnant.

In the end, for all the usual reasons women give (low self-esteem, fear, "how will I make ends meet on my own?"), I stayed with John, and we had two sons and a daughter together.

Jeremy is my firstborn. He was extremely colicky, and I couldn't soothe him properly. We took him to an infant development program where they diagnosed him as having attachment issues. John and I went for therapy, but John thought the problems with Jeremy were all in my head. John came from a family where "you made your bed, you lie in it" and talking about family issues was taboo.

Later, we discovered that Jeremy had delayed fine motor skills, was very anxious, and couldn't focus. I also learned that Jeremy was hypersensitive to the feeling of different types of clothing fabrics on his skin. I thought he might have Asperger syndrome or some kind of autism (today we would say he was "on the autism spectrum"). But I did not really know what he was experiencing. I read a lot, tried to diagnose him myself, and felt even more confused by it all.

He was always a very intense child, and an avid reader. Once he honed in on something that interested him, he was off in a world of his own. As a toddler, I attributed it to a high level of intellect and focus. Which I thought was a good thing. In hindsight, it was not such a great attribute when I did not have the skills or training to know how to help him be able to multi-task or socialize better.

John and I divorced when Jeremy was seven, his brother was four and his sister was newborn. The divorce was so traumatic: John tried to say I wasn't competent to take care of the children, so there was a protracted custody battle. It was a nightmare. John's macho attitude and "your-mother-is-a-no-good whore" kind of indoctrination really poisoned the kids against me over the years. Everybody felt it; as they grew up, they all knew what John thought of me, even if he didn't say it out loud.

At the time of the divorce, Jeremy was old enough to express a desire to live with me; he said he felt safer with me. He'd experienced his father's physical abuse: he'd even been hit over the head with a shovel by his dad. He had also experienced the lack of emotional support from his father. Later, he struggled with his father's new partner who despised Jeremy.

Long story short, we ended up with joint custody of the children.

At that time, I tried to get Jeremy into long-term counselling and to get him an Individualized Education Plan, but John would not agree to any counselling. John hated me more than he loved his children. He flat out prevented them from getting help because that would mean outsiders would know the dirty family secrets and of the abuse going on.

In his early years, Jeremy demonstrated a real propensity for learning and loved to read, always questioning life and facts. In school, from a very early age, he was considered a "geek" and was frequently bullied. What I remember most, around grades 5 to 7, was him standing alone in a corner at recess reading a book. He struggled making friends, and with being accepted for who he was and is. He has never been able to "fit in." School—for kids who are differently abled and intelligent—is often a cruel place. As he approached high school, when the time to really fit in is high on a young teen's mind, he experienced even greater alienation. In hindsight, I wish I had home-schooled him, because his relish for learning, quest for information, and love of reading was outweighed by the bullying he experienced and the lack of acceptance he felt.

When Jeremy was eight years old, I met a man I'll call Eric, who later became my second husband. Eric also had children from his previous marriage. They were older than my children, and also in joint custody. Eric was very supportive of Jeremy and my other children, thank goodness. Eric and Jeremy had a very close relationship from the get-go, maybe because they were alike in many ways, both being introverted intellectuals.

Jeremy was about ten when his father remarried—his second wife had children of her own, so that further complicated the already-complicated family dynamics. And then, on top of everything else, John and his new wife were physically and emotionally abusive to Jeremy. As a result, Jeremy now refuses to see his dad. Yet deep down, I know he really craves John's approval and acceptance. This additional trauma added to what Jeremy had already experienced growing up with his abusive father and being pulled this way and that during the custody battle.

Jeremy's siblings

After Jeremy told the court that he wanted to live with me, John was furious and gave up on Jeremy, but then he constantly tried to get the younger two children to go against me. When my second-born was 12, John and his wife coached him to say he wanted to move out and live with them. And then the same thing happened with my daughter. I couldn't believe it. And the children moved out.

The pain I felt was indescribable.

I recall crying myself to sleep many times as their father and stepmother made it impossible for me to see my two younger children or have any contact with them.

My second-born son is now in his mid-twenties, and for the past decade has been completely estranged from Jeremy and me. I believe he's been poisoned against us by his father. I have no idea how he's doing, or if he has any mental health issues of his own.

For a long time, I was very, very sad about this. I used to hold on to hope for a relationship with him. But now I wonder, how would it even be, after so many years apart? Maybe this is how a biological mother feels, waiting for her adopted child to come and find her one day. They'd be total strangers, at a loss about where to even begin forming a meaningful relationship. "Who are you? What do you enjoy in life? Have you missed me?" It must be so hard …

I tried for years to reach out to him, but he never responded. So, after several years, I just became so sad that I resigned. But even as I type this, I'm crying. So, I'm obviously not over it … I mean, just imagine the trauma of such estrangement, such searing alienation between a mother and child.

Then, as I mentioned, my youngest child, a daughter, also went to live with her father and her older brother when she was a young teen. She moved back in with me a few years later, and she's now old enough to be out of the home, living independently. She's had periods of depression and even some suicidal thoughts as a teenager, but she's hypervigilant about what she'll share with me or anyone else. I believe her father's "teachings" about keeping family issues within the family have made her fearful to talk about her feelings to anyone.

These days, I don't worry too much about her, thank goodness: she does talk to me when she has something really pressing, and asks for my input. But—not surprisingly after all she's been through—she doesn't trust easily. She shuts down her feelings to protect herself.

I can appreciate that for so much of my younger children's lives, I was severely distracted by Jeremy's overwhelming needs for care and support. I often wonder how much the younger two resented the fact that I was always Jeremy's staunch advocate, his only real cheerleader in life. As well, I was struggling with my own depression and feelings of loss. Through all of this, I likely was not there enough for my other children.

As a parent, I feel a tremendous amount of guilt and shame. I guess it's like being the parent of a disabled child. The focus of attention will always be on that child. I don't know if that impacted their decision to go and live with their dad. It would make sense. That—and the constant distractions of Jeremy's problematic behaviours—must also have negatively impacted his siblings and created this trauma in our family where nobody really trusts anyone. Family counselling was needed long before now to help create a safe place. But again, that was never permitted by their father.

I realize all of this may sound very bleak, but I also recall that as a single mom, I did many things with my kids that I think were super-positive. We played a lot of games; did puzzles; went to music and arts festivals, and museums; and one place we went to a lot was a regular family open-mic night. I exposed my children to culture and some pretty unique experiences.

Jeremy's youth

Like any young adult who wants to be accepted, Jeremy did what any other person would do. He was drawn to a group of teens who did accept him. Sadly, those tended to be the kids who had absent parents or had been labeled troublemakers. He tried so hard to be liked and to fit in that over the years he did not always pick the right crowds to hang out with. It makes perfect sense to me; he was an outlier by nature with extremely low self-esteem and could therefore easily be lured to a problematic crowd.

I noticed from the time Jeremy was around ten to twelve (somewhere around the time of his father's second marriage), he would take things of mine without asking. Just small things, like a hair barrette or a box of chalk. And he would hold onto things, hoarding them. He was quite obsessive about keeping things orderly and colour coded. He had enormous difficulty sleeping. I let him use earphones at night, and he'd eventually fall asleep listening to *Under the Covers* on CBC radio. (When he was at his dad's house, he wasn't allowed to use the earphones, so that caused problems.)

He had a lot of anxiety, and a short temper. He got very easily frustrated and had big emotional swings. Looking back, I wonder whether these were early signs of his bipolar disorder. He was also hypersensitive to skin sensations, as I mentioned: I had to be very careful when we went shopping for clothes so that he could tolerate the feeling of the various fabrics against his skin. He was also hypersensitive to activities going on around him: he would get easily stressed by different environmental stimuli. He struggled being in big crowds and with noise but was drawn to video gaming and downloading pornography, which troubled me very much. I talked to him about it but with great difficulty.

I look back at all the things I thought made him different and realize that was a huge amount for one young person to be dealing with. And for his exhausted mother, needless to say!

As I said, all those issues started becoming evident to me when Jeremy was around 12 years old. Then, he became quite obviously depressed at about age 14. I remember reading his journals at the time and finding statements such as "I wish I weren't alive." I was petrified reading those things. I talked to Jeremy and tried hard to give him a safe place to share. But young teens don't open up much to their parents at the best of times—let alone when they are filled with trauma.

Despite all the difficulties, throughout his teens Jeremy and I were very close. He would talk to me a lot, about his dreams and plans; and about whatever topic was of interest to him at the time. He could talk on and on and on. I remember driving long distances to visit Eric before we moved in together, with Jeremy beside me and my two younger kids dozing in the backseat, and he'd stare up at the stars and tell me all kinds of details about this or that constellation. They were real adult-to-adult conversations. It felt so close and friendly and safe, being together in the bubble of the car, with Jeremy away from his everyday stresses and fears.

Talks like those don't happen so much now that he's older. I really miss them. The warmth, the companionship, the trust we had with each other.

Jeremy's bipolar diagnosis and first suicide attempt

Grade 12 came long. Jeremy was hanging out with a bad crowd; they got into drugs and marijuana. One night, Jeremy left the house in the middle of the night. I don't recall any particular event that might have precipitated his actions that night.

I found a convoluted note from him. A "Sorry I can't be the person I want to be …" kind of thing. I didn't see it as a suicide note, to be honest. But he went off into the woods and called his dad to say that he was going to kill himself. (His dad, of all people! They were totally estranged!) His father called the police, who traced his phone. Thank goodness they found him in time and took him to a mental health facility a few hours away from home. It was there that they diagnosed bipolar disorder. He was in there for about three weeks.

A suicide attempt. I couldn't believe it. It shook my world. I was scared, I was angry, and I was worried all the time after that.

Jeremy was prescribed bipolar medications, but he only took them sporadically. He says the prescribed meds "don't work." Instead, he began self-medicating with alcohol and later, in his mid-twenties, with street drugs.

I looked back at the time and realized that he'd been displaying bipolar-like symptoms (e.g., mood swings and depression) for about four years before he was diagnosed. I'd been grasping at straws; I knew there was *something* wrong with Jeremy, but what? It was like watching the tide coming in slowly, slowly, until suddenly we were all under water.

I felt so helpless. And where could I go for competent and reliable services? We lived hours away from a big city. The mental health services in our small town were non-existent. On top of that, I felt that this burden fell solely on me—after all, his father and I were estranged, and I felt I had to keep secret what was going on in our lives as my ex-husband would use any information to take the kids away from me.

It wasn't until Jeremy's suicide attempt that I grasped the extent of his despair and desire to be accepted. Only then did I realize he had turned to drugs and alcohol to cope with his feelings of loneliness. Although I knew he'd been using, I did not then make the connection between his mental health issues and drug use.

I have been his strongest advocate through all of this. I have stood by him, lifted him, cried with him, been angry at him, but always, always unconditionally loved him.

Eric, his stepdad, was very worried about Jeremy at the time. They were closely connected. So Eric was understandably distraught. And of course, Eric was concerned about how I would react to this latest stress in our lives.

Since that first suicide attempt, there have been others. True attempts, at least five. And many, many other times that Jeremy has openly said he doesn't want to live. It's hard for me to know sometimes: was this a proverbial cry for help, or an actual attempt? Also, I'm aware that he sometimes tries to manipulate me by throwing the "suicide card" at me. One of the signs of bipolar disorder and borderline personality disorder is this immense fear of abandonment. So Jeremy would threaten suicide if he ever felt I was not going to be there for him.

I can never relax and assume that suicide is completely out of the question for Jeremy.

I wish, wish, wish I could.

Jeremy's adulthood to date

After Jeremy was diagnosed with bipolar in his teens, a psychological assessment picked up that he had borderline personality disorder as well. More, difficult news. And of course, there's tons of PTSD from his childhood. And I have also long thought he may have some Asperger's: he doesn't read social cues and signals well; he never has. Hoarding. Obsessive tendencies. Maybe a bit of OCD that he exhibited in earlier years, but less so now? Talk about a complicated mental health picture.

I said that Jeremy and I used to be very close when he was a teenager. But now, he sometimes just goes AWOL. He just ghosts me. I'm left to worry. Has he been picked up by the police again? Has he accidentally overdosed? Has he attempted suicide again? Is he injured somewhere? Where the hell is he?

I feel really hurt and worried when he does this. I'm chronically anxious and on edge. I can't sleep. I live in dread of getting a phone call with bad news. For a while, I tell myself that no phone call is a good thing; but then the silence leads to more fear that he has gotten into trouble, is depressed, or is manic.

I find his habit of ghosting me so confusing. For a person who fears abandonment, why would he not want to stay connected with the one person who has been his constant advocate? Could it be that my own obsessive compulsion—about making sure he is okay—actually makes him feel even less worthy? If I don't trust that he is okay, how can I expect him to believe that he is? It's a Catch-22, for sure.

I just want him to be honest with me, to trust me. Not that awful silence. I really just want a relationship with him. I want to feel like I matter too. And I want him to understand that his behaviours have a huge impact on me.

He tried attending university but dropped out twice. He does some menial work, and he has a couple of friends. But mainly I'd say he's lonely and feels overwhelmed a great deal. Just like when he was as a schoolboy. He doesn't know what to do with his life and he ruminates on this so much that he ends up freezing, not doing anything for fear of failure or not fitting in again.

He's had a couple of girlfriends, but those relationships have always ended badly. He tends to gravitate toward people with mental health problems of their own, so it becomes difficult. He's single now.

Then, with no warning, one of Eric's children died by suicide. This huge tragedy affected our whole family, including Jeremy; very deeply so for him, as he had always hero-worshipped his older stepsiblings. To this day, Jeremy thinks that he should have died, not his much-loved family member.

So much trauma. It's a lot for one family to bear.

Feeling helpless and unsupported

I want to explain what it's like as a mother who lived through all of this with Jeremy and did not—and could not—find the supports needed. My son has been struggling with mental health issues since the age of ten. What services existed? What supports could I access? Where could I turn? I felt helpless, often frustrated, and always afraid.

And I was lucky: I have formal training in the field of addictions and mental health, for god's sake. I knew how to push back. If I get overwhelmed, how would an average parent feel, trying to navigate the mental health care system?

Bizarrely, we expect people with mental health issues to make their own appointments, arrange for follow-ups, buy and take their medications with no supervision, navigate the complex in-hospital and community-based mental health system alone, apply for disability support, get legal aid when needed (Jeremy has been in jail twice so far), arrange for affordable housing, get food from a food bank, you name it. And all this while they're too sick to function, really.

The system just pushes you from one place to another. It's so infuriating! No one wants to address the actual problem.

One time, I drove Jeremy to a major mental health institution in a big city several hours away and said, "This is urgent. I'm not leaving until we see someone."

Well, six hours passed, and finally a social worker came out and said, "He's not in imminent danger; go home."

Can you imagine? I've since coached him that if he's ever feeling suicidal and needs help, to tell them "I am suicidal, and I have a plan to kill myself"—even if he doesn't have an actual plan at the time. I'd much rather he deceive them so he can be admitted and get services, than take a chance and be at risk of dying by suicide.

If I oversaw designing appropriate mental health services for young people like Jeremy, I'd get rid of the ridiculous silos where clients get shuffled from one agency to another. I would want wrap-around youth mental health centres with all relevant services in one user-friendly building—mental health clinic with access to a psychiatrist, family physicians, pharmacy, food bank, social services office, legal aid clinic, and more. These services must put the client at the centre.

And I'd want home visits by social workers or psychiatric nurses. Don't expect ill clients to make their way to some far-off institution. And in all cases, I'd want continuity of care. Jeremy got so sick of repeating his long, convoluted, and painful story to one professional after another!

Also, my province's Mental Health Act basically excludes parents and family members from being active members of the client's care team. We are kept in the dark; there is no disclosure of crucial information that could help us to support our loved ones when they're back in the community. Come on! I am his last remaining advocate! Why would you not want me on his team?

Back when Jeremy was hospitalized after attempting suicide the first time and was diagnosed with bipolar disorder, he saw a social worker in the youth psychiatry department. But before she would provide any counselling to him, she insisted on getting signed consent from both his parents. Requiring consent from both parents in a family like ours where my ex-husband and I were utterly alienated proved to be another form of health care abuse, if you ask me. Why would you ask the abuser to be part of the mental health process when trying to build trust with a young client? As I've said, John had consistently refused to allow Jeremy to get counselling all through his school years, even though I had seen the need for this from the time of our divorce when Jeremy was only seven years old.

The current system is not client-focused at all. Jeremy simply couldn't manoeuvre through all the individual well-guarded doors the existing deeply flawed system put up in his way. I have a great deal of anger toward the system that allowed Jeremy to slip through the cracks so badly.

As for me finding support for myself as the parent of a child with mental illness(es), in our little town, the only counselling and support groups for parents were offered during the day. Well, I work during the day! If there'd been access during the evenings, I would definitely have gone for individual counselling. Maybe not for a support group though. In a small town, people are reluctant to air their dirty laundry in front of others. I guess the stigma around mental illness is still alive and well.

How far do the ripples spread?

If you ask me whether Jeremy's struggles have impacted the rest of our family, my answer is an overwhelming, exhausted "Yes, of course!"

His biological siblings were hugely impacted. (His stepsiblings a bit less so, only because they were older and moved out sooner.) As I said, Jeremy's brother has isolated all of us completely, and his sister is wary of him, having seen some of his very unpredictable behaviours over the years.

Jeremy really trusts his grandma (my mom). She's been a great help. For example, she's picked him up from jail, and when he's at risk of being homeless, she lets him stay with her for a while. But it's not easy for her because her husband, my stepdad, is an alcoholic and an abuser, so she has her hands full just coping with her own dramas.

I obviously can't speak for my ex-husband and his second wife. But I do blame Jeremy's father a lot, for the hell he put us through over the years. If he had accepted and supported Jeremy, I'm convinced Jeremy could have been helped. He would have been able to seek out and receive support.

I know that early childhood trauma has a huge impact on brain wiring, but I believe Jeremy could have learned the coping skills he needed. Unconditional, loving support makes a huge difference in a child's life. It would definitely have helped his situation. Just look around in our jails: I've heard that as many as 50 to 60 percent of inmates have mental health and/or addiction issues. Go figure.

I feel really blessed in many ways that my second husband Eric was so supportive of both me and Jeremy over the years. But now there's definitely some tension between Eric and my son. Fair enough, really, because Jeremy has burned some bridges. Eric gets understandably fed up with the excessive amount of energy it takes from me to advocate for and take care of Jeremy. I am Jeremy's only advocate. Eric feels helpless and wants to protect me from the pain and stress of constantly trying to care for my son. But of course, he can't fix it.

No one can fix it.

I guess it's fair to say that Eric has been severely burned, even burned out, by Jeremy's behaviour over the many years they've known each other.

That's hard for me, of course. I often feel like I must choose between them. Or I must keep secrets. For example, if I decide to give Jeremy some money for groceries or whatever, I might not tell Eric. I can't even invite Jeremy for dinner without prior negotiation with Eric.

I've tried to have Jeremy come back home to live with us from time to time, thinking that if he has a stable base, he might improve.

But when he does stay with us, it always ends in a disaster: a fight of some kind; so the police are called. So now Eric says he's not welcome anymore.

The other day, I said, "I wish Jeremy were less volatile; then he could come and stay ..." But Eric cut me off before I could even finish my thought. That's just not an option any longer.

Eric would love for me to detach from Jeremy and just let him do his own thing. I get it. I mean, on paper, Jeremy is an adult and all, but mentally, emotionally, and socially, he's really not. Deep down, he's still just ... well, he's still just an anxious teenager, looking for love and approval.

A teenager with all kinds of complex and untreated mental health issues, what's more.

And once again, typing this, I'm weeping.

And finally, there's the impact on me. All those years, there was deep shame and embarrassment: I was always having to make excuses for Jeremy, and I often felt that people in the community, and society in general, were judging me as a "bad mother." As if to say, "What did she do wrong to have a child with so many problems?"

My own mental health has obviously suffered a lot. (More tears.)

Conclusion

My biggest hopes for Jeremy are that he finds a caring and supportive partner that he can build a life with, and that they can lean on each other. And that he can have a family of his own. Work-wise, I'd love for him to find something stimulating and creative. The menial jobs he's been doing are no fun. Mainly, I just long for him to feel worthy and loved, and to be happy.

As for my own future and dreams? Nothing really; not anymore. To be honest, I don't want to live a long life; it's been way too painful so far. Writing that brings me to tears. Why do I have to feel so chronically sad? But in case you're wondering whether I feel suicidal or not, I can say "no." I would never take my own life. Even if Jeremy were to overdose accidentally, or to die by suicide, I still wouldn't consider suicide myself. I would reach out and get the support I need.

I'd say my biggest struggle with Jeremy these days is never knowing the truth. I never know who I'm talking to. Is he truly having an episode? Is he playing me? Is it his profound trauma speaking? Is it one of his own distorted, unhealthy coping strategies? I wish I knew.

What I do know, with a deep dread, is that I live in hypervigilance that the phone will ring one day, and he's overdosed, or in jail again, or my worst nightmare: I'm going to have to bury my much-loved son. After all of this, after everything I've tried to do for him, after everything our entire family has tried to do, he may not make it.

He may not make it.

But let me end on a positive note. My hope is that our whole family—including Jeremy himself—will find a bit of peace. After all, we deserve it. And most days, I think there is still hope.

Because if Jeremy were to find some peace, I would find it too.

I was born in Ontario, Canada in the 1960s and completed a variety of post-secondary studies including a Diploma in Addictions and Mental Health and a Bachelor of Education. I enjoy painting, gardening, and advocating for social justice. I live with my husband in Ontario.

Mum on the Line

Janet Scott*

** This is a pen name.*

"Hello, darling. No, it's okay, I wasn't asleep. What's the matter?"

"We've talked about this before. I can't. No, I don't have it."

"You can't ask her. Not them either, you still owe them! I'm sorry, I really am."

"Can you sell something? Okay, how about $50? But it's just to buy groceries, nothing else! Then will you be alright?"

"Yes, I'll have to sign the loan for the car because you were refused, and you really need to get one. But you must get a small reliable car, not a Jeep Safari. That's not a good idea."

"Perhaps they needed to go somewhere, or she hung up accidently. Your sister doesn't understand. She just sees all the attention I give to you, and she gets mad. Don't take it personally, she was just having a hard time with the baby."

"Look, you need the money! That course was so expensive, and you've got all those loans. Why not go part-time for now? No,

I really think it's better that you just work for a regular company and get a steady paycheque."

"I know it's boring. Boring is good. It's just for now, until you get out of this hole. Accept the offer and if it goes well, you can ask for a raise next year. I know, but some money is better than no money, right?"

"I think that is a very good decision. Why don't you write it down and post it somewhere so that you remember it tomorrow?"

"It's not that I don't believe in you. That's not fair. It's just that it takes a lot of very hard work to start your own business and it's very risky. Your coach said that because she doesn't know you."

"Of course, you can, and you will! One day …"

"But if you move to California, you won't have a green card, a place to live, or any medical insurance."

"It's normal for some hair to fall out. It's a seasonal thing. How much hair?"

"I don't know. Just get the generic brand. If it says organic isn't that okay? Shampoo is just shampoo, isn't it?"

"Perhaps it's the eggs, you eat a lot of them. I've never seen anyone else eat six eggs and a banana for breakfast every morning. How did the Paleolithic people manage?"

"Maybe you should eat less raw food and try some more carbs. Yams, you should eat those, they're very grounding."

"One day, in the future it will get better, I know it will. I've been praying for you, a lot. We have so much to be grateful for."

"Hello there. I didn't hear from you yesterday, so I assumed that life was going well! Give me the good news also, sometimes!"

"Yes, I agree, the Baptism was a good thing for you. You have a new life to create that is more in alignment with your goals and dreams now. You see, you are maturing!"

"Well, yes, I like Jesus, but I don't think I need him inside me for now."

"Of course, love is the most important thing, although you do need money and quite a bit of it if you want to stay in the city. You've been to some lovely weddings but those friends of yours have very wealthy families."

"I still think the best way to meet someone is to find them in your network. The whole thing of online dating scares me."

"Yes, I know I'm old-fashioned."

"Wow. That's a lot of interest. How many accounts do you have?"

"Well, he looks nice, but I can't tell much from the picture. It sounds like he has a good job but is he a good person? Is he kind?"

"Well, if you don't know anyone who knows him then I guess you'll just have to find out."

"Hey! Wow, that's amazing! He did! Really, so soon? Congratulations!"

"Why Jamaica? Why now? No, I cannot let you use my credit card anymore."

"No, I don't think plastic surgery will make you feel better about yourself, and you have a lovely face, full of light and love. Why would he say something like that?"

"I don't think that's fair, and I have never thought of you as a selfish person. You don't earn enough to splurge on bottles of wine and dinners the way he and his friends do—and please don't. Alcohol is bad for you; I thought you realized that by now."

"Why do you always feel it's your fault when things go wrong?"

"Let's just be grateful that you didn't quit your job like he wanted you to."

"I just want you to know that you are loved. That I love you unconditionally (and it breaks my heart). It is perfectly alright for you to walk away and that is a sign of sanity, no, I mean health. It doesn't mean that you'll never have a good relationship; it just means not this one. When he upsets you so much it is the right thing to leave him. You're not to blame and I don't think it's fixable."

"If you can't get hold of her, leave a message. Don't forget to leave your number, then the secretary can call you back with an appointment."

"You should always have some left over, in case of a time like this. Why did you stop taking them?"

"No, feeling okay means they were working, not that you didn't need them anymore. Call the pharmacist at your old place and ask for a renewal; even if the prescription has run out, she can give you some for now. You need your meds!"

"Why are you in the Emergency room? What's the matter? Oh God! I wish you weren't so far away."

"Your heart? But you're so healthy! What have you been taking? How can you have a heart condition? You're so healthy!"

"It's going to be alright. Everything's going to be okay. I'll send you the ticket."

"Please, please just come home, I can take care of you, I'm your mum."

"Okay, that's your choice. I know you're a grown up, you'll be 34 next birthday. You still have plenty of time to reach your dreams."

"But if you move to California, you will not have a green card, a place to live, or any medical insurance. Please realize that."

"I love you. I love you. Yes. Always. Unconditionally."

"Hello, darling. What's the matter?"

I was born in England in 1965 and after studies and travel, emigrated to Canada in 1986. I now live and work in Montreal, and am the mother of three adult daughters, one of whom was diagnosed with bipolar II in her teens. My family life has been shaped by mental illness. My family of origin was broken apart by it and as a mother and wife I learned all that I could, from professionals and from organisations like Friends for Mental Health (asmfmh.org/en/) and the National Alliance on Mental Illness (nami.org). Now that my children have left home, I stay in touch through phone calls and precious time together. Like all families, we have struggles and conflicts, but our essential relationships are braided by diagnosis, self-discovery, and love.

Traversing Volcanoes

Gail Windsor

Editor's note: Gail's daughter, Tracy Windsor, has written about her experiences as someone living with bipolar disorder in a piece titled A Bumpy Road to Recovery: Worth the Ride *in part 1. Sections of Gail's piece was generated in a joint interview I did with her and Tracy. Tracy's comments and clarifications are included below, as they occurred in that conversation.*

As a young girl, my daughter Tracy met all the usual developmental markers. She was intelligent, quick-witted, cheerful, and fun, interspersed with intense grumpiness when she was tired or frustrated. Around age 8, when my ex-husband and I were getting divorced, Tracy developed a hair-pulling disorder (trichotillomania) for a while.

Years later, she experienced a depressive episode during her first semester at university in Vancouver in 2006. After a visit to Nova Scotia in the summer of 2007, her dad advised me that Tracy was exhibiting some bizarre behaviour: she was irritable and quick to snap at people; not herself. We knew that Tracy sometimes drank alcohol and smoked marijuana so he thought she may be doing street drugs, but he could find no concrete evidence of that.

I hadn't observed any extreme out-of-character behaviours myself but kept my eyes open when Tracy returned to Vancouver.

Over time, she became more and more ill-tempered; she was often cranky for no reason, impossibly snarky. Her moods and behaviour were unpredictable. Sometimes her speech was rapid-fire staccato, but her words were surprisingly succinct and clear even at such a fast pace. Many of her comments were hyper-critical and unrealistic.

At the time, Tracy had a casual job in the same company as me. One day, I walked past her office and saw her lying on the floor, feet resting up on a stability ball. Very strange behaviour in a work setting. When I spoke to her about it, she brushed it off: "I'm just taking a break." She didn't see anything inappropriate about it. I was convinced she was stoned at work, which she vehemently and repeatedly denied.

When we walked together, Tracy would walk on tiptoes like a ballerina, almost floating, and she leaned very close to me or even against my shoulder, as she would have done as a child who felt fearful. Perhaps she was looking for comfort or needing to ground herself.

She became very difficult to be around. Her irritability lurked just below the surface, waiting to pounce. I approached her with caution, on eggshells.

Tracy's bipolar diagnosis

On Mother's Day, 2008, Tracy and I went to buy flowers for my mom. I asked Tracy to help choose the flowers. She would not answer me. She just stood there silently, looking intently into my eyes. Later, she said she had been trying to contact me telepathically.

Her unusual and bizarre behaviour had to stop. I had been updating Tracy's dad and he was concerned for her, too. I called him from the car, and we both agreed that Tracy must be regularly stoned and needing help for substance abuse. On his suggestion, I took her to hospital for drug testing. Tracy immediately agreed to going for testing: she was eager to prove that she was *not* using any drugs.

The triage nurse asked Tracy why she was there. She matter-of-factly replied: "I have bipolar disorder."

I was dumbfounded by this pronouncement. With brow furrowed, I said: "This is the first *I've* ever heard of it."

Tracy said she had self-diagnosed after reading up about her symptoms, and she was correct, as we soon learned.

She tested negative for drugs and was referred to a psychiatrist in the hospital. He said it looked like a manic episode of bipolar disorder. (Later, the term *bipolar I with psychotic features* was used.)

I knew nothing about bipolar disorder or its long-term ramifications. In fact, I was completely ignorant about mental illness in general and also felt the ugly prongs of stigma. I knew I had to educate myself to understand and help my daughter. So I immediately threw myself into what would become a very long journey into bipolar research. My learning curve was steep and rocky and is still ongoing.

I was diligent to study only accredited, science based websites. Among other things, I learned that bipolar disorder is a serious mental illness and can include crushing depressions, sky-rocketing manias, and high suicide rates. Some people lack insight into their disorder (anosognosia), refuse prescribed medications, self-medicate with street drugs and/or alcohol, and develop addictions. I also learned that often many, many medication changes are needed before the right dosages and combinations are found for each individual.

Tracy's first hospitalization, May 2008

The first time I stepped through the locked doors of the psychiatric ward was surreal. I was distressed by what I saw and quickly recognized that Tracy presented with some of the same unusual behaviours as other patients. I could see that she was with her peers, people living through similar experiences with mental illness. People are in the hospital for a reason—they need help.

Tracy didn't want to take the meds. On the first night, she refused, and the hospital staff had to call security to hold her down. They gave her a shot to calm her. I explained that the staff are experienced with mental illness and have the knowledge to help her. I encouraged her to follow their advice and said that I did not know how to help her at the time.

When saying goodbye to Tracy after a visit, she would grab my arm and beg me to take her home. But clearly, she needed to be in the hospital, and I lovingly told her so.

> *Tracy Windsor: I felt so oppressed by the system and the staff. I just wanted to get out of hospital ...*

Tracy was certified for 14 days. This would be the first of several hospital stays over the next few years.

After release from the hospital, psychosis continues

After being released, Tracy was referred to a community psychiatrist who she saw once a week. I drove her there and waited to take her back home. Tracy refused to speak to the psychiatrist, so about half-way through each session, the psychiatrist would ask me to go in and prompt Tracy about what was going on in her life. Eventually, Tracy would speak a few words.

> *Tracy: It was a waste of time, really. I was just telling the psychiatrist what she wanted to hear.*

Even after being in hospital, Tracy still didn't seem to be well. Most of the time her face was impassive, lacking expression. I decided to leave my job to stay home with her. I was fearful for her. She needed my help and support until she was well again. It wasn't good for her to just sit around the house or stay in bed. Instead, we went for long walks and drives, and I was there to watch out for her.

On one walk, close to the airport, we could see planes in the distance on their approach to the runways. Tracy, gravely concerned, said the planes were coming to bomb the city.

> *Tracy: I thought the planes were crashing into buildings in downtown Vancouver, and I was confused why nobody around us seemed concerned about it. I kept secret that I had "classified information" that World War III was starting.*

I explained that they weren't bombers, just passenger planes that we had travelled in many times before. She seemed to accept this explanation.

At a visit to the community psychiatrist, I was again asked to prompt Tracy to communicate. This time, the floodgates finally opened, and she explained all about her different delusions.

> *Tracy: I told her about my delusions about being a royal princess, a Saint, the Messiah, and believing I had the power to kill people with my thoughts or to raise the dead. This all poured out of me.*

Tracy's descriptions made sense to her, but her words were garbled and disjointed. The psychiatrist said, "Tracy is clearly psychotic. She needs to go back to the hospital right away. The longer psychosis is left untreated, the more difficult it becomes to treat."

But Tracy refused. There was no way she would be locked down again. I felt that over the next few days, I would have time to gently persuade her to go voluntarily. (Had I known then that the Vancouver Police Department had specially trained officers to assist with mental health emergencies, I would have called for help to take her to the hospital. When you know better, you do better.)

Tracy had only to speak a few words before it was glaringly apparent that she was not thinking properly. I was afraid that she'd try to harm herself or run away to avoid going back to the hospital.

At night, I slept fitfully on the floor of her bedroom to keep a close, protective watch over her.

One evening, she slipped out of the house. I drove around searching for her. Luckily, I saw her stepping onto a bus. The bus hadn't yet left the bus stop. I pulled in front of the bus, slammed on the brakes, leapt out, climbed onto the bus, and pointing to Tracy, said to the astonished driver in an authoritative voice: "This woman is under my care, and I am responsible for her." To Tracy, I demanded: "Come with me right now or I'll call the cops." All the passengers silently stared, and I held my ground, hoping that Tracy would come with me quietly and not make more of a scene than I already had. She cooperated and came with me without question. I think she trusted that I had her best interests at heart.

This intervention on the bus was an extreme measure, but essential under the circumstances. I didn't know what else to do. What did I know about managing a person in psychosis? I was just muddling through, taking one day at a time. I acted on instinct to protect her. She was far too vulnerable to be out in the world in her mental state.

About two weeks after her community psychiatrist diagnosed psychosis, while we were out for a drive, Tracy said she would like to go back to hospital. St. Paul's Hospital was close by, and she was admitted immediately. At last, an end to a harrowing couple of weeks for Tracy, and for me.

> *Tracy: Actually, I didn't want to go to hospital because I thought I needed treatment; I wanted to go because I hoped the hospital would keep me safe, or at least use my body and mind responsibly for scientific purposes.*

Second hospitalization, June 2008

Tracy was in the lockdown psychiatric unit of the emergency ward waiting for a bed in the Psychiatric Assessment Unit. She was in a single room, more like a cell, with only a mattress on the floor, a stainless-steel sink and toilet. Her door was thick steel with a small rectangular wire-reinforced window.

The heavy-duty latches and locks on the doors could not be engaged from inside; only from outside. Her room was one of several on either side of a corridor, all behind an even thicker locked steel door. The nurses' station, where I had had to leave my purse for security reasons, was safely situated on the other side of the secure door to the patients' quarters.

One day while visiting Tracy, I suddenly heard a huge clamour in the corridor. I cautiously peered through the small window and saw a solid-looking man storming up and down the hallway, screaming a non-stop stream of obscenities, all the while causing thunderous clangs when opening and slamming shut other patients' doors. He was out of control.

The only thing in Tracy's room I could possibly use to defend us was her toothbrush. I shakily clutched it in both hands and stood, hardly breathing, heart pounding, right by the door, out of view of the small window, poised to protect my sedated, defenceless daughter and myself.

After what seemed like an interminable amount of time, several security guards spilled into the corridor and subdued the rampaging man. Fortunately, Tracy's door was not breached, and I slowly regained my equilibrium.

According to hospital protocol, only security can deal with dangerous behaviour in the ward. Apparently, the nursing staff had watched the drama unfold via the security cameras in the unit and in Tracy's room. They had been holding their collective breath, hoping I would remain quietly inside and not confront the unruly patient.

As soon as a bed became available, Tracy was transferred to the Psychiatric Assessment Unit.

Transfer to a specialized hospital

Every spare minute I had since Tracy's bipolar diagnosis was spent researching on the internet. Eventually, I found a small article about a long-term inpatient psychiatric unit at the University of British Columbia (UBC) Hospital for young people experiencing a first episode of psychosis. Afterward, patients were released to the Early Psychosis Intervention (EPI) Program for up to three years of outpatient treatment. I was jubilant about finding specialized long-term treatment close to home and asked the psychiatrists at St. Paul's if this could be an avenue of treatment for Tracy. They said that Tracy met the criteria, and she was transferred to UBC Hospital the next day. After a couple of months in UBC Hospital, Tracy appeared to be somewhat stable, and was released to the EPI Program.

Referral to Early Psychosis Intervention (EPI)

At Tracy's first EPI appointment in mid-August 2008, she stormed out of the room, saying, "This is bullshit!" and bolted from the office. I ran out, caught up with her, held her by the arm and begged and pleaded with her to return. Chasing after her was risky, and I just went on instinct. I didn't know if I could convince her to continue with her appointment: Tracy may never agree to go back to EPI, but it was a chance I had to take. EPI is the gold-standard for care, and I saw this as her best path to wellness. I explained all this, and said I was only trying to do what I thought was best for her. I was relieved that she agreed to give it another try and went back in to continue her session. Again, I think she trusted my judgment.

> *Tracy: Mom caught up with me and begged me to stay. She was always very supportive of me, so I relented and went back. I can't remember exactly what happened in there to upset me in the first place. Maybe I felt patronized.*

Tracy needed intense treatment, so she went to EPI at least twice a week. She attended therapy sessions with a psychiatrist, clinician, occupational therapist, and dietician. EPI staff would see Tracy or speak to her over the phone as often as she needed. Tracy and I lived in a virtual bubble in those days, with just the various therapists, psychiatrists, and doctors she had to see.

Tracy's energy level was extremely low. Often, I would have to drag her out of bed. I may have to dance around the room, pull on her ankles, and sing loudly about whatever group activity or appointment was scheduled for that day. I'd say that I would drive her there and then drive her back home; all she had to do was attend the activity. Sometimes, I would wrap my arms around her shins, like a horse pulling a cart, until she slithered down onto the floor. Another risky move to pull a grown person, much bigger than me, out of bed. She could easily have kicked me in the face. I counted on her accepting that what I was asking was the right thing for her to do. Again, I was just feeling my way, going on instinct. And relying on the trust between us.

Throughout, it was Tracy's job to get well, and it was my job to help her. I cannot stress that enough.

What I learned from psychoeducation

At EPI, I learned invaluable knowledge from the psychoeducation they provide to family members.

Staff explained that Tracy had had what they called a *brain attack* which had resulted in cognitive and psychological deficits; it would take time to recover from this bio-medical illness. To illustrate how her neuropathways were currently misaligned, they showed the outstretched fingers of their two hands trying to mesh with each other, but not interlocking smoothly. I found that image helpful: it explained why her brain was not functioning properly.

We also learned that the brain of a young person cannot mature properly when it's unwell. So as parents, we would need to make allowances for social and emotional—as well as cognitive—delays.

One psychiatrist described Tracy's bipolar I with psychotic features as "a pneumonia variety of bipolar disorder, not a common cold variety." It's serious.

> *Tracy: I remember in the psychoeducation sessions for patients, they addressed the issue of self-medication and how many patients use booze or drugs to cope with anxiety, irritability, and other bipolar symptoms. We also learned about exercise, meditation, and mindfulness. And how to deal with day-to-day life with a mental illness. At EPI, they diagnosed me as an alcoholic, so I started attending Alcoholics Anonymous (AA) meetings.*

I attended a few AA meetings with Tracy and made the decision to quit drinking myself—at first in solidarity with Tracy, and then because I realized that I, too, used alcohol in many situations in my life and didn't want to do that anymore. I haven't had a drink for almost a decade now.

They said Tracy would need to gain insight into her disorder and learn new coping strategies for the nuances of her particular illness. (Individuals have different symptoms, and react better to certain medications, and have different recovery trajectories.) They said that rest and sleep is good for a healing brain, but too much is not.

They advised that Tracy would have to reinvent herself as a person *living well* with a mental illness, and that adapting takes time.

EPI encouraged Tracy to attend various group therapy sessions. Apart from AA, she attended an art studio for creative works, and learned public speaking skills through the Mood Disorders Association of British Columbia. She has since spoken about her lived experience at many public events.

When she wasn't attending groups or other therapies, EPI asked me to prompt Tracy to talk about her thoughts, feelings, and insights, and to encourage her to use her newly learned coping strategies.

They emphasized that recovery is not only possible but expected. That was so reassuring. Of course, this assumes that the affected person uses the tools they're given, and follows the lifestyle-related guidelines, taking prescribed medications, avoiding drugs and alcohol, and so on.

> *Tracy: They also emphasized that my illness does not define me. It was hard to see that at the time, before I was stabilized, but it's a key concept. I am so much more than my illness.*

EPI advised us to focus on personal strengths and not deficits. They knew that Tracy enjoyed sports, so they appealed to her sports mentality to motivate her—like a coach would push and encourage an athlete to excel.

They said it may take many different attempts to find a combination of medications to control her symptoms. In the first few years after her diagnosis, there were so many medication changes that I stopped reading about the side effects of each one. It was crucial that she attain wellness, or she would have absolutely no quality of life.

EPI helped us develop a safety plan for suicide prevention. They were upfront about the fact that suicide is a serious issue among individuals with a mental illness, and the risk for suicide and suicide attempts is higher when someone is in the early stages of diagnosis and treatment.

In the evenings and on weekends, when EPI was not available and I did not have the right words to help, if Tracy was in distress, feeling hopeless, or dealing with suicidal ideation, we'd call the Vancouver Mental Health Emergency phone number and either one or both of us would speak with them. Their strategies were helpful, and an excellent resource at that time.

EPI staff taught that families are *not* to blame for mental illnesses. EPI had many meetings with our immediate family members to understand the family dynamics. Family involvement is welcomed and encouraged. I was part of the care team. When required, I would sit in on Tracy's therapy sessions, to prompt her to talk more. And I'd always ask the staff: "What can I do to help?" I wanted her to get the most out of every opportunity EPI was providing.

In all Tracy's time at EPI—over three years in all—there was only one thing the staff asked of me that I could not do: to try to get Tracy to change her mind about wanting to become an orca (killer whale) trainer. They wanted her to plan for a more practical, sustainable career path. But Tracy loves orcas and had dreamed of doing this since she was a very young child. I did not wish to break her heart over this—not after all the other disappointments and changes brought on by bipolar disorder. So I told the staff: "Whatever career she chooses, I will support her. It's her decision to make; her life." I wanted Tracy to feel respected as an independent adult, free to make choices for herself. I felt that when her brain had healed sufficiently, she would eventually find her own way.

Tracy's suicide attempt, January 2009

Unfortunately, even after her months-long hospital stay and several months of intensive time with the EPI team, Tracy remained deeply depressed. Her brain still wasn't functioning properly, and she was unable to absorb, recall and retain the strategies that EPI had provided. Her facial expression was blank and disinterested. Her whole world seemed dark, and she felt isolated, bleak, desperate. It was excruciating to see her continued suffering.

In January 2009, my daughter-in-law called as I was leaving my new job at the end of the day. Sounding concerned, she said

Tracy was slurring her speech and had gone to her room. I said I'd be home as soon as possible and would deal with it then.

When I arrived, Tracy was on the floor and went into a seizure, body convulsing, eyes rolling back so only the whites showed. I called the Mental Health Emergency number, but they said this sounded like a *medical* emergency. I immediately called 911. At first, I thought she might be having an allergic reaction to her meds, but suddenly panic set in: I had an epiphany that she had overdosed.

Part of Tracy's safety plan was to have her meds hidden, but they were not hidden well enough. We also had some medications waiting to be returned to the pharmacy because she'd had an adverse reaction to them, and she found those, too. She ingested everything she could find.

The 911 operator asked if she was breathing. She had stopped convulsing by then, but I couldn't tell if she was breathing or not. I was so stunned and shaky, I couldn't feel or see if her chest was moving, or if there was any air going in and out of her nostrils. Between my daughter-in-law and me, we thought that she was taking very slow, very shallow breaths.

Firefighters arrived first, checked her vital signs, and relayed details to the 911 operator. Next, paramedics came. They put in an IV, started oxygen, and rushed her off in a shrieking ambulance. I followed in a second ambulance, which also had lights flashing and sirens blaring. Even now, years later, my heart pounds just to remember it.

They ran with her on the stretcher into emergency and she disappeared behind closed doors.

In a private family room, my son and his wife soon joined me to wait for news. I was numb and on autopilot when I said, "Tracy might die."

Staff periodically gave updates. They said they had pumped her stomach, administered activated charcoal, and done many blood tests. Eventually, a social worker advised that Tracy would make it; she would survive. At that point, it was still unknown if there would be any organ damage, but that was of secondary concern to me at the time. (She eventually needed two six-hour sessions of kidney dialysis to flush the chemicals out of her blood.)

Tracy was transferred to the ICU late that night.

I slept in an ICU waiting room, and the next morning, went to see Tracy. She was on a ventilator with tubes and IVs everywhere. There were so many machines and monitors that I could barely squeeze in to stand beside her, so I kept vigil by the foot of her bed. When I could move in close, I'd say every positive thing I could think of. Things like, "You'll get through this. You'll get better. We're going to find the best care for you. You are precious, and you are loved. You will love life again."

I was profoundly heartbroken that Tracy had felt so desperately hopeless as to seek relief in death. But I was unimaginably thankful that Tracy had survived. She was alive and that was all that mattered. I was traumatized and exhausted. I knew we were, again, starting from the ground up and that we'd somehow cope and help Tracy to achieve wellness—whatever the future might hold.

Tracy, on the other hand, was disappointed to still be alive, though she did not say this to me at the time.

I had researched suicide and knew she might be feeling like this, so when she did disclose her disappointment, I wasn't discouraged. In fact, I would have been surprised if she'd been relieved to be alive. I tried to block out the negativity (leave all that to the professionals to deal with, I thought) and keep up a persistent stream of light and optimistic topics. When she expressed negative or depressed thoughts, I reinforced positivity and replied: "Things are going to get better." I became a relentless, committed cheerleader.

However, nothing anyone said would or could make Tracy feel any better.

Transfer to psychiatric ward

A few days later, Tracy was physically well enough to be moved from the ICU to a psychiatric ward where she stayed for three months.

I visited her on most days. She remained in a deep, dark, intense depression. Her face was vacant, her eyes dull and unfocused. It was difficult to get her to speak at all. I'd read that it can take a long time to recover from bipolar depression. She was in the hospital and was, at least, alive and safe.

After about two months, the hospital staff informed me that Tracy was to be released in a few days. But it was glaringly apparent to me that she was not ready for that: she was still acutely unwell and needed more hospital care.

I requested a meeting with the hospital psychiatrist. (When a patient is admitted, the hospital psychiatrist takes charge, so Tracy's psychiatrist at EPI unfortunately had no jurisdiction there.) I was courteous and direct: "Tracy has not improved at all since she's been in hospital; she's still severely depressed. I know she will attempt to end her life again, and in her current state of mind, would very likely succeed. Please do not release her now." I then asked: "What would *you* do if Tracy were your daughter? Is there a private clinic that could help her? Aren't there any more treatments available for her? Is it possible to collaborate with Tracy's EPI psychiatrist, who knows her well?" Finally, in a desperate conclusion: "What is the liability of the hospital if Tracy is released now and dies by suicide?"

There was a long silence. He then said he'd consult with his colleagues and get back to me, and Tracy could remain in hospital until then.

Speaking directly to the hospital psychiatrist about my concerns was the appropriate course of action under the circumstances.

Waiting for his reply, I envisioned other plans if my pleas went unheeded and Tracy was released while still so depressed. I could meet with the President/CEO of the hospital. Or contact TV news and radio stations about Tracy's plight. I could phone my local politicians and provincial and federal health ministers. I could even demonstrate by walking up and down in front of the hospital wearing a placard if it came to that. I sought legal advice. I was determined to do whatever was necessary to keep Tracy safe in hospital—to protect her life—even though she was an adult. Tracy could not fend for herself while mired in her unyielding depression.

The psychiatrist called me back a few days later and said he'd spoken with his colleagues and the EPI psychiatrist. They agreed that electroconvulsive therapy (ECT) could be an effective treatment for Tracy's "medication-resistant bipolar depression" (now sometimes referred to as "difficult to treat depression").

When he mentioned ECT, I was horrified at first. A shiver of dread passed through me.

However, since Tracy wasn't responding to her medications or other treatments, I was open to anything that might help her recover. I was genuinely grateful and thanked the psychiatrist for hearing, and acting upon, a desperate parent's concerns.

Electroconvulsive therapy (ECT)

I knew nothing about ECT at the time except what was shown in the old movie, One Flew Over the Cuckoo's Nest.

I asked the EPI psychiatrist what she thought, and she said ECT may help re-align Tracy's neuropathways, and that it does often alleviate persistent depression. She suggested that I do more research and discuss it with Tracy.

After poring over many studies and articles, and further discussions with the psychiatrists from the hospital and EPI, I was comfortable with ECT as a viable treatment for Tracy. To the best of my ability, I relayed what I'd learned to Tracy and said it could hopefully benefit her. Tracy then spoke with both doctors and agreed to try ECT.

> *Tracy: I was so desperate that I was willing to try anything that might help. The only other option, in my mind, was to attempt suicide again and hopefully be successful.*

ECT is performed in an operating room (OR) with the patient under anaesthesia for the few minutes of the brief treatment. Tracy and I agreed that it may be comforting for her if I accompanied her to the ECT sessions. At 7 a.m. on treatment days, I walked alongside as an orderly pushed her wheelchair to the OR. I waited outside while she had the treatment, and then we all went back to her ward. The wheelchair, the orderly, Tracy and I did this trek to and from the OR on several occasions. Tracy was groggy after the treatments and would then sleep for a couple of hours.

> *Tracy: I don't remember much of anything around the time that I was getting ECT treatments. I don't recall how I felt about ECT. The days while I was in the hospital all blended into each other.*

As I recall, Tracy had about nine sessions of ECT over about three weeks. Slowly, we saw small signs that she was coming back to herself. Her facial expression brightened a little, her eyes focused more and sometimes we even saw an inkling of a grin. The fog was finally lifting.

For me, too, everything opened up as Tracy improved. I was cautiously optimistic but remained vigilant for symptoms of a relapse.

Not long after her last ECT session, she was safely released from the hospital.

> *Tracy: As the weeks passed, I started to feel less suicidal and had more interest in life.*

Once released, Tracy returned to the excellent care of the amazing staff at the EPI Program. Her therapy sessions were finely tuned to her needs. Because her brain was functioning so much better, she was able to understand and absorb the coping strategies being taught. She enthusiastically took on new challenges.

Then, almost a year after the first round of ECT, Tracy was again depressed and having suicidal ideation. This time, she was open about it with me and the EPI staff, so it was dealt with quickly and safely. Her EPI psychiatrist recommended a second round of ECT. Tracy agreed as the first round had brought such positive results. Again, I accompanied her to and from each ECT session. A few additional sessions were done during the second round because recent studies had shown that these could be beneficial: this was true in Tracy's case.

Intermittent bouts of suicidal ideation

During one of Tracy's subsequent hospital stays—there were so many it's hard to keep track—she remained in a deep well of depression. Her desperation caused a serious incident of self-harm. Her psychiatrist was so concerned that a sitter was assigned to stay beside Tracy's bed overnight for a few nights in case Tracy woke and was distressed. This bout of depression subsided.

After the second round of ECT, when Tracy was again released from hospital, she was living in a house with three roommates. One night while she was out, she phoned me at about 10pm to say she was having suicidal thoughts about jumping off a bridge.

> *Tracy: This was in 2011. I had just seen a movie about a man with cancer, so that might have triggered thoughts about death and my own mortality. I left my friend after the movie and started walking toward the Lions Gate Bridge. To jump. I called my mom, crying, and said I was heading to the Lions Gate Bridge. She knew my intentions...*

I had to weigh my options: do I call the police, or do I drive 45 minutes to the city to get her? I followed my instincts and asked Tracy what she would prefer. She asked me please to pick her up so she could spend the night at my place.

We stayed on the phone while I drove, and she came by bus to meet me partway. To distract her, we talked about inconsequential things, and I regularly asked: "Where are you now? What can you see through the window?" From her replies, I knew that she was indeed heading to meet me and not going elsewhere. When I got to our meet-up spot, I found her waiting. I was so relieved and reassured that she had recognized that her disorder was acting up and that she'd known to reach out for help. She'd effectively applied one of the key recovery strategies taught at EPI.

This incident might have ended tragically. But Tracy called me, trusted me to come, and I trusted her to meet me as arranged.

She slept over at my place that night and thankfully felt much better the next day. Her suicidal thoughts had disappeared. She also had a telephone conference with EPI. (I would have taken her to hospital if she'd not felt better that morning.)

What I've learned

If I were to meet a young person recently diagnosed with bipolar disorder, this is what I'd like to share with them, based on my experiences with Tracy's illness:

- There's no quick fix, no silver bullet, no magic wand. Bipolar disorder is a chronic, relapsing illness that will demand your full attention if you want to get—and stay—stable.
- Please follow the advice of your mental health professionals and ask questions to ensure that you truly understand their advice.
- Take your medications as prescribed. If side effects become severe, consult your doctor about that, but don't just go off your meds on your own.

- Educate yourself about your condition: participate in psychoeducation courses; do online research on accredited, science-based websites; read books and articles; attend lectures in the community. Do due diligence on your own behalf.
- Learn to "live well with your disorder." In some cases, this may mean that you must reassess plans for future studies, travel, career options, living arrangements, and so on. Be flexible. Choose what's best for your long-term mental health.
- Keep a daily mood journal to monitor your mood patterns and respond accordingly.
- Ask a trusted support person (family member or friend) who is familiar with your particular symptoms to prompt you to get help when you may not have the insight that you are becoming unwell.
- Find a good peer support group where you can share with and learn from others with similar illnesses.

For parents whose teen or young adult has a bipolar disorder, I urge:

- Educate yourself about bipolar spectrum disorders. Arm yourself with information.
- Listen to what the mental health professionals advise. They are the experts, and you need their help every step of the way. Get a second opinion if needed.
- Advocate on your child's behalf when you have concerns about their treatment plan.
- Don't blame yourself for your child's illness; it's not your fault.
- Bipolar disorders are serious and unpredictable but can be managed with the right treatments and strategies. It can be a long and difficult road to recovery.

- Closely follow the advice of experts to help your loved one recover and "live well" with their bipolar.
- Having said that, though, trust your instincts. You know your child better than anyone.
- Try to maintain the trust that exists between you and your child or build trust if it is already weakened.
- Don't beat yourself up about how you handled things in the early stages. It can often take many years to get an accurate diagnosis. (I felt totally ignorant and stupid that I hadn't recognized my daughter's bipolar disorder even though, in retrospect, there were many warning signs. I simply didn't know enough at the time.)
- Remember that use of street drugs and alcohol can delay recognition of a mental illness and exacerbate the symptoms. Keep an open mind: "Is this a problem with substance use? Is a mental illness emerging? Or maybe both?"
- Try to look after yourself. This can be difficult at times, at least until stability of your loved one is achieved. Looking back, I did not get enough rest and time to myself and became exhausted. Please be kind to yourself. Just as Tracy needed to reinvent herself to live well with her mental illness, so I needed to do the same to live well with my recovering daughter. But this can be easier said than done.
- Find a support group where you feel comfortable sharing your thoughts and experiences.
- Attend accredited mental health conferences and seminars that are open to the public. The presenters may be psychiatrists, psychologists, occupational therapists, people with lived experience of mental illness, family members, and friends. You will learn a lot.

Many progressive hospital staff and mental health workers welcome family members as a natural, essential part of the care team. We are the people who love, stand by, and help our mentally ill loved ones to do well in life. My wish is that all affected families could be part of a program that respects the family's crucial role. The support of a loving, caring family together with the expertise of mental health professionals can lead to excellent outcomes.

I've met many parents who've made extraordinary efforts to support their mentally ill family member. For example, some moved across country to be with their ill young adult children. Others, like me, have taken time off work, or retired early, to support their loved ones. However, we hear about too many parents and their mentally ill children who are, for any number of reasons, completely estranged. And many of those affected people end up on the streets, or drifting from shelter to shelter, or in jail. Or they die prematurely from accidental overdoses, exposure, untreated physical illnesses, homicide, or suicide.

Of course, it's not only parents who go to great lengths to support their family members. Many spouses, partners, siblings, and teen or adult children do the same. We are all part of the vital—often overlooked and undervalued—safety net that supports loved ones with mental illnesses.

Conclusion

Following—and sometimes during—a flurry of activity, Tracy's depression can set in again. She only has so many spoons of energy on any given day. When too many spoons are used up, bipolar symptoms can reappear. To find a balance between self-care, studies, work, and volunteering, she needs to manage her time to provide structure and reduce stress. She continues to be medication-compliant and makes sure to get enough sleep. Mindfulness, meditation, yoga, biking, and hiking are regular activities in the mix.

In the past several years, Tracy has learned to manage her bipolar to the point where she can now study and work part-time, do peer support work, teach spin classes, and maintain a supportive network of friends. After completing her master's degree, she plans to get a PhD in social work. She's passionate about mental health. Tracy has found her niche, and I'm optimistic that she'll continue to thrive, forge her own path, attain her goals, and make important contributions to her chosen field.

Tracy was hospitalized seven times in the three years from 2008 to 2011 and she survived a serious suicide attempt in 2009 that landed her in the ICU. Her bipolar disorder severely disrupted her young life, and I was honoured to accompany her on her journey to recovery. I extend my heartfelt gratitude to all the nurses, doctors, clinicians, social workers, occupational therapists, art studio teachers, public speaking tutors, AA attendees, and everyone else who helped Tracy to gain and maintain stability. It does take a village to raise a child.

Tracy and I have looked back and recounted some of our deeply personal and difficult incidents from our shared experience, hoping that our honest depictions and reflections may help others cope with the challenges of mental illness.

Gail Windsor

I grew up in Vancouver, British Columbia (BC), and worked as a paralegal in a law office. I moved to Sydney, Nova Scotia, at age 29 to live with my now ex-husband. Our two children were born and raised there. Now retired, I live in Squamish, BC.

Volunteering with Marie

Dennis Barras

Editor's note: Dennis has used pseudonyms to protect the privacy of the family concerned. For the purposes of this narrative, the mother who has bipolar disorder is named Marie, her daughter is Julie, and her grandson is Kevin. Both Julie and Kevin have mental health problems of their own, but they have not been formally diagnosed or disclosed. As a volunteer, Dennis visits Marie, takes her out for coffee, and accompanies her on errands and to some of her medical appointments.

Let me introduce you to Marie, a cheerful, fun-loving, French-Canadian woman in Quebec. She grew up on a dairy farm with a large family of parents, brothers, and sisters. However, she was the last living member of her original family. Except for distant nieces and nephews living in other cities, all the others have passed away. She married—and later divorced—and has a daughter, Julie, who in turn has a son, Kevin. Julie and Kevin live thousands of miles away in Alberta.

Unfortunately, the bipolar disorder that affected Marie from age 50 onwards did not skip a generation in the way it sometimes does. Both Julie and Kevin have mental health problems but are responding well to treatment and are living together in harmony. Both are considered too ill to work.

By the time I met Marie in 2003, she was 77, overweight, and had been living in a Montreal group home for 19 years.

Neither Marie's age nor her excess weight (about 300 pounds at the time) slowed her down much, but her mental condition did. I found her disorder made her vulnerable to being overwhelmed and carried away by the system. At one point, for example, she was placed under the supervision of the Public Curator, and during that short time her apartment was emptied and virtually everything she owned disappeared, including all her cherished family photo albums. She managed to escape the Curator, but she had been stripped of her past, and her present and future were now dictated to her. I watched helplessly as she was passed from one institution to another and back again. All she could do was endure whatever loss or humiliation came her way. I'm grateful that we live in Canada and have health care and old age security, otherwise she could have been left to die, unattended, in a rooming house somewhere.

Marie was a lovely person, refined, and usually in good humour. She wanted to do everything: go to the hairdresser, visit the bank, eat at a restaurant, get around under her own steam. She could sew like a professional seamstress. One day, I saw her wearing a lovely new blouse and was amazed when she told me she had made it herself entirely by hand!

Sadly, she was very restricted by her age, her weight, some mobility issues, and vertigo that was a side effect of one of her bipolar medications.

I think she had been living isolated in a world of her own for a few years, so sometimes I found it hard to follow a conversation with her. But she had so many things to say. I think it was because she had spent several years without anyone to really talk to. She spoke French and all the other people in the group home were English-speaking. I enjoyed speaking French with her because it was my only opportunity to practise my French. She was caught in a time warp so I liked watching the news channel with her: I could explain things and help bring her up to date. She would ask questions and I'd respond.

I remember one time she received a letter from a Nigerian prince! Sound familiar? I nipped that in the bud, but it was another disappointment for her: she'd been divorced; her only child moved across the country; she became mentally ill; she lost all her possessions; she was placed in a group home. And now, the promise of great riches from some mythical "prince" was being exposed as a hoax!

Marie spent most days in a large, overstuffed chair, staring at the TV. When she moved around her apartment, she always had one hand against a wall to keep her balance and help support her weight.

One day she decided to go—shall we say—walkabout. Are you familiar with the term? She left the house on her own and, for some reason, wanted to visit the synagogue across the street. Problem was, she wasn't Jewish. Another problem was that she wasn't allowed to go anywhere by herself: she had fallen more than once and had the scars to show for it. I'm not sure how the caregiver found out about her little outing, but it earned Marie two weeks in a psychiatric ward.

Marie and me

Originally, staff at the now-defunct Volunteer Department at the Douglas Mental Health University Institute (a large psychiatric hospital in Montreal) asked me to accompany Marie to her doctors' appointments. Her caregiver from the group home couldn't go with her because she was a nurse who worked at night. During the day the caregiver's sister took care of the residents in the home. So, I made Marie and her caregiver an offer. I would go with Marie anywhere she wanted as long as it was on the day when I would normally visit her. That meant we could go places like doctors' appointments, the bank, the hairdresser, restaurants, and so on. The caregiver gave her permission.

The first time Marie and I went out it was warm, so we decided to walk. This required a certain amount of exertion from her as there were also several stairs to deal with. Just the same she was determined to make it. I had her take my arm and walk beside me. We had to walk slowly, matching our steps to remain stable. Every hundred feet or so, we would pause for a moment for her to catch her breath. We only had one long block to go, and it was about as much as she could do. The pots of gold at the end of that rainbow were the bank, two pharmacies, and three restaurants. She was delighted!

We walked up there a few more times, but she soon got wise to it. She knew that a five-dollar bill would take her up there in a taxi, so from then on, that's what we did. And so began a more cheerful chapter in her life with some freedoms and simple pleasures rediscovered.

One of the more noticeable symptoms of Marie's bipolar condition was the paranoia that caused her to make unfounded and bizarre accusations against the people around her. There were three other women in her group home and several times, I had to defend my reputation against Marie's accusations that I was having sex with one or more of them. On two occasions, she left messages saying she didn't want to see me again, and to give her back whatever I had that belonged to her! Those messages were easy to deal with: I just did nothing. Within 24 hours she would call back and say to forget whatever she had said and to please visit as usual.

But when I came face to face with the accusations while visiting her, it was a different story. She even accused her caregiver of running a brothel! At first, I found it all a little amusing, but she was dead serious, and it ended up needing a good half-hour of denials and explanations on my part to ease her mind. It was very difficult for the people around her, but as I said, she was quite refined, and her language was never vulgar or obscene. In times of considerable distress, she unfortunately would use the word *immigrant* in the presence of her Filipino caregivers. Everyone forgave her those episodes, but they didn't win her any friends.

Marie and Julie

At one point, Marie's health seemed to be failing due to a *Clostridium* difficile infection she acquired while in hospital. Marie's daughter Julie returned to Montreal to see about her mother. She found an apartment and began visiting three times a week. Marie eventually recovered and after about eighteen months was able to move in with Julie. I warned Julie that there would be difficulties—things she would find very hard to deal with—and I was right. For example, Marie had problems with her bowels due to surgery for intestinal cancer. Occasionally Julie had to clean up some nasty messes and she found it unbearable. It was this same problem that had precipitated Marie's departure from the group home.

Around this time, Marie began to resist taking her medication regularly. One morning in May 2014, Julie woke up to find that Marie, who walked slowly with a walker, wasn't in the apartment! She searched frantically for her in the hallways and lobby of the building but couldn't find her anywhere. She finally called the police only to be told that her mother had been found and taken to hospital. As it turned out, having elevators in the building and a bus stop at the front door weren't necessarily good for everyone.

The security cameras in the lobby revealed that Marie had left the building at 6:45 a.m. and taken a bus! She didn't have any money on her, but the bus driver had allowed her to get on his bus without paying, and someone gave her a seat at the front of the bus. It was rush hour, so the driver had a bus full of people anxious to get to the Metro station, so he did nothing. Instead of stopping right then and there and calling a supervisor, he drove her to the end of the line at the Metro and let her get off. Fortunately, there were two policemen on duty outside the Metro. Marie was 87 at the time so when the police saw this very elderly woman all alone and struggling to walk with her walker, they sensed something was wrong. They asked her where she was going and she said, "New York!" Perhaps she was just being sarcastic because she didn't want them to stop her. In any case, she was sent in an ambulance to the hospital of her choice where Julie found her later that day.

If this incident had been reported to the bus company that "kind" driver would have been in big trouble.

That adventure was the final nail in the coffin of Marie's personal freedom. After two-and-a-half years, Julie felt she could no longer care for her mother, so Marie spent some time at the Jewish General Hospital and then was moved to the hospital-like Geriatric Institute. Poor Marie, every time she put a foot wrong, the consequences were harsh.

Marie's final days

For the last three-and-a-half years of her life, Marie lived in the Geriatric Institute. We were told confidentially that this was where people went to die. The care she received there was quite good. I have very few complaints. Many of the staff were good, kind people. It's a good thing for Canadians that we have the social safety nets we do. I always appreciate that these institutions exist, despite any flaws, so that people like Marie can have a place to live safely.

One year before Marie passed away, she was diagnosed with tumours in her abdomen. This was a recurrence of her earlier bowel cancer: she'd had abdominal surgery for bowel cancer many years before—about two years before I even met her, in fact. Because of her advanced age and extreme lack of mobility, they decided not to treat the condition. Her doctor felt that it was time to begin giving her morphine, but Julie asked them to wait. She wasn't ready to admit that the end was near. Daily life—such as it was—went on, with meals, washing, visits, medication, naps, and sleep. When Julie and I would visit, we would always bring Marie something to eat and drink, which she usually enjoyed.

Julie and I were visiting one day when Marie's doctor came in to discuss the state of her cancer with her. "Do you have any pain?"

"Yes."

"Strong pain?" the doctor asked.

"Yes."

So the doctor said they would start giving Marie morphine.

I could feel a change in the atmosphere when the doctor said that. Julie stiffened, and she and I looked at each other. We both knew what this meant. It was the beginning of the end.

The morphine injections began, and Marie's appetite vanished: we couldn't get her to eat anything anymore. She slowly declined, becoming weaker and weaker, and more and more silent. She was drifting away from us.

Sometimes we saw fear in her eyes. She looked to us for reassurance, and we did what we could to calm her.

I don't know how she managed but she held on for another four-and-a-half months before she finally found peace.

Julie took Marie's passing quite well. She's keeping the urn with Marie's ashes in her home and finds comfort in that. I have encouraged her to take comfort in her faith and the belief that she and her mother will be reunited one day.

Conclusion and reflections on my volunteer experience

A caution: I'm not sure if my experience with Marie is representative of a typical person who has bipolar disorder, because I only knew her from the age of 77 to her death at age 92.

One thing I've learned about mental illness is that the degree of disability can vary greatly. Just because someone has been diagnosed as mentally ill doesn't mean they're severely ill, or ill all the time. Not at all. They are often very high functioning with only the occasional problem, usually observed as small errors in judgment. For example, the person may hold one or more conspiracy theories. Unfortunately, in Marie and others, I have seen this extend into blatant racism driven by unbridled paranoia.

I'd say the first step in volunteering for someone is to get to know them. That takes time, of course. Also, learn about their condition if you can. And be ready if things start to get out of hand.

Another thing that makes the relationship with a patient go better is if you're prepared to make a small sacrifice each time you meet them. Many of them have very little money and they appreciate it if someone will treat them to a coffee and a donut. It's almost a spiritual boost for them. Right away, it brings the relationship up to the next level.

It's odd but sometimes when I'm volunteering, I feel like an audience member attending a play. Things are happening before my eyes, but I'm not really involved. All I can do is maybe heckle a bit and then I must wait to meet my favourite actor at the stage door and go for coffee. When dealing with someone living in an institution, or even in a group home, it's just like that. You have to take sides with the patient. It helps to build trust and get closer to them if there's a bit of an "us against them" mentality. In fact, in some cases it's a necessity so the person feels you're on their side.

Looking back, I don't think there's much that I would have done differently in my dealings with Marie and Julie. Of course, there are specific instances that I could have handled better: a little more patience or better planning on my part could have solved most of the problems. All in all, I remember Marie very fondly, I feel good about the whole experience, and I can thank the practice of volunteering for some of the most meaningful and enriching experiences of my life.

Dennis Barras

I have been volunteering in Montreal for several years, mainly with people who have a mental illness. Volunteering is part of my lifestyle. The people I have volunteered with have remained friends, and I have developed a relaxed schedule that allows me to stay connected over the long-term. I usually see about six people a week. My motivation was originally to fulfil my obligations as a Christian, following the advice of the Parable of the Sheep and the Goats in Matthew 25:31-46 ("For I was sick and you visited me..."). Also, in the past, I had been tested by way of interactions and friendships with people who have a mental illness, and I found that I was comfortable around them and easily formed friendships with them.

PART 3

Contributions by Health and Other Professionals

… in which psychiatrists, therapists, social workers, psychologists, professors, and a professional photographer reflect on bipolar disorder and their work with affected people and their family members.

Bipolar 101

Kayla Behbahani, DO

He wore vivid green socks. He was in his twenties, barging up and down the cramped emergency room hallways, chatting with every patient, nurse, tech, and doctor along the way. What everyone noticed and talked about were his fluorescent green socks. I was a fourth-year medical student, and it was my first time meeting a patient who was manic. I quickly realized that while my textbooks gave an accurate clinical description of what mania was, they failed to capture the gravity of the illness the person is experiencing, and the family is forced to watch.

While I had met patients with bipolar I during my psychiatry block in medical school, this was the first time I found myself face-to-face with someone experiencing an acute manic episode.

Definition of bipolar disorder

Bipolar disorder was previously referred to by the now-outdated term manic-depressive illness and is sometimes referred to as bipolar affective disorder. It is known for its distinct feature of elevated, expansive, or irritable mood that lasts at least four consecutive days. The bipolar and related disorders are defined in the Diagnostic and Statistical Manual of Mental Disorders, fifth edition (DSM-5) as having some level of mood disturbance in which the person experiences varying degrees of increased energy and activity level. Although there are two major types of bipolar disorder, there are several other related illnesses, and while the criteria for each are slightly different, they all share these unique symptoms of elevated mood and energy level.

Bipolar I and mania

Put simply, mania refers to an elevated mood, and every symptom is related to that.

Individuals who are manic may experience a reduced need to sleep. They may feel well-rested after only a few hours of sleep. They may speak more than usual or faster than usual. It's often difficult for me to get a word in during my evaluation of such a patient. They may be irritable or impulsive, sometimes engaging in risky or potentially harmful activities, like sexual promiscuity, gambling, shopping sprees, and making unusual or unwise business decisions or investments. They may be easily distracted, switching from one topic to another repeatedly. They may have an inflated self-esteem or an exaggerated sense of their abilities and expertise. They may be laser-focused on specific activities, such as redecorating their house in the middle of the night or working non-stop on a book or a manuscript they'd like to publish. These symptoms are generally a significant change in the person's personality and level of function. If the person becomes suicidal or so impaired that they may hurt themselves or others, they may even require psychiatric hospitalization.

An episode of mania, lasting for at least one week (or less if hospitalization is necessary) is required for a diagnosis of bipolar I. In some cases, mania may be accompanied by psychotic symptoms, such as hallucinations or paranoia. It's also important to note that mania doesn't always present in textbook fashion nor does every patient who experiences the above symptoms experience them to the degree mentioned or for a full week.

While most individuals with bipolar I will experience an episode of major depression during their life, depression is not necessary to make the diagnosis according to DSM-5 criteria, and it is possible that a person who has experienced mania and receives a diagnosis of bipolar I will never experience depression.

Bipolar II and hypomania

Bipolar II is a bit different. The key to this diagnosis is hypomania, a word we use to describe symptoms that are similar to mania, but with a few key differences. First, individuals experiencing hypomania may have these symptoms for at least four consecutive days rather than a full week. Second, while friends and family will often notice a difference in the person's mood, personality, and level of function, the change is not severe enough to significantly impair either social or occupational functioning, or to require hospitalization. Finally, hypomania does not include psychotic symptoms such as hallucinations or delusions. (If psychosis is present, the episode is defined as mania and the diagnosis changes from bipolar II to bipolar I.)

Another significant difference is that, unlike bipolar I, bipolar II does require an episode of major depression at some point in the individual's life. Major depression is defined in the DSM-5 as a period of at least two weeks in which an individual has experienced depressed mood or loss of interest or pleasure in activities previously enjoyed, along with several other symptoms from sleep and appetite fluctuations to changes in concentration and attention, reduced energy, or even thoughts of death.

> In summary, hypomania, coupled with at least one major depressive episode, is necessary for the diagnosis of bipolar II.

Other bipolar diagnoses and specifiers

Cyclothymic disorder

Apart from the two main types of bipolar disorder described above, another bipolar spectrum illness that is diagnosed and treated by psychiatrists and other mental health professionals is cyclothymic disorder. When an adult experiences the symptoms of depression and hypomania multiple times over a two-year period but without quite meeting criteria for either bipolar I or II, a diagnosis of cyclothymia is considered. (The two-year period is reduced to one year in the case of children.) Cyclothymia is thought to be a less severe form of bipolar disorder.

Diagnoses based on cause

The DSM-5 characterizes additional diagnoses of bipolar-related disorders depending on their cause. For example, some medical conditions, drug and alcohol use, or even prescription medications can trigger changes in mood that may resemble mania or hypomania. When these disorders are seen, the diagnosis will specify what the condition is due to, such as "substance-induced bipolar disorder" or "bipolar disorder due to another medical condition." Individuals who experience bipolar-like illness due to external causes will not be diagnosed with bipolar I, bipolar II, or cyclothymic disorder, but it does not rule out the possibility that the individual may develop a bipolar spectrum illness in the future.

Rapid cycling and other specifiers for recurrent episodes

Due to the nature of bipolar illness and the likelihood of mood shifts, we use the term rapid cycling to specify an individual who has had four separate mood episodes within a 12-month period. These mood episodes can be mania, hypomania, or depression, and each of the four episodes must have a clear ending before the next one begins.

Other specifiers that define recurrent bipolar episodes include seasonal pattern and peripartum onset, that is before or after childbirth.

Specifiers for current or recent episodes

The DSM-5 lists several additional specifiers, all intended to provide a more accurate diagnosis and to clarify the severity, course, or special features of a person's disorder. Examples of specifiers that define current or recent episodes include anxious distress, melancholic features, psychotic features, and mixed features. (This last is when individuals with bipolar illness experience mania and depression at the same time. This combination can be highly distressing and can increase the risk of suicide.)

Suicide risk in bipolar disorder

The risk of suicide among patients with bipolar disorder is higher than in the general population. Some sources report as much as a 15-fold increase in the risk, which is why early evaluation, continued monitoring, and treatment are crucial.

Treatment approaches

I have worked with many patients who came to me with a diagnosis of bipolar disorder. I have also made the diagnosis in my own patients. The evaluation is complex, and the diagnosis is not always immediately obvious, but once it is made, my approach to treatment begins with education.

There are many misconceptions about bipolar disorder. Unfortunately, the stigma of mental illness—perpetuated by what we sometimes see in movies or television shows that don't accurately represent the facts—can have overarching consequences. Patients and their families don't always understand their illness, what it means and, more importantly, what it doesn't mean. They may not realize that there are a lot of very successful individuals with bipolar disorder who have achieved life goals in their careers from law through medicine, politics, and the arts to education. They may not know that bipolar disorder won't hold a person back from having friends, getting married, and having children. I sympathize with a person's feelings of loss of control, and I build a meaningful partnership with my patients so that, together, we can come up with a treatment plan.

Patient empowerment is at the heart of successful and sustained treatment of this illness. While medications will certainly help the symptoms, successful treatment isn't just about picking a pill. Medical diagnoses, whether psychiatric or not, have an emotional impact, and bipolar disorder is no different. The psychological consequences of living with a chronic illness and its effects as they pertain to each person's unique circumstances must be addressed first.

Medications are the most effective way to manage the symptoms. There are many myths about psychiatric drugs. It is true that all medications—from Tylenol and echinacea to prescription pain medications—have risks. Understanding the risks in the context of the profound benefits is essential to help the patient choose a treatment tailored to their own personal health.

Therapy can also play an important role in the treatment plan. A therapist—in combination with an evidence-based pharmacologic regimen—can help a patient accept a new diagnosis, and significantly reduce the effect the diagnosis has on that patient's quality of life by helping them to understand the importance of medication compliance and by analyzing potential triggers of an exacerbation.

Conclusion

Living with a chronic illness can be challenging, whether that illness is bipolar disorder or any other psychiatric or physical illness. But it doesn't have to be life-limiting. Following a treatment plan that you and your doctor and therapist develop is crucial to preventing relapse. Additional support can be found in resources in your community and even online. Support groups on social media have grown in popularity; use them with caution as patients advising other patients without the oversight of a medical professional can sometimes be risky. So while it may be helpful to talk with other patients who understand the struggle, be sure your medical and psychological advice comes from your health care team who have insight into your unique medical history.

Kayla Behbahani

I was born in Iran and moved with my family to the United States when I was a toddler. I've lived in Virginia, Florida, Vermont, Idaho, South Dakota, Missouri, and Massachusetts. I received my bachelor's degree in communication from Castleton University and my medical degree from Kansas City University of Medicine and Biosciences. I completed a residency in General Adult Psychiatry at the University of Massachusetts Medical Center and a fellowship in Consultation-Liaison Psychiatry at Brigham and Women's Hospital, Harvard Medical School. I am an attending psychiatrist at Brigham and Women's Hospital and an Instructor in Psychiatry at Harvard Medical School. I live with my spouse in Boston. In my spare time, I love to write, cook, and enjoy the beautiful New England weather—even the cold!

The Ups and Downs of the Bipolar Diagnosis

Janette Abramowitz, MD

As I walk into the inpatient unit, I am bombarded. I have two manic patients this week, and both are thrilled to see me. They greet me exuberantly despite getting no sleep at all the night before. One repeats "Good morning, doctor!" three times before moving on to "I need to get out of here. When can I leave?" The other stands too close to me and asks, "Are you married? Can I have your phone number?"

As a psychiatrist who absorbs the oozing negativity of depression and anxiety, patients in mania can be experienced as a welcome hiatus. Manic patients can make a provider feel welcomed, needed, and liked. It is easy to become more engaged and lighthearted with a manic patient and even run the risk of mirroring some of the manic jocularity. That energy can sometimes be quite infectious! However, this would obviously not be therapeutic for the manic patient who is typically not functioning adaptively.

Differential diagnoses: Is it bipolar or something else?

Also needing my attention that day are five other patients with an all-too-common laundry list of diagnoses including depression, schizoaffective disorder, stimulant-induced mood disorder, and of course bipolar disorder.

"Which is it?" I ask myself.

As diagnoses, these terms are mutually exclusive. Of all of them, bipolar disorder tends to be used as a general catch-all for mood instability, one to which patients often become quite attached. Perhaps this is because in some social circles the diagnosis is somewhat in vogue, or because once granted, it can be difficult to remove, as I'll explain in the next section.

The purpose of the Diagnostic and Statistical Manual of Mental Disorders (DSM) is to categorize and compartmentalize psychiatric illnesses. This ensures that clinicians use standardized diagnostic criteria and consistent terminology to communicate with other providers concerning diagnosis and treatment. Clear categories are also helpful when doing research. The most recent edition of the DSM (DSM-5, published in 2013, updated in 2017) categorizes "Bipolar and Related Disorders" as follows: Bipolar I Disorder, Bipolar II Disorder, Cyclothymic Disorder, Substance or Medication-Induced Bipolar and Related Disorders, Bipolar due to another medical condition, and finally other specified and unspecified Bipolar.

Although not in the DSM, some psychiatrists use the term "bipolar spectrum disorders." From a clinical perspective, I find this more accurately captures the lived experiences of patients with bipolar disorder, more so than the more rigidly defined diagnostic categories in DSM-5.

A large part of my job as a health professional is trying to figure out which diagnosis fits best. This involves taking a careful history, which is multi-tiered and involves the following:

- interviewing the patient and the close family members who've observed the patient's mood swings,

- getting a family history (for instance, asking "Does anyone else in the family have a bipolar diagnosis?"), and
- screening for other contributing factors such as substance use, a brain tumour, and so on.

"Un-diagnosing" bipolar disorder

Despite the DSM categories above, there are many overlapping grey areas between different categories of bipolar disorder, as well as between bipolar disorder and other psychiatric diagnoses. One of the greatest challenges I face as a psychiatrist, therefore, is not so much diagnosing bipolar disorder but "un-diagnosing" it.

Often an individual with the bipolar label has not in fact experienced a true manic or hypomanic episode. Instead, the description of their mania involves episodes of uncontrolled anger or mood lability (instability) lasting minutes to hours, as can often be seen in patients with personality disorders (especially borderline personality disorder), trauma histories, and of course during substance intoxication or withdrawal.

There are many drawbacks to a misplaced diagnosis of bipolar disorder, likely the most profound of which is being prescribed mood stabilizers or antipsychotics or both without an appropriate indication. Another drawback is not having other psychiatric symptoms properly addressed because the focus is on the misplaced bipolar diagnosis.

I have seen many patients diagnosed with bipolar disorder who rather are suffering from debilitating anxiety and/or irritability associated with post-traumatic stress disorder (PTSD). Such individuals may be well served by taking a selective serotonin reuptake inhibitor (SSRI) antidepressant, but if they are misdiagnosed with bipolar, they are less likely ever to have received SSRIs because these medications must be used with caution in people with bipolar disorder.

A misplaced diagnosis is a double whammy for the patient. First, they receive inappropriate treatment for their misdiagnosed symptoms. And second, they suffer much longer from an undetected and, therefore, undiagnosed condition that could be effectively treated once correctly diagnosed.

Medications and side effects

Once a diagnosis of bipolar disorder has been confirmed, however, proper treatment depends on the current phase of the illness (e.g., acute manic episode, hypomanic episode, depressive episode, or maintenance treatment).

For each phase, there are different medications to choose from that are considered first-line ("best or optimal treatments") or second-line (treatments prescribed only when first-line therapies don't work well). These medications fall into one of two categories: mood stabilizers and antipsychotics. These can be used alone or in combination, and in varying doses, and each has its own side effect profile and particular benefits.

If there are no psychotic symptoms—such as visual or auditory hallucinations, delusions, or paranoia—mood stabilizers are indicated, because the risk of certain side effects is lower with mood stabilizers than with antipsychotics. Such side effects may be sensorimotor (such as muscle stiffness, tremors) or metabolic (including high cholesterol levels, poorly controlled blood glucose). However, there are many caveats to treating with mood stabilizers. For example, one should use certain mood stabilizers with caution in women of childbearing age because of the risk of birth defects.

Some mood stabilizers cause weight gain and others can help with weight loss. Some mood stabilizers (e.g., Lamictal, Topamax, lithium) also require either careful titrations or drug monitoring with regular blood tests as they have what we call a narrow therapeutic window. These medications are generally not good choices for patients who have trouble taking their medications consistently. Some mood stabilizers such as Depakote are also excellent at treating migraines and seizures, so if these conditions are present as well, a mood stabilizer either alone or with an antipsychotic may be the appropriate choice.

On the other hand, if the patient is exhibiting psychotic symptoms (e.g., hallucinations, delusions), prescribing antipsychotics is a good treatment because mood stabilizers do not generally treat symptoms of psychosis, whereas antipsychotics can be excellent mood stabilizers at the same time as they control psychotic symptoms. Unfortunately, the side effects described above—which are clearly included in package inserts and conveyed on the internet—can be quite intimidating, despite many of them only occurring in very few patients and others being extremely rare across all patient groups. The more commonly seen sensorimotor and metabolic side effects are monitored with blood work and regular patient exams, reducing overall risk. Therefore, another challenge a psychiatrist faces is conveying to a patient that the side effects of *not* being treated can far outweigh the potential side effects of a medication.

In summary, the choice of the correct medication(s) for a patient with bipolar disorder depends on the phase of the illness and many patient-specific characteristics such as gender, age, desire to have children, and comorbid conditions, among many other factors.

Conclusion

Treating bipolar patients can be very rewarding for a psychiatrist since individuals with bipolar disorder can be highly responsive to the right medication; they can regain mental stability and get on with their lives.

For each unique patient, it often takes some time for the correct combination of medications and doses to be found, and for an initial period of adaptation to the medications to pass. I urge people with bipolar to exercise patience: bipolar is a major assault on your brain, and it will necessarily take time for you to recover.

I have seen that the right medication(s) will allow people to achieve their life goals by maintaining the creativity and love of life that are very common in individuals with bipolar disorder. Such a medication will not "numb" a person's personality—which is so often a major fear of patients—but will rather help them to become the person they would like to become by channeling their creative energy and enthusiasm in a productive rather than a manic manner.

As a psychiatrist, if I see a former patient out in the community, I am trained to maintain confidentiality and to act as if I have never met them before. However, if the patient initiates communication, a reunion of sorts is possible. When patients are hospitalized for mania, they are both (1) out of their element and (2) typically at a very low point of functioning in their lives. Nothing is more gratifying than seeing the person—no longer the "patient"—in a recovered state outside the hospital, functioning at his or her best. At these moments, I do not accept apologies for unpleasant behaviours during mania while hospitalized; again, those memories are not a good reflection of who that person actually is. However, I do accept, appreciate, and enjoy the "Thank you, doctor" I get from time to time.

Janette Abramowitz

I was born in Southfield, Michigan in 1976, and studied medicine at the University of Massachusetts Medical School, graduating in 2014. I then did a combined residency in neurology and psychiatry at the same university, graduating in 2020. I moved to Hawaii that same year and now work in the Department of Psychiatry at the University of Hawaii. In my free time, I enjoy being with my two young children.

Reflections on Bipolar Disorder from a New York City Psychiatrist

Diana Samuel, MD

As a child, I always knew I wanted to become a doctor. In college, I loved my major in psychology: learning about how people think and behave. Developmental psychology was very fascinating to me. Later, in medical school, I considered all the options for specialties, and was most interested in either surgery or psychiatry. I especially loved my rotation in child psychiatry.

The choice between surgery and psychiatry was, in the end, an easy one as I found the challenge of each person's story and presentation and how they responded to psychiatric treatment in a unique way to be very interesting.

Some people ask me if I have any personal experience with mental illness in a family member or friend, for example, that might have influenced my decision. No, none at all. My interest in psychiatry simply grew from my prior fascination with psychology.

What I would like people to consider about how they manage their bipolar disorder

Confirming a diagnosis of bipolar disorder is not always easy for the clinician. When I worked in an emergency room setting, for example, I often evaluated and treated patients who presented with mania. They often spoke very fast (known as "pressured speech"), were easily distracted when I tried to speak with them, had difficulties with their sleep, and generally behaved in ways that were very different from how they would normally act. Sometimes, these were people who did not yet know they had bipolar disorder. In these cases, the medical team and I would first have to ensure they had no medical issues that could cause their manic symptoms, such as a brain tumour, substance abuse, delirium, or hypothyroidism. We would also screen for and rule out other mental health disorders such as anxiety disorder, attention deficit disorder, and borderline personality disorder that might have some symptoms in common with bipolar disorder. Only then could we help them become stabilized on bipolar treatment.

As well, in many people, bipolar disorder presents initially as depression, and they may go for years thinking that *depression* is their diagnosis. Perhaps hypomanic episodes were missed or were so mild that the affected person never even thinks to mention them. Or perhaps at first the mood swings fluctuate between normal mood, mild depression, severe depression, back to normal mood, and so on, without ever going up into (hypo)mania. These are some of the common reasons for a delayed diagnosis, all of which can cause devastation to patients and their families, because until the correct diagnosis is confirmed, the most effective treatment cannot be prescribed.

A second consideration—after a person gets the diagnosis of bipolar disorder—is to accept that bipolar is a chronic illness, just like high blood pressure or diabetes. It's going to be with you for the long-term. For life, really. Understanding and accepting this reality is absolutely critical.

A third step is for the patient to learn as much as they can about the illness in general. The health care provider can answer questions about psychoeducation (educational sessions) about bipolar disorder. Community organizations may offer psychoeducation courses. (Some offer courses for people affected, and some for the family members and caregivers of affected people.)

Fourth, a patient can ask, "What can I do to get this disorder under control and make it something manageable; something I can live with?" Of course, bipolar medications are vital, but there's so much more: exercise, sleep, diet, talk therapy, family support, eliminating the use of alcohol. All these things make a huge difference, too. My bipolar patients who are doing really well and maintaining stability use all of these strategies, together. It's a whole package deal!

A key part of a patient getting their disorder under control is learning to identify their own triggers. Are there particular stressful situations that may affect your mood and trigger an episode? Are there red flags or warning signs? For example, a patient may notice that their sleep drops from eight hours per night, to six or five or even fewer. Next thing, they will be in a full-blown hypomanic episode again. Stress can often trigger an episode, so it's essential for a patient to learn and use stress management techniques and effective coping strategies.

Fifth, I advise my patients not to let their bipolar diagnosis consume them. "You don't want bipolar to become your whole identity: you are so much more than your diagnosis!" We all have many identities. For example, I am a mother, a psychiatrist, a daughter, a friend, and many more, all at the same time. So, too, I encourage my patients to see their bipolar disorder as just one part of their whole identity.

Therapy can really help people come to terms with the shock of their diagnosis. I'd say about 99 percent of patients need talk therapy as well as psychiatric care. People often need to talk about what a particular episode was like for them—the experience of mania, the shock of psychiatric hospitalization, their family's reaction, and so on. Therapy can frankly be life changing. However, therapy and treatment can be costly as it can be challenging to find providers in a network with insurance and, depending on where a person lives, there may not be many accessible providers.

Bear in mind that the illness can be very traumatic, depending on how the symptoms present, its impact on family members, on employment, on personal finances, and so on. I've had patients who lost their jobs. I particularly remember one elderly woman who went out and spent her entire life savings during a manic episode. She also gave away all kinds of personal belongings to people she didn't even know well. Her husband was devastated by the financial loss, but there was unfortunately nothing the couple could do to recover the funds. Mania can have a huge impact for a long time.

Some people in depression can become suicidal. I've seen that many times. And their poor quality of life while in depression is a major concern.

As a psychiatrist, I don't often see people when they're hypomanic: they don't often come in for this. In fact, many patients enjoy hypomania: they feel more productive, and happy. I tend to see them when the hypomanic episode passes, and they either go up into mania, or crash down into depression.

To summarize, the key point is for a patient to find a path for themself where they can successfully navigate through the mental health system as a person with a chronic, severe mental illness and—at the same time, somewhat paradoxically—as someone for whom bipolar is just one aspect of their unique and complex identity.

Role of family members and caregivers

I often engage with family members as well as my patients. This includes partners or spouses, parents, siblings, adult children—it depends on the patient's age and specific family situation.

I have found that involving family members can be a significant turning point in the patient's treatment and recovery. Family members are often able to identify precipitating factors and early warning signs of an impending episode. They can bring those signs to the attention of the patient, encourage the patient to get help at the first sign of trouble, and inform me as the psychiatrist, so we can all be mindful of the mood swings and react appropriately. It's obviously so much better to be proactive and *prevent* an episode than to be reactive and have to treat it. In extreme situations, family members need to be aware of when hypomanic symptoms become manic ones, needing emergency intervention to protect the affected person, or when they fear that the person may be suicidal.

What I would like my medical colleagues to consider

I fully respect the special relationship between patients and general practitioners (GPs), and I've often found that a patient will tell their GP more details than they tell me. This should not be surprising, because they've had a much longer relationship with their GP and have therefore developed deeper trust. However, GPs need to understand when they may need more help to manage a complex mental illness or to stabilize a newly diagnosed person. They should feel entirely comfortable to reach out for help from a psychiatrist at those times.

Exactly the same advice applies to my fellow psychiatrists. We all need to recognize when a patient needs more help that we personally can provide, or when we need a second opinion about the best course of treatment, and so on. We need to collaborate. For example, new medications are being developed all the time; maybe another colleague could recommend a medication or a combination of medications that I would not have considered on my own.

Here in New York, we're very fortunate to have so many excellent resources nearby: it's very easy and common for psychiatrists to work together.

Closing reflections

Earlier in my career, I worked in Africa and in Saint Vincent and the Grenadines as part of my Global Mental Health training in residency. In those places, well-trained resource people are stretched so thin that the kind of collaboration with colleagues I now enjoy in New York could only be dreamed about. It would be an absolute luxury.

Other major challenges I saw in treating people with bipolar disorder—and other mental health concerns—when I worked abroad were that resources were often limited. The shortage of resources applied to both human and material resources. There would not be enough doctors or nurses to treat those who wanted help; also, medications that the patient and care team found helpful to stabilize a person's symptoms would often run out so the patient would have to go without effective treatment until the supply was replenished. As well, stigma around mental health treatment was pervasive in the places I worked abroad and thus many people did not feel comfortable receiving treatment and, if they did, their support system was often limited by them feeling that they could not be honest with others in their family or community about what they were experiencing.

People should be aware that bipolar disorder can start in adolescence or even childhood. The bipolar diagnosis is often missed in these age groups because many young people start with depression alone. The symptoms of juvenile bipolar are often difficult to decipher, but it's worth getting an opinion if you're concerned about a child's or youth's moods and behaviours being more extreme than the average for that particular age. I don't deal with these cases myself: they are best referred to a child psychiatrist.

Women, too, may be at a higher risk for bipolar disorder, especially during the childbearing years. They may have an episode during pregnancy, or during the postpartum period. Where I work, here at ColumbiaDoctors, we now have a new specialty, Women's Mental Health. Of course, treating pregnant women with bipolar medications must be done with great caution in case the meds adversely affect the developing fetus. Generally, psychiatrists weigh up the risks of continuing psychiatric medications against the risk of suffering bipolar episodes if meds are withdrawn for the duration of the pregnancy. Another complicating factor is that many pregnancies are unplanned, and the woman may be some months into a pregnancy before she realizes the fact.

I love my work as a psychiatrist. The profession is very diverse in terms of age, gender, ethnicity, and so on, and I'm pleased to say that I've never had a problem being accepted as a young, racialized female in this field. The rapidly growing field is so interesting, and each patient is unique. There is still so much to learn about the mind and its functioning. I can honestly say that I've never been bored as a psychiatrist! And I very much appreciate knowing that I can contribute to a field that continues to grow and develop, and that has such a positive impact on the lives of people affected by mental illness—whether they be patients or family members.

Diana Samuel

I was born in New York in 1983, studied medicine at the Virginia Commonwealth University School of Medicine, did my internship at St. Vincent's Medical Center, my residency at Mount Sinai Medical Center, and my dual fellowship in Emergency Psychiatry and Public Psychiatry at the NewYork-Presbyterian Hospital, Columbia University Irving Medical Center. I have published articles about such topics as patient well-being in a psychiatric ER, disaster and global psychiatry, and suicidal behaviour. I have extensive experience evaluating and treating a variety of psychiatric symptoms and illnesses. I'm an Assistant Professor of Psychiatry at Columbia University Irving Medical Center, and also have a private practice at ColumbiaDoctors. I'm a member of the American Association of Community Psychiatrists, the Indo-American Psychiatric Association, and a Fellow of the American Psychiatric Association. I live in New York with my family.

Bipolar Disorder from the Perspective of a Licensed Clinical Social Worker

Beverley Watkins, PhD, MSW, LCSW

Editor's note: This is the author's real name, but some details in the case studies have been changed to protect people's identities.

I initially decided to become a social worker because I wanted to help people, to make a difference somehow. But I also knew I wanted a successful career. This was back in the mid-1970s, and I was definitely influenced by the philosophies of feminism concerning career goals and higher education: I got an advanced degree, and ultimately a second one.

So, I guess you could say it was a combination of these two factors: I had clear humanitarian ideals, being concerned about giving back and contributing to the greater good; but I was also aware that social work would be a personally rewarding career in which I'd be helping people.

My mother's first cousin, whom I'll call Mary, had what I now assume was severe bipolar disorder. She was in and out of state hospitals. After a long battle, she died in the 1970s. I have also assumed that Mary's mother, a great aunt of mine, had borderline personality disorder. There were also some other relatives whose mental health conditions went largely untreated. I'm not sure whether these experiences affected my initial decision to go into social work, but they have influenced my desire to work with people who have severe mental illnesses, including bipolar disorder and schizoaffective disorder. This is especially true since I became involved with the National Alliance on Mental Illness (NAMI).

Decades ago, when I started working, bipolar disorder was still called manic depressive disorder. We knew much less about the nature of the disorder, and none of the modern nuances had yet been identified. For example, today we recognize that even children and youth can experience bipolar symptoms, and recently some children are being diagnosed with a pediatric mood disorder known as disruptive mood dysregulation disorder, which has many symptoms in common with bipolar disorder.

Editor's note: Please see the contributions by psychiatrists Dr. Kayla Behbahani and Dr. Janette Abramowitz above for more details about the diagnosis and treatment of bipolar disorder.

What people with bipolar need to consider about how they manage their disorder

Before I can optimally work with a client who has bipolar disorder (or any other severe mental illness), I want to facilitate their being stabilized on the appropriate medications. This is an important part of the work. This can sometimes be a long and arduous process before the right medication (or combination of medications) and the right doses for each particular client are found. It could take one to four months or longer. But I ask my clients not to give up: persevere! Helping clients to learn skills to manage mood issues and other symptoms can be especially useful during periods when they are not stable on medications.

A part of my job is also to encourage clients to stay on their meds, or—if they insist on trying to wean off—to do so only under medical supervision.

Another part of my job entails communicating with prescribers. In our practice, we have three nurse practitioners—who consult with individual clients—and a psychiatrist. I notify the prescribers if anything relevant comes to my attention that may affect a client's need for medication adjustments, more frequent check-ups, or, in extreme cases, a need for hospitalization (for example, a job loss, a major move, an upcoming divorce, or any other social factors; or emerging side effects, changes in mood, sleep patterns, activity levels, and so on).

On that point about hospitalization, these days, we have access to very few hospital beds for psychiatric patients. But I must say, some of the intensive outpatient programs (IOPs) are excellent. People usually attend these programs for three or four days per week, for several hours at a time, over a period of four to eight weeks. Programs offer group therapy; others may offer individual therapy as well. The programs are staffed by trained therapists, and there are prescribers on hand.

I try to help a client come to terms with their diagnosis, to accept the reality of it (not deny it), and also to accept that their life with a mental illness may not be what they had hoped for. In a word, then, I advocate for acceptance. A major part of the treatment I provide is to help clients develop coping skills to identify and manage mood changes, manage anxiety and other symptoms, and work with environmental triggers and factors.

At the same time, I try to instill hope. A big part of this is referring clients to support groups where they can experience the power of peer support. The National Alliance on Mental Illness (NAMI) offers regular support groups for clients and family members. I encourage my clients to hold on to hope. (For details about NAMI and their services, please see nami.org.)

Closely linked with this concept of instilling hope is the concept of *recovery*. I want my clients to hold on to the hope that recovery is possible. My whole practice is recovery-oriented, and I like to define recovery as being able to live your best life, using the recovery principles and committing to recovery as an ongoing process.

People need to know that things can change; *they* can change; and recovery is possible.

In the USA, the Substance Abuse and Mental Health Services Administration (SAMHSA) was established by the Department of Health and Human Services. It promotes ten guiding principles of recovery: person-driven, many pathways, holistic, peer support, relational, culture, address trauma, strengths and responsibility, respect, and hope. For details, please see samhsa.gov.

I encourage my clients to be self-directed and proactive about maintaining their health and well-being. An excellent tool for self-management (including exercise, relaxation, communication, and assertiveness) that I recommend is the Wellness Recovery Action Plan (WRAP). It can be used by both clients and their family members, too; by anyone, in fact.

Developed in 1997, WRAP is now used internationally by health care and mental health systems to address all kinds of physical, mental health, and life issues. It is listed in the National Registry of Evidence-based Programs and Practices. For details and downloadable Wellness Tools, Crisis Plan and Post-crisis Plan, please see wellnessrecoveryactionplan.com/wrap-can-help/mental-health/.

I educate my clients to track their moods, using WRAP resources, self-designed daily charts, or whatever else works for them, as long as they can be aware of mood changes as soon as they start to manifest.

There are several types of therapy I use: cognitive behavioural therapy (CBT) is common, and I also find that dialectical behavioural therapy (DBT) can help manage symptoms and improve self-awareness. I also incorporate other mind-body approaches such as Somatic Experiencing into my practice as the science evolves. Then there's trauma treatment: most people with bipolar have a history of some type of trauma. And often, having a severe mental illness can, in itself, be traumatizing—even if the client has no earlier trauma. I'm trained in Eye Movement Desensitization and Reprocessing (EMDR), which is about the closest thing to a miracle I have yet seen in this field. There are specific EMDR protocols for all kinds of mental health issues and problem areas. In my experience, EMDR really helps people to process trauma and move forward.

I recently heard Bessel van der Kolk, MD (BesselvanderKolk.com), a world-renowned expert on rewiring the traumatized brain, and author of *The Body Keeps the Score: Brain, Mind, and Body in the Healing of Trauma* (2015), and he noted the same thing about the effectiveness of Eye Movement Desensitization and Reprocessing (EMDR).

Remembering one of my most memorable bipolar clients

Despite all my best intentions and hard work, sometimes treatment isn't as effective as we might hope. I remember one well-educated young man who worked in a very responsible job. He had been diagnosed with various medical problems and had been partially managing everything when he first got his bipolar diagnosis. His baseline mood was low-grade hypomania; he was very social—the life of the party—and he drank a lot.

He'd had his share of trauma, besides his physical problems. His parents divorced when he was young, his father sounded like a narcissist, and, as a young teen, he was sexually abused by a family member. When he told his father, he was not believed. Eventually, he moved to another state to be with his mother and stepfather, whom he loved very much. Shortly after, his stepfather died suddenly.

When the young man was diagnosed with bipolar, he came to me for therapy, but we were having some problems with staff turnover of prescribers at the time, so communication between me and the prescribers was impaired. This is an unfortunate reality of practice. This client fell through the cracks: he wasn't well stabilized on medication, and his lifestyle was problematic.

I think his behaviour was just so erratic that our discussions about problem-solving, self-management, and so on were helpful to a point, but all the "moving parts" of the treatment plan didn't work consistently over time. There were lifestyle issues and impaired judgments. This was an ongoing therapeutic issue, of course. For example, he'd get involved in relationships that seemed to be with healthy people but weren't. He would put on rose-coloured glasses and frame his thought processes and responses accordingly. I almost got taken in by that!

My interactions with family members

I find that my interactions with family members are very important. I educate them about their affected family member's mental illness and often refer them to the class called "NAMI Family-to-Family" and to family support groups. "NAMI Basics" is a class for parents of children under 18. Education is key, as is self-care for family members themselves. Peer support is also essential because dealing with someone who has a mental illness can be very stressful and taxing—I know this from my personal experience. Advocacy can be a way to be proactive against stigma, and to feel valued in the world.

Some family members come to me for therapy themselves. It's hard to imagine the stresses that family caregivers have to bear—sometimes for years without relief—as their family members struggle to get a correct diagnosis or effective treatment; or remain stuck in denial; or start self-medicating with street drugs; or become homeless, incarcerated, or suicidal. Living with a person who has a severe mental illness can be extremely challenging, so I offer support for them as caregivers.

Marital therapy can also be crucial. Often one partner has an undiagnosed or inadequately treated mental illness or is still in denial about their illness. People sometimes go in and out of denial, unfortunately.

Some family members can also benefit from attending Al-Anon meetings, even if the identified patient has no issues with alcohol. (Al-Anon is a support group for the family members of alcoholics and people attending Alcoholics Anonymous.) People often need to distance themselves emotionally, and to set personal boundaries to protect their own mental well-being. Al-Anon can really help with that.

Suggestions for health professionals

If I were to give a few words of advice to my colleagues who are health professionals (family physicians, psychiatrists, fellow social workers, other therapists, and so on), I would say this:

- Be proactive and educate yourself about severe mental illnesses, especially if that is not your specialty.
- Work collaboratively with clients and their families and incorporate their voices.
- Learn about recovery principles and contemporary thinking about hope and recovery.
- Surround yourself with a team you can call on and collaborate with. In my experience, organizational issues and conflicts are the most stressful elements of work—much more than the clinical work itself.
- Get organizational and administrative problems addressed in a timely way, if at all possible.

- Anticipate and deal effectively with staff turnover or you will spin your wheels and clients may get lost in the process. (For instance, you may have rotating graduate students who change every six months.)
- Communicate with your clients' family members and have clients sign releases so professionals can communicate with the families when needed.
- Finally, actively protect your own mental health and practise self-care and stress management as if you were your own therapist!

Conclusion

I hope that the mental health field can do what it needs to do to help people who need it. However, in the US, we've been dealing with shrinking resources for many years. That's largely because of the growth of conservative political agendas and policies. Mental health resources have been dwindling since as far back as the early 1980s. I'm hoping for better news with our newly elected US President. I wish we had an established national health care system to make mental health care and medical care co-ordinated and accessible to all.

I feel strongly that we need to break the stigma that surrounds mental illness. Looking back over my career, I'd say that we made some great strides in the 1980s and 1990s, but more recently, social attitudes have gone back toward the stigma end of the spectrum. Back then, people felt it was sort of "fashionable" to consult a therapist, but now, doing so is more stigmatized, which is disheartening.

I'm strongly opposed to stigma, but even some mental health professionals are themselves prejudiced and do not embrace the recovery model.

If we could get rid of stigma, we could change the world!

Beverley Watkins

I was born in Jackson, Mississippi, and received a BA from Louisiana Tech University, a Master's in Social Work (MSW) from the University of Southern Mississippi, and a PhD in social work from St. Louis University, Missouri. In 1990, I became a licensed clinical social worker (LCSW). I have a private practice in Fairview Heights, Illinois, and serve as VP of the board of a local affiliate of the National Alliance on Mental Illness. My husband and I have a son and one grandchild.
Facebook.com/Beverley.Watkins3

Supporting a Bipolar Family with Complex Symptoms

Brionna Morse, LMFT

I started out thinking I'd be a teacher: I was particularly interested in English as a Second Language (ESL) and special education. But after my bachelor's degree, I worked in a "Level 14" residential treatment program. The young people there were one step away from being sent to either juvenile detention centre for some reason, or to a psychiatric hospital with any one of a number of possible diagnoses including attention deficit hyperactivity disorder (ADHD), bipolar disorder, schizophrenia, major depression, oppositional disorder, reactive attachment disorder, post-traumatic stress disorder (PTSD), and anxiety. Many had been hospitalized over and over again.

These kids were there in the care of the state either because their homes were unsafe, abusive, or neglectful, or because their parents—unable to control or care for their high-needs kids—had signed over their rights to the state.

As you can imagine, many of these youth were quite hardened and tough. But I loved them and learned so much from them about the world beyond my limited, privileged experience.

As a result of my work with them, I decided to become a Marriage and Family Therapist, so I could be a voice for kids who didn't understand the significant adults in their lives. My interest in attachment issues and the value of providing love and a sense of felt safety through developing healthy connections grew directly from that work, and it's positioned me well to work with other clients going through difficult times.

The case of a particularly complex bipolar family

I was employed as a Behavioural Specialist at a county office in California at the time of this event. In my therapy classes, I worked with many affected young people. For the purposes of this essay, I'll focus on two youngsters and their younger half-sibling, all living with their single mother. (To protect their confidentiality, I have slightly modified the family structure, withheld specific ages, and changed some of the genders.)

The mother (let's call her Karen) herself had bipolar, and both her parents had mental illnesses: her mom had bipolar, and her dad had some other undisclosed mental health issue or issues. Now, two of Karen's three children were diagnosed with bipolar. Talk about a family history!

Karen had two children with her first husband, and a third, much younger child, with her second. (Her second marriage had ended about a year before I met the family.)

Karen still had some mood swings at the time I worked with the family, but in general she was a great mom. She always had the best interests of her children at heart. She took some parent coaching with me and was always keen to learn new skills to benefit her family. She tried every suggestion I ever made to help her kids get out of the vicious spirals bipolar can cause. They were poor, living on food stamps, and Karen was understandably overwhelmed much of the time, but she would do anything for her family. I really empathized with and admired her.

Both her older children had been diagnosed with bipolar. The eldest (I'll call him Tate) was in his mid-teens, and her middle child, Mary, was a pre-teen. Mary had been experiencing symptoms from the age of eight but—despite the strong family history—remained undiagnosed for several years. Once diagnosed and started on bipolar treatment, she responded well.

Mary was my primary client, but I worked with the whole family, too. I made weekly home visits—each lasting about one-and-a-half hours—over a period of about nine months, so I came to know them all very well. I found the home visits (covered by medical health care in California) to be very valuable. I saw a whole other side of the client and the family when I met them where they lived, on their own turf, where all their everyday interactions just unfolded naturally for me to observe. Also, home visits allow the clients to practise transferring new skills I'm teaching them in the very environment they'll be expected to apply them, with all the everyday household comings and goings—or chaos—and ingrained patterns of behaviour.

Mary took her recovery very seriously: I had her doing journal logs, tracking her moods every day, being consistent with her meds, and attending all her psychiatric appointments. In many ways, she was a model client!

However, that's not to say that Mary wasn't sometimes a real handful for Karen and the rest of the family. She could get pretty erratic and even destructive at times. These spikes of anger or rage are typical of (hypo)mania. But at least she always showed remorse after an outburst.

Mary's anger was frequently directed at her younger half-sister, Jen. So I would do role plays with the two of them:

Me: "Mary, you play Jen. And Jen, you pretend to be Mary. Now, Jen, shout at Mary just the way she shouted at you yesterday. Try to make her feel just what you felt when you ran out of the apartment; to understand how upset she made you feel."

Jen: *[Playing Mary.]* Screams, shouts, swears, storms out and bangs bedroom door. Then comes back in and continues to rant.

Mary: *[Playing Jen.]* Eyes get big, puts hand over mouth in shock, looks down in shame. Then runs from the apartment and cowers in the corridor.

Then we'd sit together and discuss the role play. What did we see happening? How did each person feel playing those reversed roles? How do outbursts like these make each of us—and the others in the family—feel? What might we each do in future to prevent, avoid, or cut short such blow-ups? What did we learn from this role play? Do we need to apologize to each other? And so on.

> *After several years, Mary was weaned off her lithium and was managed with a different mood stabilizer. She continued her cognitive behavioural therapy and graduated high school with top marks. I was so happy to hear that!*

In contrast to Mary, her older brother, Tate, was not well-controlled. He stayed in mania a lot and became very destructive as a result. There were reports of him engaging in inappropriate sexual behaviour. He made false accusations about things going on in the home, skipped school, picked fights, and made impulsive threats of violence.

I could *feel* the high drama in the house whenever I visited. Tate would fly into rages, scream, slam doors. Sometimes, he'd isolate himself for days in his room, just cry-cry-crying. He seemed stuck in overwhelming anger or sadness. It was almost as if he wanted everyone to feel the same emotional turmoil and chaos he was feeling. It must have been hell for him. And for Karen and his siblings.

At one point, Tate pulled a knife and threatened to hurt himself or his mother. I had to work with Karen on a safety plan. After all, she was responsible for herself and all three children. But as I told her, "As much as we try to keep our children safe, there are times that they need more than we ourselves can provide."

But through it all, Karen didn't want to call police on Tate. She tried at all costs to shield him from becoming part of "the system."

> *Over my years of work in the mental health system, as difficult as it may seem for a child to become part of the "system," I have to remind myself that at the end of the day it's a matter of "the one for the many." Does Tate need more structure, additional safety precautions, less possibility for triggers, and to be stripped of access to potential weapons, in order to address his needs, so the rest of the family can move on with their lives? Or does the whole family feel confined, jailed in a sense of chaos, unpredictability, and uncertainty about whether their lives are safe so Tate can continue living, untreated, at home? As unfair as it may seem, in this situation if I were Karen, I would call the police every single time.*

A big difference between Tate and Mary was that Tate showed zero remorse for his actions. It's hard for family members to "forgive and forget" when the person can't apologize for their destructive and even dangerous behaviour.

For me as a professional, Tate's lack of remorse was very scary.

> *A lack of remorse may indicate the potential for even more negative behaviour with no concern for the impacts on family members or*

others. It can also suggest the beginning of a concurrent personality disorder—perhaps borderline personality disorder.

After each home visit to this extremely complex and difficult family, I felt absolutely wiped out. Exhausted! Working on this case was a real challenge, but if given a choice, I would do it all over again. I found it very satisfying, and I hope that my care and interventions helped them.

When I started working on this essay, I tried to contact Karen again to get an update about her and her family, but unfortunately, I couldn't reach her. I would have loved to ask her these questions:

- How are you doing these days? (Bipolar control? Job? Housing? New partner, perhaps?)
- Is Mary's bipolar still well-controlled? Is she working? Studying? In a relationship? Happy? Does she feel she got the support she needed at the time?
- Is Tate's bipolar finally under control? Is he safe? Working? Studying? In a relationship? Happy? In contact with the family or alienated? Any addictions from self-medicating? Any jail time or time on the streets? Does he feel he got the support he needed at the time?
- Is Jen showing any signs of bipolar? What and/or how is she doing these days?
- Did you feel your family got the necessary support from us? (What could we have done differently?)
- Are you still receiving therapy or home visits?

I sincerely hope they're all doing well.

What I would like people with bipolar to consider

Some points I'd like people with bipolar to think about concerning how they manage their disorder are these:

- I want to invite you to be gentler and more compassionate with yourselves. (Don't be harsh or judgmental. This is not your fault!)
- Educate yourself about your disorder using reliable sources, so that you'll be in the strongest possible position to manage the ups and downs.
- Never forget that you have people in your corner who want to help you. (Sometimes they may hold back, not wanting to intrude or disturb you, especially when you're depressed. Or they may feel inadequate about how to relate to you when you're (hypo)manic. So you may need to reach out first, even when you feel least able to do so.)
- Recognize that whether you're super-depressed or super-high, asking for support is the most important thing. Living with bipolar can be so confusing. You need somebody to be part of your support system: it could be a friend, relative, pastor, therapist, and others.
- Remember that no mood or feeling ever lasts forever. This will pass.
- Weight gain is a big issue for many people on bipolar meds. Be gentle with yourself and remember that stabilizing your mood must be the first priority. Seek the help of a dietician, nutritionist, or therapist who works on emotional eating and repairing our relationships with food. People in mania just want to stay busy-busy, and eating is one easy way to do that. Ask yourself: What specific foods do you crave? Then: What healthier options can I use to replace those with?

- Include regular exercise in your recovery plan. It's great for your brain health and your body.

I have learned the sad truth that some people simply aren't willing to put in the work needed to find stability. Even if they do accept the diagnosis and take meds as prescribed, that's seldom enough to keep bipolar under control. People have to learn about their disorder, get support, and do therapy … Professionals can only help so much. At some point, the affected person has to take control of managing their own disorder.

What I would like family members of people with bipolar to think about

I'd invite family members to get well-educated about the disorder, so they'll know what to expect and how to be most helpful and supportive.

I think that what really triggers people with bipolar is when their family members and friends minimize what the person is going through. Never say things like "Oh, just get over it" or "Everything's going to be fine."

Rather, try phrasing things with more respect and empathy:

- "What do you need right now?"
- "How can I support you in getting through this?"
- "What can I do help you with this problem?"
- "Do you feel like your meds are still working well?"
- "Do we need to make an appointment so you can be re-assessed?"

Finally, I'd ask family members to give some grace to everyone concerned: don't allow understandable feelings of fear, frustration, disappointment, and impatience to overwhelm you. Bipolar is a chronic, usually lifelong, disorder so—if at all possible—you need to be prepared and stay strong for the long haul.

What I would like health professionals to reflect upon

I have worked with a lot of children and youth and have seen that many kids have to go through an initial cycle of multiple diagnoses before psychiatrists finally settle on bipolar disorder. For example, they may first be diagnosed with oppositional defiance disorder, or depression, or ADHD. It can take years before they get an accurate diagnosis and appropriate treatment. Of course, with each new diagnosis, they are prescribed new meds. And they stumble through their critical formative years stigmatized, confused, often over-medicated but under-treated for their real problem: undiagnosed bipolar disorder.

It's so unfair to them.

And of course, their rapidly developing brains are just bombarded with all these different prescribed chemicals for no good reason, while the undiagnosed bipolar disorder goes untreated, causing its own set of mental, emotional, social, and intellectual problems.

Most psychiatrists I have known prefer to wait until a child is 13, 14, or even 15 before giving a diagnosis of bipolar disorder. Often, symptoms are brushed aside with assumptions like "It could just be hormonal changes." While of course I agree that one doesn't want to rush to diagnose such a serious condition, I do think that many young people—and their exhausted families—are left for far too long coping with symptoms that, in hindsight, were clearly caused by bipolar, and could have been appropriately treated much sooner. If only there were a simple blood or other diagnostic test we could use to confirm the diagnosis!

I wish psychiatrists would warn their patients about weight gain and other side effects of prescribed meds and connect them to a dietician or nutritionist immediately, rather than waiting for the person to balloon to an unrecognizable weight, leaving them disheartened, depressed, and wanting to go off the meds that have caused such rapid weight gain.

Some psychiatrists and doctors are sometimes too quick to prescribe meds. I invite them to collaborate with therapists, nutritionists, and others who value a holistic approach that provides as much mental, emotional, and physical support as possible. Bipolar is by no means an easy disorder to diagnose, treat, and manage effectively over the person's entire lifespan. So why would we not collaborate with all the available professional resource people, community organizations, and peer support groups to do the best possible job?

Conclusion

I was interested in contributing to this anthology because, while there's a great deal of educational information about bipolar disorder, most books don't include stories. I find that stories by and about real people give us information that is practical and easy to relate to.

Also, there's often a big taboo around bipolar, but at the same time anyone who is over-emotional for any reason is randomly *mis*labelled: "Oh, s/he must have bipolar!" This not only minimizes the emotions the person is experiencing in the moment, but totally devalues what people who actually do have bipolar have to live with.

I've observed that some people with bipolar—like young Mary—learn to manage it really well. Once stabilized on treatment and perhaps with ongoing therapy, they can live highly successful and fulfilling lives. Many can study, hold down a responsible job, maintain a relationship, and even raise a family. Occasional intrusions of bipolar symptoms are dealt with quickly, and their moods become stabilized once more.

But other people—like Tate when I knew him as a teen—are unfortunately not like that. Either they stay in denial about their diagnosis, or they resist taking the medications that would help control the symptoms. Or they become unduly attached to their "bipolar identity" and believe that they could never be happy or function as well without the bipolar mood swings to fuel their creative drive.

It's up to each affected person to decide for themselves. The rest of us—family members, friends, peer support workers, and care providers—can only go so far in offering acceptance, support, and friendship or professional advice.

Brionna Morse

I was born in southern California in 1982, and moved to Weiser, Idaho, in third grade. I got my bachelor's degree from the California Lutheran University where I was a collegiate volleyball athlete, and then did a Master's in Psychology at Phillip's Graduate Institute. I was licensed as a Marriage and Family Therapist (LMFT) in California where I worked before moving to Greenville, South Carolina, in 2017. I'm an online Executive Mindset Coach, keynote speaker, and consultant who brings my knowledge of Cognitive Behavioural Therapy and Neurolinguistic Programming—as well as my insights from personal experiences of loss and self-sabotage—to my work. I enjoy the outdoors, hiking, kayaking, yoga, painting, and spending time with my friends and dogs.

BrionnaMorse.com, Instagram: @brionna_morse

Bipolar Stories

David Laing Dawson, MD

Editor's note: An earlier version of this was published on Marvin Ross's Mind You *blog, 16 September 2019 (dawsonross.wordpress.com). All case studies have been anonymized.*

Some years ago, having published my fourth novel, I was asked by a local writers' group to be the guest speaker at their monthly meeting. I accepted, and when I arrived, I found about twelve people sitting around a large table. The first half of the session went as expected: I discussed my approach to writing, and novel writing in particular, and they joined in, asking questions, and sharing thoughts. Then we broke for coffee.

A few went immediately to fill their cups, but the majority remained with me at the table. They knew of my other profession as a psychiatrist and started asking me questions about mood stabilizers and antidepressants and sharing their own experiences with these medications. And suddenly, rather than being a speaker at a writers' meeting, I became a psychiatrist in an impromptu Mood Disorders Support Group.

It is not all that surprising, I think, that bipolar disorder is overrepresented among writers, and that within this group it's estimated that about half of all poets might be affected by bipolar.

It has been said as well that depression fuels the furnace of creativity, providing the writer with anguish, despair, glimpses of hopelessness, and a wealth of existential questions; while mania—or at least hypomania—provides both the energy and optimism to put pen to paper, or fingers to keyboard.

For a psychiatrist, or anyone else who likes stories, bipolar disorder—among all the mental illnesses—provides the best stories, though not always with happy endings. Here are a few from my long career as a psychiatrist.

The case of the highly educated librarian

In the winter of 1968, a tall man was brought to the emergency of a big city hospital. In my memory, he towered over me—though that may have been his mania rather than his height. I was an intern that year, and this man would become my patient for a few hours. He was the chief librarian of a major institution and held PhDs in English and Library Science. And he was indeed manic. His eyes were alight as eyes always are in a state of mania, seeming to see in more dimensions than mine. He could not stop moving or talking and so I walked beside him and listened as we made the full U-shaped journey through the emergency ward several times that evening.

He had a revelation to share, and this revelation was literary for within his excited stream of consciousness he sprinkled a hodgepodge of quotes from poetry and literature spanning several centuries. He spoke so quickly and with such an excess of erudition that I could not follow and at the time I wished I had a tape recorder because his revelation may have been significant and would surely be forgotten by the next day.

Now and again, he paused in his stride, not so much to catch his breath as to see if I as his amanuensis was keeping up. And each time he paused I would reach into my white coat and offer him a small tablet of chlorpromazine with a Dixie cup of water and most times he would take it before he was off in full flight again.

Chlorpromazine was, at the time, relatively new. Discovered in France in 1952, brought to Canada for a trial in 1954, it found its way into general use through the 1960s. Prior to this, the only available tools for trying to control severe mania were cold-water baths and various anaesthetics and narcotics.

Eventually he slowed, both in movement and in speech, and eventually he sat. And then I convinced him to walk with me across the hospital and up in an elevator to be admitted to the psychiatry ward. He came with me, quietly now—thanks to the medications he had taken—a little wary and vigilant, and I handed him over to a nurse and wrote the admission orders.

I don't know what became of this exceptional man of letters, but I hope any future bouts of depression or mania did no irreparable damage to his brain. And I hope he stayed on his lithium.

Lithium was available for treatment and maintenance of manic depression by then but was used primarily for continuing treatment and prevention of relapse. There were no other effective mood stabilizers at the time, so I assume he was discharged on a lithium maintenance dose. By then, my internship in psychiatry was done, and I was an intern on the obstetric floor.

The case of the travelling cowboy

I had treated this young man in the big mental hospital outside Vancouver, British Columbia, in the fall of 1968, though he was from an Alberta ranch and wore the requisite Stetson and boots. He had driven straight over the Rocky Mountains and through the Fraser Valley without stopping on his way to Vancouver. He managed this, he said, by holding his foot to the pedal while pissing in a bottle and dumping it out the window. He repeated this gleefully. "Piss in a bottle; dump it out the window. Whoo-ee!"

I don't remember what had attracted him to Vancouver in the first place. The rumours of a nude beach? The hippie scene on West 4th Avenue? Feeling confined by family responsibilities and expectations back home? Who knows? What I *do* know is that at some point the Vancouver City Police found him encamped on the roof of their headquarters unfurling a banner of some sort over the side.

He didn't think much of taking medication and he thought even less of the nurses telling him to stay away from the vulnerable female patients. After a few months—a typical length of time to be hospitalized in that era—we eventually got him settled enough to send him home to Alberta and the family ranch.

A year went by, and I was then working at the brand spanking new psychiatric hospital on the University of British Columbia campus in Vancouver.

> *Those were very optimistic days in psychiatry with both new and effective medications intersecting with the idealism of the sixties. This unit—which would eventually become part of a neuroscience section and one program in a Health Sciences Centre—had no locked doors beyond the pharmacy. I noticed the earth-toned colour scheme, carpeted floors, single rooms, wide short corridors, teak furniture, comfortable beds, nurses in civilian clothing, docs shedding their white coats, all patients voluntary, community meetings every morning, even a fireplace in the lounge area, and a very nice, well-appointed auditorium on the main floor...*

"There's a call for you from Alberta," I was told. "Will you accept the charges?"

It was the young cowboy I had treated a year before. He had stayed on the ranch for a while and attended a clinic in a nearby town. But now he was off his meds and his father had sent him as a buyer to a cattle auction in Calgary, with money in his pocket.

He felt that some guys there were looking at him, talking about him, and calling him "queer, and shit like that." He was clearly getting paranoid. He was supposed to stay at the auction and bid on some good breeders, he said, but he couldn't stay under those circumstances.

> *Paranoid delusions are essentially mistaken self-explanations about one's sense of self in this world, a way of organizing and interpreting what is happening in relation to others (those others being immediate, close, and distant communities and institutions), and what it means for one within the basic parameters of life (power, control, love, hate, sex, worth, social status).*
>
> *This way of thinking about the concept of self is useful in understanding delusions because it is our relationships to others (which our brains insist on organizing, as in a mental map) that then allow us to navigate sanely and successfully in our social world.*
>
> *So, for example, my own personal sense of self contains a sense that I am of some importance to my family, and an awareness of myself by a few in my social network. To the police, however, I am merely an elderly pedestrian crossing the road; I'm of absolutely no importance to the CIA; and I am a carbon-based life form with limited lifespan to "God." So, no delusions there.*
>
> *But, with mania and overstimulation and the bombardment of information coming at one while in a very aroused and receptive state, the brain can leap to simple explanations and simple misinterpretations. The first step to many delusions is what we call an "idea of reference," which is assuming or experiencing events in other peoples' lives and relationships as being directly related to oneself. Often with bipolar disorder, the delusion is congruent with mood. That is to say: "I feel so bad, so low, and so sick that I must have cancer." Or, "I feel so good, so powerful, so creative that I must be 'on a special mission' or be a 'messenger of God.'"*

> *In bipolar disorder, when a person has protracted periods of altered mood, energy, and arousal, their mental map—or sense of self in this world—adjusts to accommodate this hyperactive state. It leaps from "that song is about me" to "I can satisfy all my aroused sexual desires with impunity" to "I deserve to own a Jaguar" to "I will write a bestseller in a month and be rich and famous" to "the world is waiting to receive my messages sent directly from God."*
>
> *Likewise, in schizophrenia and psychosis, delusions are the product of an inability to filter, read, and interpret rationally all the contextual and social messages impinging upon a person that would normally enable them to develop a simple and basic explanation of their own, a "that explains what is happening to me" moment.*
>
> *The brain is an organizing machine. And people suffering from bipolar disorder or schizophrenia do what we all do once we have developed a belief or reached a conclusion: we look for evidence to support this belief and we ignore all contrary evidence.*

I spoke with this young man for a while, ignoring the long-distance charges. I urged him to go back on his meds and/or take himself to the nearest hospital emergency room. I remember feeling some relief after he hung up, knowing that he was currently in Alberta and at least 600 miles away from being my responsibility.

My day passed uneventfully, with patient meetings, conferences, team meetings, the usual. Then, mid-afternoon, the receptionist at the main entrance paged me to say: "Your patient is here asking for you. He's wearing a cowboy hat."

And there he was, as big as life, as loud as life. He had used the cash in his pocket not to buy a heifer but a one-way plane ticket from Calgary to Vancouver. And I calculated, belatedly, that 600 miles is really not a long distance when you are manic, impulsive, and have some cash in your pocket.

A common component of mania, with its fast talking and fast thinking, is impulsivity, taking risks, living as if there is no tomorrow. This can include taking a trip, gambling, spending sprees, or risky and ill-advised sexual behaviours. Years ago, I was once on the phone trying to convince a major department store to take back at least two of the three fur coats my manic patient had purchased. Today, of course, much of the spending and other risky behaviour is happening online.

He didn't want to come up to my office. "I need open space," he said. "No walls, man, no walls!"

The auditorium was just behind the main reception desk, so I took him in there. He chose a theatre chair in the very middle beneath the high ceiling. I sat beside him. He was okay with the spaciousness of the auditorium though it obviously wasn't like the open prairies of Alberta where he could see forever and didn't have to watch his back.

Once more, he became my patient and I got him on and kept him on the right medication.

Finding the "right" medication for continuing treatment and maintaining stability in bipolar disorder is never straightforward. For any individual patient it depends on what works, what medications are tolerated, the level of side effects from each, and any specific risk factors, including those of overdose, impaired kidneys, thyroid impairment, over-sedation, poor medication management, and so on. Some patients—many, actually—adamantly refuse certain medications they have either had a previous bad experience with or have read that they cause bad reactions. For better or worse today, much unfiltered information is available for all online.

Later, as an outpatient, he expressed his disdain for medication quite dramatically. In my office, he took a vial of pills from his pocket and placed it on a solid wood coffee table. Then he drew a hunting knife from his other pocket and repeatedly stabbed at the now-scattered pills and the table, saying, "This is what I think of your goddamn pills."

"I hear you, I hear you," I said.

Even now, fifty years later, I remember his behaviour quite well. I don't recall how I reacted to his outburst at the time, but I'm sure I did what I usually do: remain calm and non-threatening, sit low in my chair, make no sudden movements, acknowledge the person's feelings, let the feelings dissipate, be very careful to not provoke, and then get back to the job at hand when the person calms down and signals they are ready. (I could write a whole other essay on crisis management and de-escalation …)

But eventually, again, he became well enough to long for the open sky. His parents sent money and he flew home to the ranch once more.

Today I'm sure I would be involved with the parents themselves if they lived anywhere nearby, and I would certainly see them as a major factor in my patient's future wellness and stability. At the time, I remember talking with them on the phone at least once, but they remained in distant Alberta.

The case of the star salesman

Five years ago, I was working at the mental health clinic of a town near Toronto. One day, the receptionist came to my office. "There's a call from Toronto," she said. "A Dr. Philpott. He insists on talking with you and says it's urgent. Do you want me to put him through?"

"I don't know a Dr. Philpott, but sure, why not?"

When I answered, the voice on the phone said, "Hi, Dr. D. It's Frank Rivers (a pseudonym). Remember me?"

Twelve years before, I had been working as a psychiatrist for children and adolescents, when Frank, in his late teens, had become my patient after admission to hospital in an acute manic episode. For the following six years, he took his lithium diligently and remained stable and successful. But neither Frank nor I were ever sure his episode had not been a one-off thing: a manic episode fueled or triggered by some party drugs he had used at the time. So, we discussed the risks associated with staying on the lithium indefinitely, and the risks of going off it. He opted to stop the lithium and soon I lost him as a patient.

I know in the ensuing years he became a star salesman for a major telecommunications company, his hypomania being a source of his success. I also knew he was sometimes in trouble. But because he was now an adult, he was not referred back to me.

Now, he was calling from Sutton Place, a rather expensive hotel in Toronto. He had absconded from the Mood Disorders Program at Toronto's Centre for Addiction and Mental Health and booked into a penthouse suite. His employer had put him on sick leave, and he wanted to come back to see me.

"Would you take me on as a patient again?" he asked.

"Of course I will."

"Dr. Philpott" has been stable now for five years, and we have had the time and space to discuss all his problems, and the nuances of having bipolar disorder. On the edge of mania, he has the gift of reading people and persuading them to buy, to sell, or to make a deal. When a little depressed he feels guilty about this. When thinking clearly and calmly he is embarrassed by some of his antics when manic, and then gets anxious about meeting colleagues who have encountered him in that state. And stigma is a constant worry for him. Should he hide his disorder, or wear it like a badge?

He is aware of the harm and embarrassment he has caused others when manic, and he suffers some symptoms of post-traumatic stress disorder (PTSD) from his hospital admissions, which sometimes included seclusion rooms and forced injections. He says he wonders, "How much of my current lack of ambition is caused by my fear of relapse?" And we discuss all the stresses and situations that might put him at risk of relapse: parties, travel, late nights, drinking and use of non-prescription drugs—especially stimulants, affairs, the corporate life … And we discuss his warning signs. I ask, "Can you recognize the warnings signs when you are having a good time?" We talk of the absolute necessity of sleep, exercise, routine, and solid relationships to maintain a stable mood.

We have also talked about the benefits of having bipolar disorder: the bouts of high energy and accomplishment, fearlessness, confidence, creativity, and persuasive powers.

Today he takes his medication regularly, I hope, and he seeks, as I suppose we all must, the right balance in his life, which means to some extent, knowing when to leave the party, go home, take your medications, and go to bed. And when to avoid going to the party altogether.

But, like most who have experienced a period of mania, he is never absolutely sure the humdrum life of "normalcy" (the daily chores, responsibilities, the boredom and uncertainties, and the limitations and routine of taking a dampening drug) is worth the loss of those marvellous moments of mania. If only they could be harnessed!

Conclusion

I have often said, tongue in cheek, that 50 percent of my job as a psychiatrist is to convince people to stop or wean off drugs they shouldn't be taking (both prescription and otherwise), and 50 percent is trying to convince people to take medications they need. "Compliance" is a poor, inadequate word for these behaviours, for it is always a negotiation that is subject to human whim, misinformation, changing lives, subjective experiences, sometimes serious side effects or warnings, human weakness and optimism, addiction, sloth and yearning, and the latest news gathered from social media.

Bipolar disorder is obviously a huge challenge for people living with it, and for their families and friends. It is also an ongoing challenge for psychiatrists and others in the team to treat. But looking back over my long career, I can see we have come a long way in the understanding and treatment of what was then called manic depression and now, bipolar disorder—especially compared to some other mental illnesses.

The stigma of having bipolar disorder has been greatly reduced, perhaps mostly thanks to the many well-known and successful people who have talked and written about their struggles; and the number of effective medications to choose from has increased from one or two to many. Still, the difficulty of intervening in a manic person's illness—at least one who is not in imminent danger to self or others—remains. And this difficulty applies equally to family members and professionals.

Five decades ago, the social and psychological damage done by lengthy hospitalizations was underestimated. Today, the hospitalizations are often too *short* to achieve stability. Resources for the transition from hospital to community are scarce, families are sometimes ignored, and adequate resources for long-term care remain a challenge.

And perhaps the most surprising thing of all that I have seen over fifty years is that just as the number, effectiveness, and safety of pharmacotherapies for mental illness have advanced, so has social ambivalence toward psychiatry and medications increased.

Though perhaps I shouldn't be surprised. I was once in my office with an 80-year-old man who hoisted tables and chairs above me to demonstrate his vitality and prove why I should absolutely let him continue on his quest—with a shovel and his life savings in the trunk of his car—to drive across the continent to prospect for gold in the Yukon. None of us wants to believe that our sense of ourself in this world—our essence and our being—especially if it is a gloriously inflated sense of self—can be so dramatically altered by the slippage of some neurotransmitters, or indeed, by some medications I might prescribe.

David Laing Dawson

I was born in Victoria, British Columbia, in 1941. I studied medicine at the University of British Columbia (UBC), and psychiatry at UBC, the University of Cambridge (England), and McMaster University in Hamilton, Ontario. I live in Hamilton, where I was originally lured by the development of a new Department of Psychiatry. Over the years, I directed two community psychiatry programs, consulted in Northern Ontario, spent ten years as Psychiatrist in Chief of Hamilton Psychiatric Hospital, then moved back to community work, shifting to focus on Child and Adolescent psychiatry because that is where the need was greatest. I've written and published three non-fiction books, six novels, eight plays, several videos, and two small books of paintings and poetry. I regularly contribute to a blog by Marvin Ross called *Mind You.* Please visit: DawsonRoss.wordpress.com

Bipolar Disorder and Concurrent Addictions Are an Explosive Combination

Anthony Berger, MA, CCC

I am a clinical psychologist and clinical supervisor working at Dunham House, a 28-bed residential treatment centre in Quebec. We specialize in treating clients who have mental illnesses and concurrent addictions. In addition to clients with bipolar disorder, we have worked with clients diagnosed with personality disorders, depression, anxiety, and schizophrenia, among others. As you can imagine, it can be quite a challenge to create an individualized treatment plan for each client, considering the specifics of their unique mental health and addiction issues.

We have a total of six counsellors, and although we don't have a psychiatrist on staff, a local family doctor works with us if a client who needs psychiatric medications comes in without a prescription from their own care team. (Most clients come in with their prescriptions, so we know exactly what to administer. And we stay in touch with their social worker, psychiatrist, and/or therapist if they have one.)

Our program is based on an evidence-based, psychoeducational approach and uses techniques from cognitive behavioural therapy (CBT) and dialectical behaviour therapy (DBT). We offer individual and group counselling, workshops (for example, communication skills, stress management, emotional regulation), physical exercise, yoga, pottery, and music therapy. We recommend that clients stay in the program for the full six months, but of course people are free to leave whenever they choose to. As you'll see in both case studies below, when clients choose to leave early, we often see them returning for a second or third stint at the House.

A client with bipolar mania and concurrent addictions

Many of the clients with bipolar disorder who come to us have been previously stabilized on medications already.

Many, but not all.

One client in his early thirties—let's call him John—had bipolar and had been consuming alcohol, marijuana, speed, and occasionally cocaine. That's obviously a very dangerous cocktail of substances for an already-fragile bipolar brain to cope with.

As so often happens in these cases, family members get burned out by their loved one's erratic behaviour. John had a poor relationship with his mother and ended up drifting from one treatment facility and shelter to another; he was very much part of "the system."

For better or worse, it was now *our* turn to try to help him manage his bipolar and recover from his addictions.

When he arrived, John was on prescribed medications, but given his unsettled lifestyle and concurrent addictions, his adherence to therapy wasn't always the best.

John was very aware of his bipolar, and he knew that his use of substances escalated the bipolar symptoms. We only ever saw him in mania, never depression. (When people drop down into depression, they often want to self-medicate with uppers to lift their mood.)

In mania, John's self-esteem was sky high. He became very impulsive and irritable; he had rapid speech and flight of ideas; and he was full of good intentions and grand—even grandiose—plans. He showed lots of anxiety through his facial expressions. He often seemed to go off into his own world, so we'd talk to him calmly to try to engage with him and centre him a bit. Most times, this would help to ground him in reality.

John stayed with us twice, but neither time did he stay for the suggested six-month period. His first stay lasted about three months, and his second stay was just one month. There was a two- or three-year gap in between his two stays.

During his second stay, he became paranoid. He had given up smoking and switched to vaping instead, but he was convinced that someone in the House had interfered with his vaping liquid. Delusions like these were a real problem.

Unfortunately, John chose to leave the centre while he was still unstable. Somehow, he managed to convince his reluctant mother to come and pick him up. We've not heard from him since then. (We seldom do hear from former clients, most of whom are unemployed and on social assistance programs, often wandering from one temporary housing situation to another.)

You might think, "No news is good news," but in this field that is unfortunately seldom the case. John still had a lot of work to do concerning his addictions, in addition to getting his bipolar under control.

A client with bipolar depression and addictions

More recently, we worked with another man in his thirties whom I'll call Patrick. He has bipolar disorder, and his drug of choice was marijuana. When he arrived, he was deeply depressed: low energy, poor motivation, no ambition.

He had been living at home with his parents, doing little except playing video games in the basement. He was first admitted to the Douglas Hospital, a psychiatric hospital in Montreal, for depression, and was transferred to us from there. His parents basically pushed him to agree to do at least three of the suggested six months with us.

He only stayed about two-and-a-half weeks the first time, then begged his parents to come and fetch him. "I can't stand it here; I'm so bored," he said.

They refused and insisted that he stay for at least another month.

So, he jumped on a bus and went back to Montreal on his own.

Within three days, he was readmitted to the Douglas. He called us from there and asked, "Can I come back to Dunham House?"

We said, "Sure. We'll start your treatment plan all over."

But when he arrived, we saw immediately that his mood had deteriorated even more. He was now completely blank-faced, moving very slowly, with very slow speech and almost no body language. He was almost catatonic, to be honest. Something major had changed between his first time here and now.

We assumed that there might be a medication—or over-medication—component that needed to be addressed, so we consulted with his psychiatrist about that.

But Patrick had many other problems, apart from medication combinations and dosages. We could tell that he was simply going through the motions with us, waiting out the three months his parents had insisted upon and hoping to move back home. But his parents had clearly said they would *not* have him back. They didn't want to enable him any longer.

Right now, Patrick is still with us in treatment. He's at 35 days and counting.

He's clearly going to need some family involvement to look for solutions and help him improve his quality of life in the long-term. Helping him develop confidence that he can live independently is going to be a huge challenge.

What I would like people with bipolar and concurrent addictions to consider

People sometimes ask me, "What usually comes first: the mental illness or the addiction?" I have seen both, and I'd say there's about a fifty-fifty chance of either scenario occurring. On the one hand, people with an undiagnosed and/or untreated mental illness often try to self-medicate and can end up getting addicted to whatever substance(s) they are using, and on the other hand, people without an initial mental illness can use substances that then trigger a mental illness. Either way, they end up with double trouble.

To effectively manage your bipolar, you need to monitor and identify your moods and become aware of how you think and feel. Become very alert to the extremes of your moods, and the length of time each episode lasts. Learn to improve your mood, your thought patterns, and your behaviours.

Be patient with yourself! Know that "this too shall pass." Work at feeling comfortable in your own skin.

And of course, know that an addiction on top of bipolar will make your mental health even more unstable, more at risk. What is a difficult balance for anyone with bipolar disorder becomes a harrowing tightrope for people with both bipolar and an addiction.

Which is precisely why we recommend that clients complete the full six-month treatment program, of course.

A word to family members

I've mentioned that many of our clients have burned their bridges with family members who've often been pushed beyond their limits by the demands of caring for a person with both a mental illness and an addiction. In cases where there is still a salvageable relationship, and where the client agrees, we try to involve the family, especially during the final months of the program.

I always advise family caregivers to take care of themselves first: their own mental health is sometimes almost as precarious as that of their loved one, and we can each only take care of others if we ourselves are mentally strong and healthy.

I also advise families to seek out as much information as possible, and to join community-based support groups.

Finally, I ask them please to be patient with their affected family member. Recovery will not be easy, but it is possible.

To family members and the public, I try to spread the message that stigma still exists and needs to be broken. For example, not everyone with a mental illness is violent, and not every addict *chooses* to be addicted.

Conclusion

Even from childhood, I was always a good listener. I knew that I wanted to make a difference in people's lives; to give back; and offer suggestions or feedback that might be useful. Also, I do have some family members who have struggled with depression. So, I chose to go into one of the helping professions. And I'm very glad I did. I find my work very satisfying, as well as challenging, of course.

One challenge that I didn't anticipate concerns fellow health professionals. Maybe I was naïve, but I assumed that there would be professional respect and good communication between members of the different helping professions: therapists, counsellors, nurses, doctors, psychiatrists, and so on. If I could give one message to my colleagues it would be this: please be a bit more collaborative and open with the various community organizations, treatment centres, and other third parties that serve your clients and their families. We see the clients so much more intensively, and yet we often don't feel accepted as full members of the care team.

This "professional snubbing" puts us under even more stress than usual. Remember, many of these third-party organizations are severely underfunded and run with a skeleton staff, always worrying whether enough donations will be received, and wishing for funds to hire additional clinical staff to avoid burnout. I would also love to hire an in-house psychiatrist ... I can assure you, working for a non-profit brings constant stress. Financial concerns are ever-present.

But our work is extremely rewarding. Our goal is to help our clients heal and fall back in love with life and accept who they are. When a client leaves the House feeling stable and looking forward to the next steps on their recovery journey, we all celebrate with them.

Anthony Berger

I was born in Montreal in 1990 and did my bachelor's in psychology at Bishop's University and a master's in counselling psychology at Yorkville University. I am a licensed Canadian Certified Counsellor (CCC) with the Canadian Counselling and Psychotherapy Association and a member of the Academy of Naturopaths and Naturotherapists of Canada. I have a variety of clinical experiences, working in centres specializing in the treatment of substance abuse and concurrent mental health disorders. I am the clinical supervisor at Dunham House near Sutton, Quebec, where I oversee all elements of the residential treatment program and support clinical team members. I live in Montreal with my spouse and enjoy playing and refereeing soccer, reading, and doing continuing education.

DunhamHouse.ca, AnthonyBerger.ca

Let Me into Your Mind

Matthieu Zellweger, photographer

In the early days of summer 2017, the scientific journal The Lancet confirmed with me that they wanted to publish a series of pictures on a mental health issue. It was to be my third photographic contribution to that journal. As a photographer specializing in health-related stories, with a background as a research scientist, I rejoiced at the renewed opportunity to publish my work in such a prestigious medical journal.

What made it extra special is that they said they were open as to how I treated the topic, and which angle I chose. I had full freedom to do anything I wanted, a true *carte blanche* with a minor caveat only: they wanted to review the images before finally committing. That was fair, I thought; after all, the topic was not exactly ordinary or uncontroversial. Even I did not yet know what the images would turn out to be.

The difficult part about total freedom is to follow the right lead. This is especially true when the topic is delicate and promises to be challenging in terms of access to the right stories—a question that is central to any photographic project and usually differentiates a good project from a great one. The blessing was indeed disguised, but I knew that my best photographic projects were also the ones that left me puzzled in the beginning, even struggling a bit. In this case, I had to decide which mental illness I would focus on, and with which angle I would approach it.

In fact, I did not have to think for very long—it was going to be about bipolar disorder. I had spent two years on a previous project, documenting the life of a close friend of mine who suffers a relatively severe form of the disease. I felt reasonably aware of what awaited me. On the other hand, whilst this prior project was by all accounts successful, the images were unsuitable for this job because they were about my friend and his life. This new project had to be about the disorder itself. I needed to tell a wider range of stories, to meet a larger group of people, to encounter a variety of experiences.

As I mentioned, I used to work as a research scientist. So, I can dive into a topic and relatively rapidly map out what I need to know. I must add that it is always humbling to also realize in parallel how much I ignore about it. This skill proved to be a great advantage for this project. At first, I met health care providers, both world-leading and locally based. Several of them welcomed my project and agreed to collaborate.

It keeps striking me, as I shoot delicate topic after delicate topic, how affected people and those around them are extremely willing to talk. To several people whom I met over the years (and over many projects on difficult topics), silence, solitude, and ignorance seem to be far heavier burdens than any stigma that sharing their story might cause. This project was no exception. Doctors, psychiatrists, patient groups. All doors were open, with only the odd exception. Yes, there was one person—not a patient, but a health professional in this case—who went to extraordinary lengths to let me know that she strongly disapproved of my project. This happens. I can never let myself be stopped by occasional opposition. It's part of the process.

After a slow start, which is usual, I eventually found my cruising speed. I met people. I interviewed them. I listened carefully and took detailed notes. I shot many, many journalistic pictures. The body of work was growing nicely, both written and photographic.

It would not be a problem at all to send in a good submission to *The Lancet* editor.

Yet, something was missing. See, the people I met were all willing to talk to me directly. They all contacted me on their own free will after hearing about my project, either after I introduced myself in patient groups, or through one of the extraordinary people who went very much out of their way to facilitate my work. Almost by definition, this meant that the people who spoke to me were in the stable (most of the time), or in the depressed phase of bipolar disorder. I did not know it at the time, but it would be another full year before I met someone in an actively manic phase in circumstances when I could photograph them. An essential piece of the bipolar story was escaping me.

I had to find a way around this obstacle. For a journalistic coverage of the disease, it was fine to use the body of work I had. In fact, it almost worked to my advantage, because it portrayed a very reassuring facet of these people's lives, almost banal. Nothing was controversial and that would give solace to *The Lancet* editors. So much so that almost everyone could easily relate to the people I had photographed. That was good to get my message across that for most patients, life outside of crises is just like anyone else's life. A "this-patient-could-be-your-neighbour" sort of message.

But for me, to complete my story, I had to find a way to include the missing part, the manic phase. Incidentally, at around the same time, I spent a week in a very high-level masterclass with a senior member of Magnum Photo, a renowned photographic company. Under his mentorship, I pushed open a door I had never noticed previously: I took staged pictures of actors who were posing for me and whom I had to direct. Incidentally again, I had chosen to spend the week shooting about fears and dreams. Low light situations; dark corners of an invisible world; tortured stories to be told in one image only. That week unlocked more in me than anyone, my mentor included, would have imagined.

And that proved to be the key: provided I was honest about the process, I could *stage* pictures, based on reminiscences that people with bipolar would tell me about their own manic episodes. I called them one by one, expecting that some might decline. All said yes. I went for another series of interviews, this time much longer and deeper. These manic phases seemed to harbour so many elements and facets that there was indeed much to say and write.

The process was always the same: interviewing, a few days of pausing and reflecting, shooting. Sometimes several shootings, depending on how much material I was given. Some people were incredibly generous. To be absolutely clear with my audience, I decided to only shoot blurry images for the staged part. After all, I was reconstructing my personal vision of the internal mental space of a person with bipolar disorder, based on elements of recollections given by that person. It was all obviously very personal and specific. Whereas the elements in my notes and in my original pictures were from the patients, the blurred, staged picture itself was my creation, guided by their recollections. This had to be made clear and completely separated from the journalistic images, which are sharp and spontaneous.

It worked well. I shot a number of pictures, all expressing my vision of what the patients' manic phase might have looked and felt like. They all validated the pictures—to my great relief, but then again, if they had not, it would have meant that I had failed miserably. The interesting part of that body of work (which grew to be a separate project and was later published as a book titled *Worlds Beyond* in 2019) is that it has a consistency of its own. It was almost as though the people who offered to tell me their experiences took me into their inner workings during a manic phase and let me into their mind with my camera. More than anything, it was great fun to shoot and, according to the patients who participated, great fun to be part of.

A woman with bipolar disorder re-enacts what she described she feels during manic crises, in particular, the constant whirlwind of thoughts and ideas that overwhelms her during these moments. For full-colour, full-size image, please see MatthieuZellweger.com/share/ZellwegerMPE-1.jpg or scan this QR code

A woman with bipolar disorder re-enacts what she described feeling during manic crises, in particular, the burning creativity and urge to paint that she feels at these times. She is seen here surrounded by paintings she made when in crisis. For full-colour, full-size image, please see MatthieuZellweger.com/share/ZellwegerMPE-2.jpg or scan this QR code

The Lancet essay and the *Worlds Beyond* book were both published in 2019 (see list of references at the end of this book). Both publications were praised, and the book won several distinctions in photographic contests. The series got me enormous media attention in Switzerland—where I live—and way beyond. It was featured in the prestigious *New York Times* Lens Blog and got me on Merryl Hammond's radar, which explains the presence of my piece in this anthology.

Of course, all these developments were welcome and very rewarding professionally. But there was more to this project and its aftermath. There is something considerably more important than any distinction it has received: close to two years after I shot the last image of this project, I am still in regular contact with almost all the people who shared their stories with me. I am delighted to say that some have become friends.

I do not think that anyone ever expected that when I first accepted *The Lancet*'s commission.

Matthieu Zellweger

I grew up in French-speaking Switzerland. My background as a scientist in the field of health and medicine has allowed me to tell stories from a different perspective. As an award-winning photographic artist, I bring a keen eye to the human condition and my poetic insights illuminate the inner landscape of the psyche to make the invisible visible. My cinematic images and essays have been widely published and exhibited on three continents, and I have published two books: *Secrets of Rice and Water* (2017) and *Worlds Beyond* (2019). I have travelled extensively and developed a special interest in Japan's cultural traditions, particularly the world of sake, which connects the people of Japan with the world of the gods. Based in Switzerland, I work in French, English, German, and Italian. I also have working knowledge of Spanish and Japanese.

mpezellweger@yahoo.com, MatthieuZellweger.com

Bipolar Disorder and Creative Expression

Abdu'l-Missagh Ghadirian, MD

Editor's note: Please see the list of references at the back of this book for sources cited in this essay.

My interest in creativity began when I was very young. It grew through my observation of the work of visual artists. When I began my practice of psychiatry, I was interested to note that some patients with emotional disorders who had difficulty expressing their thoughts and feelings verbally could express them through the arts such as drawing, painting, writing, poetry, and music. For some, this became a second language of expression and communication and was therapeutic. I also realized how gifted some of them were, regardless of whether they were depressed or elated. I developed art therapy for individuals and groups as a complement to conventional psychiatric treatment when appropriate.

Throughout my career, I have also been fascinated by creativity and its relation to human suffering of all kinds: mental, physical, spiritual. I am particularly interested in the creative responses and resilience of some people who respond by bouncing back and overcoming hardships such as mental health challenges, and situational or existential crises; and being subject to social injustices including racism and/or persecution on religious or ideological grounds. I have published several academic articles on this topic over three decades, starting back in 1974; in 2009 I published a book, *Creative Dimensions of Suffering*.

My aim in this essay is to reflect on the relationship between bipolar disorder specifically and the enhancement of creative expression. We need a better understanding and appreciation of the gift of creativity that is often interwoven with the process of bipolar illness. Many health professionals, families, and bipolar patients remain unaware that this hidden treasure may flourish in some bipolar individuals and even their family members.

Researchers have noted that although some progress has been made in understanding the relationship between creativity and bipolar illness, there is still much to learn. There is also a real challenge concerning how best to treat gifted patients with conventional treatments without adversely diminishing their creative spark, which I will address toward the end of this essay.

Bipolar mood swings

Most readers of this anthology will be familiar with the highs and lows of bipolar disorder, either as people living with the disorder, as family members and friends, or as health professionals who work with affected people and family members. However, few have described bipolar episodes as eloquently as Kay Redfield Jamison, PhD, a renowned American clinical psychologist and Professor of Psychiatry and Behavioural Sciences at Johns Hopkins and an expert in bipolar disorder who herself has suffered from bipolar disorder since early adulthood.

> Reflecting on her own mood swings in her classic 1995 book, *An Unquiet Mind*, Kay Redfield Jamison, PhD writes, "When you're high it's tremendous. The ideas and feelings are fast and frequent like shooting stars, and you follow them until you find better and brighter ones ... Feelings of ease, intensity, power,

well-being, financial omnipotence, and euphoria pervade one's marrow ..." Then in depression she writes, "Everything previously moving with the grain is now against—you are irritable, angry, frightened, uncontrollable, and enmeshed totally in the blackest caves of the mind. You never knew these caves were there. It will never end, for madness carves its own reality" (page 67).

The link between mental illness, genius, and creativity

Creativity has been defined in different ways. It involves skillful and innovative use of talents or the creation of something unique such as artwork or an invention. Imagination plays an important role.

In my book, *Creative Dimensions of Suffering*, I explain that creativity can be a useful catalyst for healing, but it can also be misused and can cause emotional and psychological damage (page 17). For example, some ambitious, creative people sometimes drive themselves to their limit, trying to maximize creative productivity. They may neglect basic needs for sleep, nutrition, exercise, family, and social contact in an excessive creative frenzy, day after day. This of course often results in serious consequences for the individual, their family, and their employers and colleagues.

The concept of a link between mental illness and genius goes back to ancient times. Hippocrates, the great Greek physician born in about 460 BCE and known as the "Father of Medicine," described "melancholia" or what we now refer to as depression. Other Greek physicians noted a tendency in some patients to change from a state of melancholia into an agitated state of mania (Benaur, M. 2010, pages xvii–xxvi). Aristotle, the ancient Greek philosopher and scientist born in 384 BCE believed that "No great genius was without a mixture of insanity." Regarding melancholia, he said, "Those who have become eminent in philosophy, politics, poetry, and the arts have all had tendencies toward melancholia" (Aristotle cited by Rosenthal, NE. 1993, page 229).

Benjamin Rush, considered to be the father of American psychiatry, explained the relation between mental illness and creativity using this analogy in which "globe" means "brain": "The disease which thus evolves these new and wonderful talents and operations of the mind may be compared to an earthquake which by convulsing the upper strata of our globe throws upon its surface precious and splendid fossils, the existence of which was unknown to the proprietors of the soil in which they were buried" (Ghadirian, A-M. 2009, page 75).

For centuries, there was an assumption that a connection might exist between having a mood disorder such as melancholia or mania and possessing a high degree of creativity. However, since there were no psychiatrists to validate this impression, biographers of certain gifted individuals (prominent writers, poets, artists, and others) noted the possibility of a relationship between what they had observed in the creative life of such people and their mental problems. It was not until a few decades ago that researchers began to purposefully explore and study this relationship.

Recent research

Recent research shows that there is a connection between creativity and bipolar, especially during the hypomanic state of the disorder, but not for every patient. Some people seem to have a particular susceptibility to this development. Our understanding of the connection between creativity and patients with bipolar illness is growing, but the precise nature and the mechanism of this connection remains a mystery.

Kay Jamison conducted a study on a group of eminent, highly accomplished prize-winning British writers and artists to explore any relationship between intense mood disorders and creativity. Results showed that over one-third of the participants had been treated for mood disorders, most of them through medication and hospitalization. Among them, poets were most likely to be treated with medication for depression and mania. With respect to creativity, most study participants reported creative periods with intense and high productivity associated with enthusiasm, speed of mental activity, excited mood, and feelings of well-being, like a state of hypomania. They also reported experiencing more creativity during summer months when light has a stimulating emotional effect and can serve as a healing medicine for those suffering from seasonal affective disorder. By the same token, during the fall and winter, these individuals suffered more from depression and were less creative (Rosenthal, NE. 1993, pages 230-1).

More recent systematic reviews of the correlation between creativity and bipolar disorder do show a significant link between these two phenomena, with an overrepresentation of bipolar patients in creative careers and professions. And in a study of 219 bipolar patients, 82 percent reported that during their manic or hypomanic episodes they experienced increased creativity (McCraw, S., et al. 2013).

As with much of the research in this area, the researchers relied on people's self-reports rather than an objective process to evaluate the creative expressions. In other words—as the authors themselves note—creative activities were not judged for quality or originality and so may reflect common or everyday creative abilities rather than exceptional quality. (Not every creative person is necessarily a genius!) Other common problems with research of this kind include small sample sizes, difficulty categorizing patients into distinct bipolar I and II sub-groups, and the fact that bipolar patients' perceptions of their own creativity and of their motivation to be creative may change dramatically as their moods shift from (hypo)mania to depression and back again.

Another research team (Burkhardt, E., et al, 2019) recently studied and found evidence of increased creativity in people at risk for developing bipolar disorder. They concluded that mood swings are indeed strongly associated with creativity but—as above—not necessarily with exceptional creative achievements. As these researchers point out, the association between bipolar and creativity may be related to symptoms of the disorder itself, or to personality traits that were already present in the individual before the onset of the disorder.

Some people wonder: does creativity influence the development of bipolar disorder or does bipolar influence creativity? The answer is not yet clear. While research shows that some bipolar patients display heightened creativity, the mechanism causing this phenomenon remains an enigma for now.

Treating bipolar disorder in creative people: clinical and ethical considerations

The importance of research findings about the relationship between bipolar illness and creativity may have ethical implications for the current pharmacological treatment of patients with these disorders. Many visual artists, writers, musicians, and others make their living through their art while receiving treatment for their psychiatric disorders. Some of them, during their ongoing treatment, whether by not complying in taking their medication or by consuming alcohol and/or psychoactive drugs and without informing their therapist, may develop a (hypo)manic or depressive state. The consequences can be serious and costly. For example, during a manic episode, individuals are at a much higher risk for destructive behaviour, family conflicts, significant financial loss through overspending, or moral indiscretions that could damage their credibility and well-being.

One of my bipolar patients was a gifted artist who from time to time would miss her appointment for weeks. Then she would show up at the emergency room in a relapse. When I inquired about her periods of absence from treatment, she told me that she had stopped her medication to regain her excitement and elation to be productive and thus better able to earn her living. She would work hard but unfortunately would also neglect her need to sleep. This, in addition to her non-compliance with treatment, led to her relapse. Nevertheless, she felt that she had no choice for otherwise she was unable to work, a situation that would result in financial difficulties and an accumulation of debt. Relapse was the price she paid for non-compliance with her mood stabilizing treatment.

Patty Duke, a famous American actress and health advocate who suffered from bipolar disorder, wrote, "You can have manic-depression without having an ounce of creativity." She also said, "I know that without treatment I would have never been able to harness my creativity in such a successful way" (McCraw, S., et al. 2013, page 831).

Treating a creative bipolar patient is a daunting intervention both clinically and ethically. A patient's agitation, delusional thoughts, mood changes, and other symptoms are believed to stem from biological disturbances in brain function. All these factors point to a crucial need for adequate treatment. The challenge for a physician is to find the right balance between using a medication that regulates mood swings, such as lithium and other mood stabilizers, and enabling a patient to maintain their creativity. Occupational therapy including art therapy can be beneficial, especially for those who have an artistic interest and background. Depending on the stability of the patient, art therapy may be combined with other therapeutic approaches such as supportive or interpersonal therapy.

Conclusion

The emergence of creativity in bipolar patients can be therapeutic and may complement conventional treatment when a patient is stabilized. In fact, the subjective feeling of satisfaction and accomplishment brought on by creative expression can itself be an important element in the treatment of bipolar patients as it boosts a patient's positive sense of self. It can also reduce the stigma of the illness, causing patients to feel valued and increasing their self-esteem.

Having said that, a word of caution is necessary. We should be careful not to romanticize the emergence of creativity and its development in bipolar patients. As well, although research suggests a higher prevalence of creativity in bipolar patients who are poets, artists, musicians, and who practise other arts, this phenomenon cannot be generalized to all of them. Nor do we know the mechanism of its development. Is the creative spark a compensation for having the illness or are there other factors such as genetic predisposition, personality traits, or other elements? How can these patients be efficiently treated without adversely hampering their creativity or be adequately treated so as not to aggravate the illness? Finally, not every manifestation of creativity is necessarily in the best interests of a patient's well-being. In brief, understanding this exciting creative phenomenon is still a work in progress, but healing the disease remains the highest priority.

Abdu'l-Missagh Ghadirian

I was born in Iran and studied medicine at Tabriz University, then psychiatry with an MSc degree in the United States. I taught at Queen's University and McGill University, both in Canada. I am a professor emeritus at McGill's Faculty of Medicine, and a Distinguished Life Fellow of the American Psychiatric Association. As a physician, author, and researcher, I have published extensively in scientific journals and spoken internationally on social, psychological, and current issues. Among my publications are fourteen books, including *Creative Dimensions of Suffering* and more recently, *Alzheimer's Disease: An Eclipse before Sunset* (2016) and *Materialism: Moral and Social Consequences* (second edition, 2017). My research also includes the relevance of the Baha'i Faith's teachings to contemporary social issues, and I wrote a chapter on "The Role of Religion and Spirituality in Mental Health" for *Innovations in Global Mental Health* (Springer Nature, 2021). I live in Montreal with my wife; we have two children and three grandchildren.

Involvement of Family and Caregivers of People Living with Bipolar Disorder

Jens Peter Eckardt, BSW, MSc

Throughout my professional and personal life, I have met many wonderful people with bipolar disorder and their loved ones. I have listened to their heartbreaking stories and the honest and brave accounts of their experiences; heard about their hopes but also their challenges; and observed the successes and failures of their various struggles. All this has made a large impact on me. As a result, I am continually trying to demystify this so often misunderstood mental illness in the hopes of enlightening the public and helping to eradicate the ignorance, stigma, and prejudice attached to the illness. Hopefully sooner rather than later; once and for all.

A colleague once told me, "Becoming a caregiver for a person with bipolar disorder is like riding an emotional rollercoaster and never knowing when it will stop."

And one does not have to read too many textbooks before available research confirms the substantial long-term adverse effects on caregivers.

Becoming a caregiver for an individual living with bipolar disorder often leads to dramatic and complex changes in life with no possibility of returning to "normal" for a long time. Just think how people living with someone who has bipolar disorder can be adversely affected by:

- acute disruption,
- the constant risk of turmoil,
- severe bipolar symptoms and sometimes extremely disturbed behaviour,
- the possible risk of relapse and readmission to hospital, especially when the illness is most severe.

Thousands of family members and caregivers struggle every day with the ambiguity of bipolar disorder, its often-deteriorating course, the challenging symptoms, their own caretaking roles while at the same time trying to maintain a sense of normalcy. This is an inconvenient truth that has been scientifically studied over the last couple of decades and it unquestionably demonstrates the deep impact on the whole family's well-being, closeness, and quality of life. Editor's note: Please see the list of selected references about caregivers at the end of this book.

Subjective and objective experiences of caregivers

On the subjective side of the caregiver's experience, extensive research has shown how caregivers identify losses such as hopes, dreams, and shattered expectations combined with emotional reactions like grief, shock, disbelief, anger, withdrawal, hyperactivity, irritability, worry, despair, loneliness, guilt, shame, and, not least, stigma by association. In other words, these are predictors of a perfect storm for caregivers. In a more clinical sense, evidence repeatedly reports that caregivers experience higher than average levels of insomnia, psychological and psychiatric distress, depression, anxiety, and post-traumatic stress disorder.

On the objective side of the caregiver experience, it is not uncommon for caregivers to experience poor family functioning, marital or family breakdown, separation, and interpersonal conflicts. In addition, many studies have highlighted the economic impact of caregiving, including reduced work activities, increased time off work, reduced income, financial difficulties, job insecurity, loss of vacation time, and legal implications. These effects combine with often disrupted social and leisure activities and less support from one's social network.

The level of subjective and objective impact depends upon many variables such as gender, age, cultural factors, severity of the disorder, relationship with and closeness to the person with bipolar disorder, and the specific role of the caregiver. But overall, there is indisputable and substantial scientific consensus that caregivers who live with a person who has bipolar disorder can experience severe negative and long-term consequences.

These consequences include the well-known caregiver experiences of suicidal ideation and attempts, and involuntary admission for acute mental health treatment. All this combines with barriers to collaboration caused by patient confidentiality policies. In addition, researchers have argued that the burden of bipolar disorder on caregivers may even impose a substantial economic cost on society.

And just imagine how the pressure of caregiving might increase due to external circumstances such as the current COVID-19 restrictions. As I wrote in my 2020 article in *The Lancet Psychiatry*:

> *The pandemic could lead to substantial deterioration of family functioning caused by the unimaginable pressure inflicted by COVID-19 restrictions and precautions.... There is scarce research on the effect of COVID-19 on caregivers and I am concerned that the current public health messaging might be leaving out this important at-risk population who are underutilised in the treatment of people with mental illness.... [T]he importance of caregivers needs to be recognised more than ever before. The health-care community cannot afford to lose the aid of caregivers, engagement with whom offers a unique*

opportunity to ensure healthy lives and overall wellbeing for people with mental health disorders.

Benefits of caregiver involvement

On the other side of the caregiver experience, the family and caregivers also play a central role in the treatment and the recovery process of people with bipolar disorder according to the literature.

During the last couple of decades, significant evidence has proven that active involvement of the family (for example, family interventions, educational initiatives, and interpersonal factors) could be beneficial and may improve comprehensive and good long-term outcomes for patients and caregivers.

Other research on family interventions highlights positive outcomes such as fewer relapses, reduced readmissions, and less family burden combined with improved medicine compliance, better response to treatment, reduced symptoms, positive social and/or family functioning, and improved attitudes and quality of life.

Studies attribute these changes to families and caregivers learning to change their thinking and interactional behaviour patterns. Over time, family interventions have been modified to include more education about bipolar illness, coping strategies, communication training, social involvement, and problem-solving skills training; all in typical psycho-educational sessions. The rationale is that caregivers cope better and perceive less burden when they understand that the problematic behaviour is caused by the illness and not by willful misconduct. Clearly, these studies demonstrate that families and caregivers can benefit from short-term as well as long-term interventions like these, resulting in extensive improvement of caregivers' burdens.

By all accounts, then, caregiver engagement must be an essential component of an optimal treatment strategy for people with bipolar disorder.

However, despite substantial and growing evidence that shows the effectiveness of family interventions, it is still not routinely provided in clinical practices, nor widely implemented in mental health services. As a result, many families' needs go unmet every day—and even right now while you are reading this sentence, too.

Solutions and recommendations

Research shows that organizational difficulties represent a major barrier or gap in clinical practice for family involvement, even in many developed countries. Implementing family involvement and addressing the unmet needs of caregivers might be one of the most urgent challenges and a major concern for mental health care services of bipolar disorder today.

And the solution?

Caregiver involvement must be addressed at a decision-making level according to the literature. This includes everything from a clear structure to cultural and organizational shifts, as well as having the necessary "top-down" support, clear policies, guidelines, staff skills, training, and supervision combined with a whole-team approach.

It is not easy, and we are faced with many challenges given the variation in resources and cultural contexts. But it is vital for the future successful treatment of bipolar disorders.

In other words, if we want family members and caregivers to be competent and committed partners in the treatment of people experiencing bipolar disorders, the only way is to ensure high quality mental health services are built on evidence-based approaches and well-documented research into the lives of family members and caregivers. This also means sustainable holistic support and recognition of the underutilized benefits and potentials of caregiver involvement and commitment.

To conclude this section, let's consider future mental health care management for a moment. Allow me to address my colleagues in psychiatry and other mental health professions and to summarize some key recommendations from the literature about engaging caregivers who live with people with bipolar disorder.

1. Believe that it is both desirable and possible to involve caregivers in mental health care.
2. Consider your own basic attitudes toward caregivers and the care and treatment you offer them.
3. Try to see caregiver engagement in a prevention perspective and as a benefit for the person with bipolar disorder.
4. See the lack of caregiver involvement as high-risk and failed-care situation.
5. See caregiver engagement as a professional and managerial challenge, not as something that comes from above, for example, from politicians who do not know the daily life in a psychiatric ward. In other words, take ownership of the task.
6. Keep updated on recent research about caregiver involvement and family interventions.
7. Ask yourself, what is the ability of our organization or department to implement and maintain new initiatives? Make resources available for transition and learning.
8. Recognize that since change can be accomplished in other countries, hospitals, and departments, then it is also possible to implement change in your organization!
9. Strive to achieve results and be proud of what you achieve.

Conclusion

Many years of research and increased knowledge has first of all underlined that continued involvement of caregivers and the family of an individual living with bipolar disorder is crucial to the recovery process. Second, the presence of bipolar disorder in a family and among caregivers often represents a significant burden but it is not given the requisite attention.

One must remember that over several decades, the health care of people living with bipolar disorder has undergone major changes as a consequence of deinstitutionalization policies. As a result, families and caregivers have become more exposed and even more involved in providing informal care.

Clearly, then, it is time to look at ways we can engage and empower caregivers. The time for words is over; it's time for concrete action now.

Editor's note: This author provided a list of suggested readings about this topic; please see references at the back of the book.

Jens Peter Eckardt

I was born in Haderslev, Denmark, in 1983 and studied social work and sociology at Aalborg University and University College Copenhagen. I am a chief analyst at *Bedre Psykiatri* ("Better Psychiatry"), the Danish national association of caregivers of people with mental illnesses. I have worked in the field of caregiver research, analysis, and policy work over the past ten-plus years and have written several articles on the topic. I am a member of the National Board of Health's Committee for Psychiatry, The National Board of Health and Welfare's Follow-up Group for Strengthened Quality in Social Psychiatry, the Danish National Partnership for Suicide Prevention, Denmark's Council for Human Rights, and the Danish Government's working group for an upcoming ten-year mental health action plan. I live in Copenhagen with my wife, Signe, a child psychologist, and our six-year-old son, Elliot and a newborn girl named Nora.

See the Person, Not the Disorder

Sheryl Bruce, MA

I have worked for non-profit community organizations in Montreal for the last twenty-five years, ten of which were with people who had mental health challenges. For the last fifteen years, I have counselled the family members of affected people. I hope to give an idea of the difficulties that emerge when bipolar disorder enters the picture.

Diagnosis and symptoms

Families are turned upside down when bipolar surfaces in a loved one. In the beginning, no one knows what is happening. Suddenly there is a shift of mood and new, uncharacteristic behaviours appear.

Symptoms of bipolar disorder most commonly begin in the late teens or twenties, although they can start in childhood ("juvenile bipolar") and as late as middle age or even later. I have a distant relative who was only diagnosed at the age of 70! (All we knew—as her family members—was that she had always been flamboyant and "odd." She had endless energy and a big heart. In retrospect, I can see that she had periods of hypomania over the years. To the extended family, the negative effects of the illness were hidden. At seventy, when she announced her diagnosis at a family birthday, she actually seemed quite relieved that after all these decades, her condition had a name, bipolar II, and she had medication to help.)

Getting a bipolar diagnosis can sometimes be delayed for years because there is no laboratory test or X-ray to reveal its presence. Recent brain scan research may be helpful, but for now, health professionals have to rely on a comprehensive medical history looking for patterns that reveal the classic bipolar signs and symptoms of (hypo)mania with depression.

Kay Redfield Jamison, PhD (author of *Touched with Fire: Manic-Depressive Illness and the Artistic Temperament* and *An Unquiet Mind*) is a renowned expert on bipolar disorder from Johns Hopkins School of Medicine who herself has the disorder. She noted in an interview with NBC News on April 12, 2018, that the average length of time between a person's first bipolar episode and getting the correct diagnosis is eight years.

Some might assume that the problem of delayed diagnosis is the doctor's fault. This is not so. The doctor will identify the problem only if the person accurately describes their symptoms. For this reason, it is important for families to keep a journal of the signs and symptoms they observe, and to note how long they occur. You can then assist the treating professionals by giving objective, accurate information to supplement what the affected person conveys from their perspective.

While getting a bipolar diagnosis can clearly be stressful and deeply upsetting, it can also be very helpful. At least appropriate treatment can then be started. Bipolar will not simply "go away" if it's ignored or denied. It is a chronic, relapsing condition, and with each additional episode, there is a psychological toll on the person. They start to feel defective when they lose control and get themselves into trouble. Early diagnosis and treatment can greatly lessen the impact of the disorder on individuals and their families.

During the manic phase the person will often have unrealistic, grandiose ideas (e.g., about world travel, achieving excellence in sports, having exceptional business acumen, and so on). Impulsive behaviours are typical: too much partying, gambling, speeding and dangerous driving, risky sex, use of alcohol or street drugs, and/or excessive spending. Often the person does not realize they need help until they start suffering the consequences of their behaviours: increased debt, job loss, speeding tickets, accumulations of goods, drunk driving incidents, or sexually transmitted diseases are all signs that the person has lost control. These consequences can motivate them to accept treatment.

The family's response

Family members have told me about the chaos that mania creates for the family. In talking with clients who experience hypomania, they suffer as well. Even when families have genuine compassion for the affected person, individual family members often have different ideas about how best to respond to their loved one. This creates problems as they try to decide what to do and how to intervene.

For example, families may need to reach a consensus about such difficult questions as:

- Do we call for an ambulance, or not?
- Should we call the police?
- Should we lend the person money?
- Are we helping or enabling them?

Mania is a phase during which the affected person has no insight into their condition; they often don't realize that their grandiose plans are not realistic. So, it won't help for family members to simply say, "You're not well and you need help." The person cannot understand this if they lack insight. Until family members understand this, they will only create more tension and conflict. The more the family insists, the worse the situation can get.

The only way to find out if someone lacks insight is gently and respectfully to say something like this: "We are all really worried that you may have a problem. Let me take you to see the doctor." I get that you have to try to reason with them, I would too. However, do not keep repeating this if it does not work.

I recommend that you work with your loved one to find out what issues are troubling for them. Partnering with them and being on their side works better in the long run for maintaining the relationship. This method is best described by Dr. Xavier Amador in his recently updated 2020 book, *I Am Not Sick, I Don't Need Help: How to Help Someone Accept Treatment.*

It can also be hard when the family does not yet realize that there is a problem. Sometimes the person has access to money (personal or business). What sometimes happens is that one parent—out of misguided kindness—keeps lending more and more money to the adult child. Debt can build up very fast.

I remember one parent who just didn't realize at the time that their adult child—who was highly functional when well—had no control when manic. The parent ended up thousands and thousands of dollars in debt due to the various business ventures that were started and failed. Many families eventually put up a barrier and cut off the flow of money. I can understand this: it's not fair that one member should bleed the family's collective assets that have been accumulated over many years, decades, or even generations.

Everyone says that family members must be on the same page, but I see that the person with the illness needs a family member or friend who will listen. As you listen, you develop trust, and then you can help or possibly convince, because you will have shown that you have the affected person's best interests at heart.

Some families are understandably concerned about the unity and well-being of the extended family, the security of the family business, and their reputation in the wider community. Bipolar disorder can threaten all this.

Court orders and involuntary treatment

I recall two clients who were a considerable danger to themselves and others due to their impulsive actions and excessive speeding. The families tried to take away the car keys or control access to the cars. Another option is to inform the psychiatrist or doctor who will withdraw the person's driver's licence. Lastly, if the person is likely to put someone or themselves at risk in the very near future, then families can get a court order.

A court order is a serious matter because it interrupts other court processes to say that this is an emergency. The person requesting the court order must indicate danger, by documenting the actions or words (for example, dangerous driving, suicidal thoughts, death threats, carrying a weapon, intimidating and/or aggressive behaviours. Perhaps the person with bipolar disorder is at risk of losing their apartment or job due to out-of-control behaviours. It is also possible to say they are creating chaos in their personal or financial life due to their spending behaviour.) It is up to the judge—not the family—to decide whether to take away the person's liberties.

Note that danger is a temporary condition and even though someone made suicidal or death threats, they may have calmed down by the time they see a psychiatrist, and no longer be a risk.

If a court order is granted, the police take the person to hospital for assessment. If the psychiatrist thinks the person themselves or anyone else is in danger, they are kept and reassessed. The person will only be hospitalized after a second psychiatrist evaluates them and concludes that they are still a danger to themselves or others. If this continues then they could be admitted for stabilization or to keep them safe. (Sometimes they are sent to a crisis centre instead.)

In Quebec this does not necessarily mean that medication is given right away. The person has the right to refuse medication under certain circumstances. (A family member cannot get a court order for treatment; only a psychiatrist can.) However, medication may be given under duress if the person is not stable or is out of control. The whole issue of helping the person understand that they have an illness comes into play again. Once the person is in the hospital, the nurses and doctors will help to explain the illness and what is going on. But they want to establish trust. Sometimes, more than one stay in the hospital may occur and each time the staff members try to help the patient understand their illness and see that the team wants to help—not fight—them.

One common scenario when a person lacks insight is that they take the bipolar medications at the hospital and maybe for a short while after, but when they feel well, they go off their meds. They do not understand the nature of the illness. Bipolar is chronic and cyclical, and it will likely need lifelong treatment.

People have the right to stop treatment and test out the theory that they no longer need meds. This process is usually painful to watch but it helps the person understand the cyclical nature of the disorder and then they are much more likely to believe the doctors. It is part of the learning process that many people go through. (It's a rare individual who immediately listens to medical advice and follows the treatment plan compliantly.)

Stigma and self-stigma

People in the community need to get past their own stigmas and understand that bipolar is a medical problem like any other.

Stigma presents in many ways. For example, employers often won't hire people with a history of mental illness. Neighbours may exhibit a "not in my backyard" attitude when organizations plan to build day centres nearby. Health professionals are not always free of stigma, either: many clients say they have felt mistreated by medical staff. And families may feel ashamed that their loved one has been diagnosed, or they may not want their children to date or marry a person with a mental illness, as I discuss in the next section about relationships.

We psychologists work to identify barriers to progress and development, so we ask family members to examine their own attitudes critically, and work through things. A therapist can help people find resolution and come to a healthy understanding of their role as the family member of a person with mental health challenges.

When I worked at a day centre, I met many clients who felt they had been tossed aside by society. But perhaps the most disheartening form of stigma is when the affected person self-stigmatizes. For example, some of my clients felt great shame when they heard how they'd behaved during a (hypo)manic episode. And they were devastated when they recognized that they'd done it again during a subsequent episode, or that their colleagues or family members did not want anything to do with them anymore.

It breaks my heart when I see people who feel broken and incapable due to their disorder, and who then stigmatize themselves as less worthy, less deserving, less acceptable, or less human than others, simply because they have a mental illness.

Stigma—this cruel prejudice—must be uncovered and treated to help people feel whole and ready to face the world, even with their challenges.

Relationships

Many who are affected by mental illnesses feel that they will not find love or a partner to share their lives because they have an illness. This does not have to be true. It may represent the self-stigma:

"I am not good enough" or "I am too damaged." I have seen that it is possible; it may just be harder, and people need support.

Some families are critical of who their bipolar relative marries: "That person is not good enough for our loved one." I have also seen stigma on behalf of a person with bipolar against a potential partner because that partner also had a mental illness: "They are going to hold our loved one back" or "Our family already has too much to deal with, with just one person being mentally ill; two would be too much."

To be fair, though, I have also seen many family members be very helpful by giving the right support and guidance. When families provide encouragement, a person with a mental illness can definitely have meaningful and lasting relationships.

Work and volunteering

One big prejudice I have seen in families is that they sometimes expect the affected person to work and be productive. I believe that everyone has a right to pleasure and work. Work can in itself be therapeutic, but our society puts pressure on individuals to fit in and do a full workweek without accommodations.

Our work-oriented society can actually make some people's conditions worse. The stigma that they are "lazy" and have no value if they don't work has to be seriously questioned. People with mental illness are not lazy: they are working twice as hard as others just to stay stable. People who don't live with a mental illness do not see how hard it is to manage a day, never mind how much effort it takes to manage a workweek.

Once in recovery, people with a mental illness can also study, create or volunteer—to an extent that allows them to maintain stability. When working with very ill people, I have found that they need purpose in their lives, and they usually want to work in some capacity. They want to contribute and feel of value. Volunteers are highly valued in our society and a flexible schedule can be found.

Doing mental health advocacy work can also be therapeutic for people in recovery, and for family members.

It's a shame that there are not enough companies that understand mental illness and offer flexible positions for people with mental illness. However, changes are happening: work programs are being developed and some companies realize that some employees have mental illnesses and need certain accommodations.

> *Some Montreal-based programs that offer positions to people with mental illness are L'Équipe Entreprise; L'Arrimage; and Centre Bienvenue, L'Atelier. Please ask community-based mental health organizations in your area about local resources.*

Role of the family

Family members of affected people have shouldered the burden alone for far too many years, and they want that burden lifted.

Families are often stuck. They see the potential of their loved one and want them to succeed. There is a period of grieving that happens when it is so painful to realize the losses for the individual, for their dreams for this person and for their family. So sometimes to avoid all this pain, family members fight to get the loved one to accept their diagnosis, take their medications, and get on with the life program for whatever stage they are at. Families often do not realize that adapting to bipolar disorder can take years and years, not mere months. If a family badgers them in a way that makes them feel broken, then they won't buy into the process of moving from denial and anger to acceptance. You need to partner with them.

Family members can help their loved one identify the triggers that cause them stress so that they can seek help for those issues: anxiety, fear, problems with sleep, disturbed circadian rhythm (day and night switched around), spending excessive amounts of money, losing a job and/or relationship.

Remember, you're in it for the long haul, so you need to take good care of yourself. Prioritize your rest and keep yourself healthy. Learn how to manage your stress and get exercise. Develop your relationship with your loved one. Have conversations and activities that are not centred on the illness but on other things that help you to bond. And as I discuss below, please seek support from your local family association for mental health.

Role of community organizations

Community organizations exist to support the families of people who have a mental illness. This support is crucial because families often feel excluded by the psychiatric treatment team who must respect patient confidentiality.

For example, a patient in hospital may feel angry with or alienated from their family members who called the police or got a court order. The patient may then refuse to grant access to their family, and the family ends up with very limited access to the psychiatric team. They may only be asked for information and history about the patient's illness, but not get any information about the diagnosis or treatment in return.

This can leave families feeling helpless, undervalued, and excluded. It can be enormously reassuring to have a safe space to share their concerns with other families who have experienced similar struggles.

Family support can also be really helpful with getting people with undiagnosed mental illnesses into treatment. Experienced families can help newcomers effectively access and navigate the often-fragmented mental health system to get the best possible care for their loved ones.

> I highly recommend that you reach out to your local family association for mental health. They can help you understand how to work with your affected loved one's lack of insight and

provide support for you as a family member. Sharing ideas with and learning from other families is extremely helpful. Your association may also offer workshops and training courses about various mental illnesses. The National Alliance on Mental Illness (NAMI) also offers a course which runs over eight to ten weeks.

Family members often disclose that they feel shame about how they reacted to an out-of-control loved one in the heat of a crisis. Seek support and reassurance from your community association if this is the case for you. Dealing with undiagnosed and/or untreated bipolar (and other mental illnesses) can result in extreme stress, shock, and exhaustion for you, regardless of how loving and understanding you were before the crisis. The ill person may become uncharacteristically verbally abusive, aggressive, or even physically violent, and this may push you beyond your limits. In a supportive and confidential setting with other families, you can vent, be reassured that these are perfectly human reactions to extreme situations, and then get ideas about how to take care of your loved one—and yourself.

In conversation with other families, people can consider fundamental questions like these:

- What are the rights of the affected person versus my rights?
- Does a person rendered incompetent by their untreated disorder have the right to determine their own life?
- What constitutes dangerous behaviour (e.g., impulsive overspending versus threats of suicide or homicide)?
- What are the constraints and realities affecting my role as a family caregiver in the short- and long-term?

Families can also share insights and learnings about what we call the "helping dynamic." You need to decide how much help you can give to an affected loved one, and whether your help is actually helping. For example, sometimes a family member's help only teaches the ill person to be helpless. This is called "learned helplessness." At some point, we must step back so our loved one can start managing on their own.

There is a very fine balance in the helping dynamic. Before you leap into action, ask: "Can my loved one do this for themselves?"

The goal of a community organization that aims to support affected families is to help the *whole* family. When one member of a family gets a mental illness, the whole family can be severely affected. It can cause major divisions. Not everyone will agree on the best course of action, and arguments and opposing perspectives can burn up a lot of emotional energy that would be better spent looking for solutions for the ill person.

For example, to protect themselves or to help the ill person move toward a goal, some family members may want to set limits or even remove the affected person from the home. Others may disagree and want to be more "protective." Some members may be beyond their limit, and they cut the person out of their lives. Others may find this too harsh. The resulting rifts then cause even more stress within the family.

Conclusion

Everyone I have met in my career has been interesting and has enriched my life. I see the person, not the disorder. I try to convey that they are not their illness: they are people and personalities first. I have learned that people with bipolar disorder are people living with a medical condition just trying to have a life worth living. They have times when they suffer greatly, and the stigma makes things much worse. They struggle every day to deal with so many things that others just don't see. They have their own preconceived notions and self-stigma: questioning their own worth and contribution to society and fitness for family life, managing children, and holding down a full-time job.

Behind the person with bipolar, there is a family often dealing with confusion, shock, and grief. Families deserve much greater recognition as a crucial part of the affected person's care plan, and they need much greater support. Dealing with an ill family member can be mentally and physically exhausting. Families need understanding and support, and they need access to resources. Please remember that there are many competent psychiatrists, there are effective medications, and new research is being conducted all the time. More medications and treatments are coming. The medical system and the support systems for both patients and families are getting better.

I would like to see more families acknowledge that their loved one is trying. Love them and help them to live the fullest possible life, recognizing the limitations that their disorder puts on them. Sometimes it is through struggle that we realize what is important. Each person has something to offer this world and they need to find a niche where they can contribute and feel valued. The most important place to start is within the family. They can always be of value to the family.

I challenge you to see your loved one who has bipolar as a human being first! They can love and be loved as children, parents, siblings, grandparents, aunts, uncles, nieces, nephews, and friends.

Sheryl Bruce

I was born in Sudbury, Ontario in 1958. I got a Bachelor of Arts in Honour's Psychology from the University of Waterloo in 1985 and studied Applied Social Psychology with a specialty in Community Mental Health at the University of Guelph, receiving an MA in 1988. I was a foster care caseworker in California and then moved to Montreal in 1990. I volunteered at the Douglas Hospital (now Douglas Mental Health University Institute) and Citizen Advocacy, then worked for Community Perspectives. From 2007, I worked at Friends for Mental Health, a non-profit organization supporting family members of people with mental illnesses. I was initially a counsellor and then clinical supervisor from 2017 until my retirement in 2021. I live with my husband, and we have three adult children and one grandchild.

Epilogue: Looking Back; Looking Forward

Merryl Hammond, PhD

Thank you for reading this anthology. A few final points to wrap up.

How I gathered contributions for *Navigating Bipolar Country*

At the time I started thinking about compiling a bipolar anthology, only a very few such anthologies were available, all either poetry or essay collections by a single author. The only collection with multiple authors I could find was *Voices of Bipolar Disorder: The Healing Companion* (2010), edited by Gore and Garey. I cited this groundbreaking volume in my 2018 memoir, and highly recommend it to you, too. To my knowledge, no other bipolar anthologies exist that have contributions from multiple authors. So the wide-ranging, multidisciplinary collection in *Navigating Bipolar Country* is truly unique.

To seek contributions for this anthology, I first developed a detailed document, "Guidelines for Contributors," which I posted on my website and emailed to as many bipolar, mental health, and writers' organizations as I could think of, asking them please to publicize this project. Numerous contributors contacted me from these efforts, and I'm proud to include the works of some of them here.

As well, I tried to track down some high-profile "bipolar celebrities": people who have published a successful bipolar memoir, self-help guide, workbook, or textbook. I also contacted famous actors, singers, or celebrities living with bipolar themselves or related to someone with the disorder. You may know some of these "big names": Kay Redfield Jamison, Margaret Trudeau, Julie A. Fast, Bassey Ikpi, Natasha Tracy, Victoria Maxwell, Amy Dodd Pilkington, Tara Mandarano, Candida Fink, David Miklowitz, Monica Ramirez Basco, William R. Marchand, Marya Hornbacher, Glenn Close, and Terri Cheney, among others. In many cases, my efforts yielded no response at all. (The COVID-19 pandemic didn't help: many were out of the office for months at a time.) In other cases, I was successfully blocked by various agents and their assistants, who simply made it impossible for me to invite the person concerned to even consider participating. But in the end, several previously published authors submitted a piece that is included.

My role as editor

A word about my role as editor and compiler of this book. Of course, working with 42 individual contributors, some of whom preferred to do interviews rather than submit written pieces, took a lot of time. And even when writers—even previously published ones—submitted articles, it often took several emails back and forth before we were both satisfied with the final version included here.

But this initial screening, accepting, and editing work was so much easier than the subsequent job of sorting, organizing, and compiling this final version of the book. I wavered for weeks once all contributions were finally in hand. Apart from considering the variety of topics and word counts for each piece that range from about one- to almost seven-thousand words, I wondered how best to weave it all together to provide a logical flow for the reader, while also carefully placing each piece to its best possible advantage. "Should Piece A go before or after Piece B? Or should Piece A in fact close the section, rather than open it?" And so on, endlessly. I felt like a quilter determined to sew a beautiful heirloom quilt using all the precious pieces of fabric she'd inherited. Just one big problem: the pieces were all different textures, colours, sizes, and shapes. Each one was unique and priceless, and my job was to stitch them together in a way that would do justice to each, and to the quilt as a whole. I felt the weight of the expectations of all the contributors on my shoulders, and I felt I owed it to the entire global bipolar community to produce a worthy final product.

No wonder I was overwhelmed!

Mindful of my own always-fragile mental health as a person living with bipolar, I took a couple of weeks off. When I returned to my desk, I started writing the preface and doing some other small administrative tasks for the book. Finally, I felt ready to return to my spreadsheet of contributions and make some decisions, resigned to the fact that another editor might use very different criteria and reasoning and, therefore, make very different decisions about the sequencing of contributions.

Limitations of the collection

First, there are many more essays from people living with bipolar (19) than from family members (12) and from health and other professionals (11). On the one hand, I was delighted with the positive response from others in the same bipolar boat as me. But as an editor whose original vision was for a compilation with more-or-less equal contributions from all three groups, I was somewhat disappointed by this imbalance.

Second, a glaring shortcoming is the lack of gender balance: many more women contributed than men. Despite my best efforts, not a single husband, brother, or father contributed to the section by family members. In total, only ten of the 42 contributors (24 percent) are male, most in the professionals' section.

Third, there are many more contributors from Canada and the US than from other parts of the world.

Fourth, and again despite every effort I made over an 18-month period of seeking contributions, part 3 of this collection lacks the perspectives of several key groups including occupational therapists, art therapists, lawyers, housing advocates, people working in the correctional system, and others who regularly work with people who are living with bipolar, and our families.

Are you aware of any other limitations?

A second edition?

Some people who only heard about this book after the deadline for submissions had passed have asked if there might be a second edition that they could submit to. It's way too early to decide, but I have started a "tentative waiting list" for people who would like to be contacted if ever I do proceed with a second edition. If you're interested, please use the contact form on my website at MerrylHammond.com and just indicate: Second edition of *Navigating Bipolar Country*. No promises on my end; and no commitments on yours!

Please review!

Please help us to reach more potential readers by rating this anthology on Amazon or Goodreads. Every extra review is vital and really helps!

Acknowledgements

To all the contributors

My sincere thanks to each contributor whose work is included here.

To those who decided to publish under your own name for the first time, a massive high-five to you! I know that for many of you, going public with your story was a real challenge. I hope this represents a key step on your journey through bipolar country.

To those who have previously published under your own names, thank you for adding your valued voices to this anthology.

To the few who chose to use a pen name (a small minority of nine contributors or just 21 percent of the total), I fully understand your need to protect yourself or your loved ones from prejudiced employers, and even family members and friends. One day, let's hope, we'll all be free to speak out without fear of judgment.

To the professionals who participated, thank you for helping us gain insight into what it's like for you, working with and seeking to help individuals and families affected by bipolar disorder.

To Dr. Candida Fink, thank you for writing the foreword for this anthology. I am truly honoured that you accepted my request.

Finally, I'd like to acknowledge the contributor, "Wayfarer," who tragically lost his battle with bipolar depression less than two years after being diagnosed. His poignant contribution to this anthology serves to remind us of the desperate need for more effective treatment options, and of the profound seriousness of a bipolar diagnosis.

To those who helped shape this book

A huge thank you to Geoff Affleck, my production and publishing consultant at AuthorPreneneur Publishing Inc. To my daughter, Tami Hammond-Collins, an editor (who also contributed two poems to part 2), and did a fantastic job of editing the first half of the manuscript, after which her COVID-related work intervened; and to Nina Shoroplova who took over as editor. (I thought I had a beady eye, but Nina put me to shame; thank you!) Amit Dey did the book design and typesetting, and Pagatana Design Service designed the cover. My thanks to you all.

To my family

As always, thank you to my family who have bushwhacked with me throughout my journeys in bipolar country. My husband, Rob Collins, has been my most loyal champion and cheerleader. I wish everyone had a life partner and advocate like him in their lives.

To our five children, and to all my other family members, near and far, a thousand thanks for your love, acceptance, and support.

About Me, the Editor

My background

I was born in Johannesburg, South Africa, in 1956, and did a bachelor's degree in nursing and honours in sociology at the University of Natal, Durban. I then did a master's in sociology and a PhD in community health and adult education at the University of the Witwatersrand, Johannesburg. My husband Rob Collins and I immigrated to Montreal, Canada, in 1988. I'm a public health consultant for Indigenous clients and have published widely in both countries.

Writing in my Montreal-area backyard.

My memoir, *Mad Like Me: Travels in Bipolar Country*

In the mid-1970s, I was a student nurse, and I—like most people—judged, blamed, and stigmatized my patients who had a mental illness. Fast-forward several decades. It's 2008. I'm a wife, mother, and health professional. I have never experienced any hint of mental illness. In early menopause, boom! "Bipolar disorder," they said. What? For me this meant exhausting episodes of outer-space-high (hypo)manias interspersed with blacker-than-black depressions.

So at age 51, with this diagnosis, I flipped from researcher and health professional to locked-ward patient. I'd come full circle: now I was the mental patient, being stigmatized by others—and myself.

I disappeared from the stage of my own life for years.

When I had recovered sufficiently to think straight, I wanted to share what I had endured and decided to write a memoir. In *Mad Like Me: Travels in Bipolar Country* (2018), I disclose what my family and I confronted on our unplanned journey deep into bipolar country and ultimately to recovery. The memoir fights the stigma of mental illness and gives readers sincere cause for hope.

As I write in the prologue of *Mad Like Me*, I got the idea for my memoir during a manic episode: "Despite the wild fizzing in my brain, I kept a detailed paper trail of post-it notes with scribbled ideas and insights that enabled me to look back with startling clarity and allowed me to capture realistic recollections of my lurching journey through Bipolar Country. My goal is not merely to bring you along for the ride, a passive observer of the crazy antics of one particular bipolar sufferer. Rather, I hope to bring you into my stormy mind, so you can experience what I went through as a bipolar patient. Whether you're 'mad like me' or a carer, I hope you find sustenance for your travels in Bipolar Country here" (page 13).

When the mania dissipated, depression would descend like a garage door rumbling shut, trapping me inside in the dark. As I write: "When depressed, sleep was my only solace, offering brief oblivion. More than that: sleep was a clandestine lover from whom I couldn't bear to be separated. I wanted only to be wrapped in his protective arms, and have the world eclipsed by his tender attentions. Wakefulness was the ultimate enemy. With wakefulness came people. Responsibilities. Commitments. Guilt. Energy-draining chores. Forget it; just roll over and try to blot it all out" (page 31).

After many such episodes and two hospitalizations, I gradually clawed my way back to stability. Thankfully, I am now back from that wild bipolar country. I've been stable—on medications, using a variety of self-care strategies, and with the unfailing support of my family—for many calm years. "I'm here to tell you that things can get better, and that you can, piece by piece, build a life where bipolar no longer controls you. You can tame this tiger!" (page 13).

In my memoir, I explain how bipolar feels from the inside, and I advocate for these anti-stigma messages:

- Every person with a mental illness deserves dignity and respect.
- If you have a mental illness, maintain hope: recovery is possible!
- Mental health and mental illness are on the same continuum, so please take active steps to protect your own mental health.
- When relating to anyone who has a mental illness, remember: "It could be me ..."

What reviewers say about *Mad Like Me: Travels in Bipolar Country*

"Wow; bullseye! The definitive book for bipolar sufferers and everyone around them. I was mesmerized. Read this!" ~Laurence Potgieter

"Amazing! Compelling. Infused with humour yet filled with serious research, it permits the reader to enter the incredible labyrinth of the human brain. A must-read." ~Anne Vrana

"One word: Wow! What an incredible resource. It allows us to peek right inside the mind of a bipolar sufferer. The appendices are especially helpful. Indispensable." ~Pierre-Julien Mazenot

"The book helped me identify my triggers and manage my bipolar."
~CourtF (Amazon reviewer)

"I was sucked right in. It gave me a deeper understanding of what my family members with bipolar have dealt with, and how we can support a loved one dealing with it." ~Sue Canfield

"Very helpful as I learn to support my husband."
~"Pizzercat" (Amazon reviewer)

"Really lets the world know what it's like to LIVE the diagnosis of bipolar disorder. Should be compulsory reading for all health professionals."
~Barbara Webster, RN, BScN, MSc.

"Helped me understand what my clients may experience but can't explain so eloquently." ~Anne (Amazon reviewer)

"Informative, clear, and very personal. And frankly very brave."
~Dr. Sturla Bruun-Meyer, Psychiatrist

Contact me

Instagram: @MerrylHammond

Facebook: MerrylHammondAuthor

Or please visit MerrylHammond.com for videos (including brief interviews with my husband, and with two of our adult children), blog posts, information about memoir coaching, and to subscribe to my newsletter. You can also use the contact form if you're interested in a possible second edition of *Navigating Bipolar Country.*

References

Selected references about photographing people with bipolar from Matthieu Zellweger's essay

Zellweger, M. 2019. "Picturing health: living with bipolar disorder," *The Lancet*, Vol 393: 119-126.

Zellweger, M. 2019. *Worlds Beyond*. InFolio Editions, Switzerland. ISBN 978-2-88474-425-6. matthieuzellweger.com/en/livres

Selected references about bipolar and creativity from Abdu'l-Missagh Ghadirian's essay

Benaur, M. 2010. "An introduction to bipolar disorder," *Voices of Bipolar Disorder: The Healing Companion: Stories for Courage, Comfort and Strength*, eds. R. D. Gore and J. Garey, xvii-xxvi. New York: LaChance Publishing.

Burkhardt, E., A. Pfennig, G. Breitling, et al. 2019. "Creativity in persons at-risk for bipolar disorder: A pilot study." *Early Intervention in Psychiatry* 13(5):1165-72.

Ghadirian, A-M. 2009. *Creative Dimensions of Suffering*. Wilmette: Baha'i Publishing.

Jamison, K. R. 1995. *An Unquiet Mind*. New York: A.A. Knopf, Inc.

McCraw, S., G. Parker, K. Fletcher, et al. 2013. "Self-reported creativity in bipolar disorder: prevalence, types and associated outcomes in mania versus hypomania." *Journal of Affective Disorders*. 151(3): 831-36.

Rosenthal, N. E. 1993. *Winter Blues: Seasonal Affective Disorder*. New York: The Guilford Press.

Selected references about family and caregivers from Jens Peter Eckardt's essay

Access Economics and SANE Australia. 2003. Bipolar Disorder: Costs. An Analysis of the Burden of Bipolar Disorder and Related Suicide in Australia. Melbourne: SANE Australia.

Baruch, E., N. Pistrang, C. Barker. 2018. "Psychological interventions for caregivers of people with bipolar disorder: A systematic review and meta-analysis." *The Journal of Affective Disorders*. 236:187-198. doi: 10.1016/j.jad.2018.04.077.

Bordbar, M., S. Soltanifar, A. Talaei. 2009. "Short-term family-focused psychoeducational program for bipolar mood disorder in Mashad." *The Iranian Journal of Medical Sciences*. 2009:34.

Clarkin, J. F., D. Carpenter, J. Hull, et al. 1998. "Effects of psychoeducational intervention for married patients with bipolar disorder and their spouses." *Journal of Psychiatric Services*. 49:531-33.

D'Souza, R., D. Piskulic, S. Sundram. 2010. "A brief dyadic group-based psychoeducation program improves relapse rates in recently remitted bipolar disorder: a pilot randomised controlled trial." *The Journal of Affective Disorders*. 120:272-76.

Dean, K., H. Stevens, P. B. Mortensen, et al. 2010. "Full spectrum of psychiatric outcomes among offspring with parental history of mental disorder." *Archives of General Psychiatry*. 67(8):822-29. doi: 10.1001/archgenpsychiatry.2010.86.

Dirik, A., S. Sandhu, D. Giacco, et al. 2017. "Why involve families in acute mental health care? A collaborative conceptual review." *BMJ Open*. doi: 10.1136/bmjopen-2017-017680.

Eckardt, J. P. 2020. "Caregivers of people with severe mental illness in the COVID-19 pandemic." *Lancet Psychiatry*. 7(8):e53. doi:10.1016/S2215-0366(20)30252-2.

Fiorillo, A., G. Sampogna, L. Gaudio, et al. 2013. "Efficacy of supportive family interventions in bipolar disorder: A review of the literature." *Journal of Psychopathology*. 19:134-42.

Justo, L.P., B. G. Soares, H. M. Calil. 2007 "Family interventions for bipolar disorder. *The Cochrane Database of Systematic Reviews*. 4:CD005167. doi.org/10.1002/14651858.CD005167.pub2.

Jönsson, P. D., I. Skärsäter, H. Wijk, E. Danielson. 2011. "Experience of living with a family member with bipolar disorder." *International Journal of Mental Health Nursing*. 20:29-37. doi:10.1111/j.1447-0349.2010.00704.x.

Keitner, G. I., C. E. Ryan, A. Heru. 2005. "Families of People with Bipolar Disorder." *Families and Mental Disorders*, eds. N. Sartorius, J. Leff, J. J. López-Ibor, M. Maj, A. Okasha. New Jersey: Wiley. doi:10.1002/0470024712.ch4.

Madigan, K., P. Egan, D. Brennan, et al. 2012. "A randomised controlled trial of carer-focused multi-family group psychoeducation in bipolar disorder." *European Psychiatry*. 27:281-84.

Marshall, T., P. Solomon. 2003. "Professionals' responsibilities in releasing information to families of adults with mental illness." *Psychiatric Services*. 54(12):1622-28. doi: 10.1176/appi.ps.54.12.1622.

McFarlane, W. R. 2002. Multifamily Groups in the Treatment of Severe Psychiatric Disorders. New York: Guilford Press.

Miklowitz, D. J., D. A. Axelson, B. Birmaher, et al. 2008. "Family-focused treatment for adolescents with bipolar disorder: results of a 2-year randomized trial." *Archives of General Psychiatry*. 65:1053-61.

Miklowitz, D.J., E. L. George,J. A. Richards, et al. 2003. "A randomized study of family-focused psychoeducation and pharmacotherapy in the outpatient management of bipolar disorder." *Archives of General Psychiatry*. 60:904-n12.

Miklowitz, D. J., D. O. Taylor. 2006. "Family-focused treatment of the suicidal bipolar patient." *Bipolar Disorders*. 8(5 Pt 2):640-51. doi: 10.1111/j.1399-5618.2006.00320.x.

Miller, I. W., D. A. Solomon, C. E. Ryan, et al. 2004. "Does adjunctive family therapy enhance recovery from bipolar I mood episodes?" *The Journal of Affective Disorders*. 82:431-36.

Murray-Swank, A. B., L. Dixon. "Family psychoeducation as an evidence-based practice." 2004. *CNS Spectrums*. 9(12):905-12. doi: 10.1017/s109285290000972x.

Onwumere, J. 2020. "Informal carers in severe mental health conditions: Issues raised by the United Kingdom SARS-CoV-2 (COVID-19) Pandemic." *The International Journal of Social Psychiatry*. doi:10.1177/0020764020927046.

Östman, M., L. Kjellin. 2002. "Stigma by association: Psychological factors in relatives of people with mental illness." *The British Journal of Psychiatry*. 181(6):494-98. doi:10.1192/bjp.181.6.494.

Perlick, D. A., D. J. Miklowitz, N. Lopez, et al. 2010. "Family-focused treatment for caregivers of patients with bipolar disorder." *Bipolar Disorders*. 12:627-37.

Perlick, D. A., R. A. Rosenheck, J. F. Clarkin, et al. 2004. "Impact of family burden and affective response on clinical outcome among patients with bipolar disorder." *Psychiatric Services*. (9):1029-35. doi: 10.1176/appi.ps.55.9.1029.

Perlick, D. A., R. A. Rosenheck, D. J. Miklowitz, et al. 2007. "Prevalence and correlates of burden among caregivers of patients with bipolar disorder enrolled in the Systematic Treatment Enhancement Program for Bipolar Disorder." *Bipolar Disorders*. 9:262-73.

Pompili, M., D. Harnic, X. Gonda, et al. 2014. "Impact of living with bipolar patients: Making sense of caregivers' burden." *World Journal of Psychiatry*. 4(1):1-12. doi.org/10.5498/wjp.v4.i1.1.

Poon, A. W. C., W. Kung. 2020. "An Overview of Social Work Approaches in Working with Families of People with Serious Mental Illness." *Mental Health and Social Work*, eds. R. Ow, A. Poon. Singapore: Springer. 10.1007/978-981-13-0440-8_8-1.

Reinares, M., C. M. Bonnín, D. Hidalgo-Mazzei, et al. 2016. "The role of family interventions in bipolar disorder: A systematic review." *Clinical Psychology Review*. 43:47-57. doi: 10.1016/j.cpr.2015.11.010.

Reinares, M., F. Colom, J. Sanchez-Moreno, et al. 2008. "Impact of caregiver group psychoeducation on the course and outcome of bipolar patients in remission: a randomized controlled trial." *Bipolar Disorders*. 10:511-19.

Reinares, M., E. Vieta, F. Colom, et al. 2004. "Impact of a psychoeducational family intervention on caregivers of stabilized bipolar patients." *Psychotherapy and Psychosomatics*. 73:312-19.

Reinares, E., F. Vieta, A. Colom, et al. 2006. "What really matters to bipolar patients' caregivers: Sources of family burden." *The Journal of Affective Disorders*. Vol 94, Issues 1-3:157-63, ISSN 0165-0327. doi.org/10.1016/j.jad.2006.04.022.

Rusner, M., G. Carlsson, D. A. Brunt, M. Nyström. 2012. "The paradox of being both needed and rejected: the existential meaning of being closely related to a person with bipolar disorder." *Issues in Mental Health Nursing*. 33(4):200-08. doi: 10.3109/01612840.2011.653037.

Solomon, P., M. Molinaro, E. Mannion, K. Cantwell. 2012. "Confidentiality policies and practices in regard to family involvement: Does training make a difference?" *The American Journal of Psychiatric Rehabilitation*. 15(1):97-115.

Van Gent, E. M., F. M. Zwart. 1991. "Psychoeducation of partners of bipolar-manic patients." *The Journal of Affective Disorders*. 21:15-18.

Wolff, N., D. A. Perlick, R. Kaczynski, et al. 2006. "Modeling costs and burden of informal caregiving for persons with bipolar disorder." *The Journal of Mental Health Policy and Economics*. 9(2):99-110.

Made in the USA
Coppell, TX
18 April 2023

15761496R00249